Maria
Septe

SUBPERSON

THE PEOPLE INSIDE US

JOHN ROWAN

Routledge
Taylor & Francis Group

HOVE AND NEW YORK

First published 1990
by Routledge
27 Church Road, Hove, East Sussex, BN3 2FA
Simultaneously published in the USA and Canada
by Routledge
a division of Routledge, Chapman and Hall, Inc.
711 Third Avenue, New York, NY 10017

Typeset by LaserScript Limited, Mitcham, Surrey

British Library Cataloguing in Publication Data

Rowan. John. 1925–
Superpersonalities: the people inside us
1. Psychology I. Title
150

Library of Congress Cataloging in Publication Data

Rowan, John.
Subpersonalities: the people inside us/John Rowan.
p. cm.
Bibliography: p.
Includes index.
1. Personality. 2. Self. 3. Identity (Psychology) 4. Multiple personality.
5. Psychotherapy. I. Title.
BF698.R8872 1989
155.2—dc20   89–33104
CIP
AC
ISBN 978-0-415-04329-8 (pbk)

HOUSE OF CHANGES

My body is a wide house
a commune
of bickering women, hearing
their own breathing
denying each other.

Nearer the door
ready in black leather
is *Vulnerable.* She lives in the hall
her face painted with care
her black boots reaching her crotch
her black hair shining
her skin milky and soft as butter.
If you should ring the doorbell
she would answer
and a wound would open across her eyes
as she touched your hand.

On the stairs, glossy and determined
is *Mindful.* She's the boss, handing out
punishments and rations and examination
papers with precise
justice. She keeps her perceptions in a huge
album under her arm
her debts in the garden with the weedkill
friends in a card-index
on the windowsill of the sittingroom
and a tape-recording of the world
on earphones
which she plays to herself over and over
assessing her life
writing summaries.

In the kitchen is *Commendable*
The only lady in the house who
dresses in florals

she is always busy, always doing something
for someone she has
a lot of friends. Her hands are quick and
cunning as blackbirds
her pantry is stuffed with loaves and fishes
she knows the times of trains and
mends fuses and makes
a lot of noise with the vacuum cleaner.
In her linen cupboard, new-ironed and neatly
folded, she keeps her resentments like
wedding presents – each week
takes them out for counting not to
lose any but would never think of
using any being a lady.

Upstairs in a white room
is my favourite. She is *Equivocal*
has no flesh on her bones
that are changeable as yarrow stalks.
She hears her green plants talking
watches the bad dreams under the world
unfolding
spends all her days and nights
arranging her symbols
never sleeps
never eats hamburgers
never lets anyone into her room
never asks for anything.

In the basement is *Harmful*
She is the keeper of weapons
the watchdog. Keeps intruders at bay
but the others keep her
locked up in the daytime and when she escapes
she comes out screaming
smoke streaming from her nostrils
flames on her tongue
razor-blades for fingernails
skewers for eyes.

I am *Imminent*
live out in the street

watching them. I lodge myself in other people's
heads with a sleeping bag
strapped to my back.
One day I'll perhaps get to like them enough
those rough, truthful women
to move in. One by one
I'm making friends with them all
unobtrusively, slow and steady
slow and steady.

This book is dedicated to the memory of
Jacob Stattman
who first taught me about my subpersonalities.

CONTENTS

ILLUSTRATIONS

ACKNOWLEDGEMENTS

I would like to thank the following people for their help in answering questions about various matters: Ian Gordon-Brown, Tom Greening, Anthony Greenwald, Rom Harré, John Kihlstrom, David Lorimer, Dan McAdams, Alvin Mahrer, Joseph Redfearn, Seymour Rosenberg, Howard Sasportas, Richard Schwartz, and John Watkins.

INTRODUCTION

This book tries to put subpersonalities on the map. At the moment this concept is not there, and it ought to be.

We all use the concept in our folk psychology, but it has escaped the notice of orthodox academic personality theory. What I want to argue is that academic personality theory is going to have to take notice of it in the future.

It is obviously convenient for someone trying to construct a personality test to assume that there is just one personality. But that is all it is – an assumption, a convenience. It would be more inconvenient if we had to admit that people could have one personality in one frame, and another in another. The whole idea of a personality test might have to change.

So this book is partly addressed to psychologists working in the field of personality, and of the self, and of identity – all those kinds of questions. It is also addressed to psychotherapists, encouraging them to look outside the walls of their training institutes at what is going on elsewhere to deal with the self-same problems they are tackling themselves.

It is also addressed to the general reader, who would like to know how brilliant people can be in this field, and how stupid. For anyone just interested in human beings (including people working in the human sciences) and how they function and act, this book is full of illuminating examples and accounts.

Because this book is a pioneering effort, it mainly consists of simple descriptions of what is going on, of what people are saying and doing. In that sense it is a very concrete, down-to-earth book.

It does not profess to put forward a complete theory reconciling all that is known about subpersonalities. That is a task for later,

1

when the field is better developed, and there are more connections between the different parts of it. At the moment it is very disconnected, with most people not knowing that the person next door is working on the very same problems, perhaps with a slightly different vocabulary. So all I want to do is to show that there needs to be a fuller and better theoretical structure, and that all the materials are there for anyone who wants to construct it.

Part One

WHAT ARE SUBPERSONALITIES?

Chapter One

SETTING THE SCENE

In writing a book like this, it seems to be important to make it clear where I am coming from. What school do I represent? What is my philosophy? What biases do you have to allow for?

STARTING POINT

When I was twenty I discovered Spinoza: his philosophy seemed to take me up on to a high mountain from which I could see everything very clearly. Then when I was twenty-five I met Harold Walsby, a deeply versed Hegelian who later went on to create a dialectical algebra: he initiated me into the philosophy of Hegel, and particularly into a version which emphasized that nothing is absolute. It was a devastating intellectual experience, which seemed to strip away everything I had believed up to that point, and then to build up again from nothing. (Then I came across a text which said, 'No one can be a Hegelian who has not first been a Spinozist.') Through Walsby's insistence, I learned how Hegel's dialectical thinking came into Marxism, and acquired a thorough education in that way of thinking about the world. Also I made some study of Polish many-valued logic. I also discovered that certain psychologists were dialectical in their thinking, and particularly valued Krech and Crutchfield, whose 1948 ground-breaking book on social psychology was not long out, and Mary Parker Follett, whose book *Freedom and Coordination* had only recently appeared.

I was a long time finding out what I wanted to do in life, and it was not until 1959, when I was thirty-four, that I embarked on my first degree (in philosophy and psychology) under Richard Peters at Birkbeck College in the University of London. Four years later I graduated, and went on to become a social psychologist, specializing in consumer research. From there, after a personal revolution in my whole attitude to the world, I discovered humanistic psychology and found it very congenial, and also became interested in radical psychology. The whole field of group work opened up, and interested me very much, as I have explained in more detail elsewhere (Rowan, in press). Later, in 1974, I took the Diploma in Applied Behavioural Science under John Southgate at the Polytechnic of North London, became an organizational psychologist specializing in research and group work, and joined the Occupational Psychology Division of the British Psychological Society. And from there, after another traumatic turn-round, I became a counsellor and psychotherapist, joining the British Association for Counselling (and later becoming part of the committee dealing with the accreditation of individual counsellors) and the Association of Humanistic Psychology Practitioners, where I became part of the membership committee. Later I helped to found the Institute of Psychotherapy and Social Studies, where I had to work with psychoanalysts in an integrated course, and learned a great deal about Freud and the object relations school. It was out of this experience that my book *The Reality Game: a Guide to Humanistic Counselling and Psychotherapy* emerged in 1983.

My own experience in psychotherapy started in groups (encounter, psychodrama, Gestalt, Tavistock, T-groups, psycho-synthesis, bioenergetics, movement, marathon, and so on), moved into co-counselling (where I became a teacher with the Barefoot Psychoanalyst school), and from there into psychotherapy after I had trained with Dr William Swartley in the approach known as primal integration (see Rowan 1988), which is in many ways very close to the object relations school in psychoanalysis, represented by people like Balint, Fairbairn, Guntrip, and Winnicott. At present I am seeing a Jungian analyst, and this represents the longest period of one-to-one work in my experience. I find much in the Jungian approach which helps to integrate the humanistic and the psychoanalytic.

This puts me in the position of coming from a basically humanistic orientation, but being able to see and use material from the psychoanalytic schools and also from academic philosophy and psychology. With this much as preamble, let us embark on a quest which will take us into all these areas and more.

DEFINITIONS

Most of us have had the experience of being 'taken over' by a part of ourselves which we didn't know was there. We say 'I don't know what got into me.' This is generally a negative experience, although it can be positive too. The way in which we usually recognize the presence of a subpersonality is that we find ourselves, in a particular situation, acting in ways which we do not like or which go against our interests, and unable to change this by an act of will or a conscious decision. This lasts as long as the situation lasts – perhaps a few minutes, perhaps an hour, perhaps a few hours – and then it changes by itself when we leave this situation and go into a different one. As long as fifteen years ago it was possible for a good and quite uncontroversial text on social psychology (Middlebrook 1974) to say things like 'Thus the individual is not a single self, but many selves, which change somewhat as the individual shifts from situation to situation and person to person. We are, in short, what the situation demands.'

The question of whether there are parts of a person which can be talked to and worked with as if they were separate little personalities with a will of their own is one which has fascinated nearly everyone who has had to work with people in any depth. Phrases like 'On the one hand I want to . . . on the other hand I don't', 'I don't know how I could have done it', 'It was as if a voice was telling me off' are so common that they inevitably give a counsellor or therapist the cue that more than one system is at work. Internalized mothers and fathers are so common that it has almost become a joke. All these are examples of ways in which the idea of subpersonalities presents itself very patently and obviously.

It is an extraordinary fact that there is at present no systematic book on subpersonalities, and the word does not appear in any text on personality theory known to me. It is not in the dictionaries of psychology nor in the dictionaries of psychotherapy. Yet the thing itself is used by virtually every clinician who has ever written about working with people, and by more and more psychologists paying attention to what is there as opposed to what is supposed to be there. Whether with Freud we talk about the ego, the id and the superego; whether with Jung we talk about the complexes or the archetypes; whether with Federn or Berne or John Watkins we talk about ego states; whether with Lewin we talk about subregions of the personality; whether with Perls we talk about the topdog and the underdog, or retroflection; whether with Klein or Fairbairn or Guntrip we talk about internal objects; whether with Balint we talk about the child in the patient; whether with Mary Watkins we talk about imaginal objects; whether with McAdams we talk about imagoes; whether with Hilgard we talk about the hidden observer; whether with Tart we talk about identity states; whether with Denzin we talk about the emotionally divided self; whether with Winnicott or Lake or Janov or Laing we talk about the false or unreal self; whether with Gurdjieff we talk about little I's; whether with Goffman we talk about multiple selfing; whether with Stone and Winkelman we talk about energy patterns; whether with Mahrer we talk about deeper potentials coming to the surface; whether with Mair we talk about a community of self; whether with Ornstein we talk about small minds; whether with Gazzaniga or Minsky we talk about agents and agencies within the mind; whether with Gergen or Martindale or O'Connor or Shapiro we talk about subselves; whether with Strauss or Rossan we talk about subidentities; whether with Markus we talk about possible selves; whether with Kihlstrom and Cantor we talk about self-schemas; whether with T. B. Rogers we talk about prototypes; whether with Beahrs we talk about alter-personalities, or whether with Assagioli or Redfearn we talk about subpersonalities – all the time we are talking about the same thing: this thing which is not mentioned in the textbooks of personality.

My own working definition of a subpersonality is *a semi-permanent and semi-autonomous region of the personality capable of acting as a person.* This goes further than the definition offered by Brown (1979), who says that subpersonalities are 'patterns of feelings, thoughts, behaviours, perceptions, postures and ways of moving which tend to coalesce in response to various recurring situations in life'. And I think it is an improvement on the definition of an ego state (which we shall see later is another name for a subpersonality) of Watkins (1978) where he says that it is 'a coherent system of behaviours and experiences with boundaries more or less permeable which separate it from other such systems within the overall Self '. It is very close to the definition which Tart (1986) gives of what he calls identity states: 'a unique *configuration* or system of psychological structures or subsystems . . . to which the sense of "I!" is given'.

But perhaps it is best of all to say with Beahrs (1982) that dissociation is not an either/or phenomenon, but exists along a dissociative continuum. At one end of this continuum are fluctuations in mood, interpreted as a state of mind organized around a particular emotion. Moods can be transient even when they seem quite long-lasting; basically they can come and go, leaving no trace behind. Similarly with hypnotic altered states of consciousness, or the altered states due to drugs: these too can be powerful and impressive at the time, but vanish as though they had never been: they are basically transient.

Further along the continuum, but still well within the range of normal experience, are the roles and ego states and sub-personalities within which individuals perform state-specific tasks and life activities. It is this region of the continuum with which we shall be concerned in this book – a particular set of circumstances will call forth a particular identifiable and relatively long-lasting subpersonality, which existed before that moment and will continue to exist after it.

Marie-Louise von Franz has suggested in an interview on film that subpersonalities themselves have a range of relative dissociation, such that they take us over sometimes mildly and sometimes more forcefully:

> I could give you a whole list of the persons I can be. I am an old peasant woman who thinks of cooking and of the house. I am a scholar who thinks about deciphering manuscripts. I am a psychotherapist who thinks about how to interpret people's dreams. I am a mischievous little boy who enjoys the company of a ten-year-old and playing mischievous tricks on adults, and so on. I could give you twenty more such characters. They suddenly enter you, but if you see what is happening you can keep them out of your system, play with them and put them aside again. But if you are possessed, they enter you involuntarily and you act them out involuntarily.
>
> (Boa 1988: 241)

9

She goes on to say that possession by the *animus* is a common problem for women and the men who live with them. We shall come back to this later.

Further along again, and now I think outside the range of normality, are the states of possession detailed by Crabtree (1988), where a family member, who may be alive or dead, can somehow enter into a person and influence them, often against their will.

At the far end of this continuum are the very dissociated states, characterized by fugue and amnesia, which come under the heading of psychiatric states of dissociated personality. These have been dealt with in terms of standard psychiatric categories, because they are very serious and disabling. But we are not concerned in this book with multiple personalities as such, because they are too extreme. In this book we are dealing with people who are as normal as you and I.

The fact seems to be that there are many researchers and practitioners using conceptual systems which bring in the idea of subpersonalities in some form, all working independently of one another and using different terms and different ways of thinking about the matter.

It seems, then, that there is room for a full-scale book which will deal with the matter fully, showing how important it is for any truly adequate personality theory, and how relevant it is both in psychotherapy and in everyday life; and sorting out the varied terminology which makes the field difficult to grapple with.

One possible source of confusion needs to be dealt with at the start, though it will recur at various points within the whole treatment of the subject. This is that it is important that on the one hand we want to reify the subpersonalities – turn them into solid objects, as it were, by the process of personification – but on the other hand to remember always that we are not talking about things, but about processes which are actually very fluid and in change, and may be much bigger than we understand at first. On the one hand it will be very useful for us to think in terms of homunculi – little people within the person – but on the other hand we must beware of giving them a status which they do not deserve and which would not be proper; they are in fact moments in a process of change and development which is lifelong. We have to hang on to the dialectic of this ability to handle these apparent contradictions and paradoxes.

HISTORY

It is not easy to discover the history of the idea of subpersonalities. It is one of those concepts, so common in the field of the human sciences, which has a long past but a short history.

Most primitive cultures, both ancient and modern, have been aware of altered states of consciousness and spirit possession, both of which are forerunners of the modern idea of subpersonalities. Priests, witch doctors, and shamans have made these ideas a stock-in-trade since early in the history of the human race. There were 'sleep temples' in ancient Greece and in Egypt where patients were encouraged to go into altered states of consciousness, were actually hypnotized, or were talked to during their sleep and given curative suggestions. Gods and goddesses, as we shall see later, can sometimes usefully be thought of as projected subpersonalities. The Druids, the Celtic priesthood, are supposed to have been experts in the use of these methods. In primitive cultures, these changes have often been brought about through the use of trances, and trance induction has been brought about by means of rhythm, drums, dancing , chanting, and so on.

The earliest example I have come across of someone actually talking to a subpersonality, and being answered back, comes in an Egyptian document of approximately 2200 BC – a dialogue between a suicidal man and his soul. This is quoted in full and explained at length by Barbara Hannah (1981), who makes some very interesting comments on it.

In *The Republic*, Plato speaks of three parts to the psyche: the rational, the appetitive (concerned with bodily needs such as hunger and thirst), and the spirited one. In the *Phaedrus* he speaks more concretely of a three-part psyche, imaged as a charioteer and two horses. One horse is a lover of honour, modesty, and temperance, who seems to be prudent and restrained; the other a crooked, lumbering animal with insolence, pride, and impulsiveness, who seems very much the voice of instinct.

Many later thinkers had different versions of this type of approach, and in the Middle Ages we find this sort of thing:

> The problem of the unity of personality had already been pondered over by St Augustine in his *Confessions*. Considering the change that had taken place in him since his conversion,

Augustine remarked that his old pagan personality, of which nothing seemed to remain in his waking state, still must exist since it was revived at night and in his dreams. He wrote: 'Am I not myself, O Lord, my God. And yet, there is so much difference between myself and myself within the moment wherein I pass from waking to sleeping or return from sleeping to waking.' This brings Augustine to discuss the problem of the dreamer's moral responsibility for his dreams. Later the analogous problem of the individual's responsibility for actions committed by his 'secondary personality' would become the subject of similar investigation.

(Ellenberger 1970: 126-7)

Augustine also emphasized the fact that memories from early infancy, which we had thought to be entirely lost, can reappear, and that our brains retain traces of all that we have previously experienced.

Barbara Hannah (1981) also gives us a very full example of a twelfth century dialogue with the soul, coming from Hugh de St Victor. And she points to a quotation of Jung from the early Church father, Origen: 'You will see that a man who seems to be one is not one, but as many different persons appear in him as he has attitudes' (Jung 1946: 197).

More dramatic, of course, is the idea of spirit possession. For centuries this was the only way of explaining how someone could be 'taken over' by another spirit, another personality. In possession the appearance of the person could change, the voice could change, and the whole emotional range of the person would extend. As Oesterreich (1974) points out at length, possession in its fullest sense exists only in countries and at times when there is an implicit belief in the devil, or at least in demons.

The phenomenon of possession, so frequent for many centuries, could well be considered as one variety of multiple personality. We have already mentioned the two forms of possession: lucid possession (in which the subject feels within himself the two souls striving against each other), and somnambulistic possession (in which the subject loses consciousness of his own self while a mysterious intruder seems to take possession of his body and acts and speaks with an individuality of which the subject knows nothing when he returns to awareness). We may note the parallelism between these two forms of possession and the two main forms of multiple personality. Moreover, just as possession could be manifest or latent, multiple personality can be manifest (that is, appear and develop spontaneously), or it may appear only under the influence of hypnotic maneuvers or automatic writing.

(Ellenberger 1970: 127)

Of course, we in this book are not concerned with possession, although, as we have said already, the more neurotic the subpersonality the more it may approach the nature of possession. Possession is of course a fascinating subject: in an interview von Franz has said:

I have a book on Haitian states of possession in which there is a photograph of three male mediums incorporating the same god, *Legbe*. In the trance all three mediums make exactly the same movements. When they are possessed they all behave in the same way. They are, as we would say, possessed by an archetypal figure.

(Boa 1988: 240)

In this book, however, we shall not be dealing with these phenomena, nor with the equally fascinating subject of multiple personality, which entails a much higher degree of dissociation than that with which we are occupied here, but it is an historical fact that the idea of subpersonalities evolved out of the findings about dual and multiple personality. It will not always be easy to draw this line, because much of the reasoning about multiple personalities also applies to subpersonalities, and clearly it is a matter of degree of dissociation rather than any real difference of principle. But there does seem to be a qualitative divide which is evidenced in the fact that multiple personality is a much more serious disturbance of the person, and classifiable in psychiatric terms. The standard psychiatric classification (usually known as DSM-III) has a section for Dissociative Disorders (and also for Hysterical Neuroses, Dissociative Type), which includes psychogenic amnesia, psychogenic fugue, multiple personality,

13

depersonalization disorder (or neurosis) and atypical dissociative disorder. Similarly with possession, which, as Crabtree (1988) has argued so eloquently and with a wealth of detail, is by no means dead today, and may have to be much more seriously and intensively investigated at some point. But in this book we are not concerned with any of these. We are strictly within the bounds of the normal variations which may be found in anyone.

Similarly, in this book we are not much concerned with hypnosis, but it is a fact that the unconscious was explored by hypnotists (mesmerists, magnetizers, and others) for 150 or so before psychotherapy as we know it came on the scene.

As has been pointed out by Carlson (1986), the concept of the unconscious had to come first, and the concept of dual personality actually came before the idea of subpersonalities considered as something within the normal range of variation for human beings. We can even pinpoint a year, 1784, when the idea of the unconscious came into the sphere of psychology, through the work of the Comte de Puységur (Chertok and de Saussure 1979). At the start of the nineteenth century, the philosopher Herbart (with whose work Freud was well acquainted) was already talking about the psychology of internal conflict, the unconscious, and repression.

All through the nineteenth century what Henri Ellenberger calls the first dynamic psychiatry was growing up. In this body of work

a new model of the human mind was evolved. It was based on the duality of conscious and unconscious psychism. Later, it was modified to the form of a cluster of subpersonalities underlying the conscious personality. . . . In the latter part of the nineteenth century the concepts of the autonomous activity of split fragments of personality and of the mythopoetic function of the unconscious arose.

(Ellenberger 1970: 111)

We shall see in Chapter 8 how the mythopoetic function is very central to what we are talking about in this book. So it is worth while to take notice of what Ellenberger says about this important aspect of the unconscious and its working.

The *mythopoetic* function (a term apparently coined by Myers)
is a 'middle region' of the subliminal self where a strange
fabrication of inner romances perpetually goes on. Its great
explorer was Flournoy with his research on Helen Smith and
other mediums. In this conception the unconscious seems to
be continually concerned with creating fictions and myths,
which sometimes remain unconscious or appear only in
dreams. Sometimes they take the form of daydreams that
evolve spontaneously in the background of the subject's mind
(a fact hinted at by Charcot). Sometimes, these functions are
acted out in the form of somnambulism, hypnosis, possession,
medium's trance, mythomania, or certain delusions.
Sometimes the mythopoetic functions express themselves
organically, and this suggests one of the possible concepts of
hysteria. It is surprising, however, to see that the notion of the
mythopoetic function of the unconscious, which seemed so
promising, was not more fully investigated.

(Ellenberger 1970: 318)

It is hoped that the present work will help to redress this injustice,
and show how important the mythopoetic function is, and how it
can be an enrichment to the whole way in which we conceive of the
normal personality, as Mary Watkins (1986) more than anyone else
has shown.

The first psychologist I can find who dealt with the idea in a way
which seems to throw off the historical distortions was William
James, but he really said very little about exactly where
subpersonalities came from or how they worked. He started
working on his great book *The Principles of Psychology* in about 1878,
and it was published in 1890. In it he talked about social selves, and
reckoned that people had many social selves, each of which could
be called up in an appropriate situation.

Starting with the discoveries of Richet and Taine, the
unconscious became an active part of the personality as well
as a reservoir of the emotions and of forgotten or repressed
facts. Tarde, in particular, showed that the unconscious loses
none of its dynamism and that the past experiences of a child
may in some cases influence his actions in adult life. We have

here a very different conception of the unconscious, one
which is remarkably close to the Freudian concept.

(Chertok and de Saussure 1979: 168)

All through the 1890s Charcot and Janet and their colleagues were
working on the problems of hysteria, and linking them with the
phenomena of hypnosis. They talked about secondary personalities, dissociated from the primary personality, but saw this as
something definitely in the area of the abnormal.

In 1892 the famous psychologist Binet published a book on
alterations in personality in which he says:

One observes that in a large number of people, placed in the
most diverse conditions, the normal unity of consciousness is
disintegrated. Several distinct consciousnesses arise, each of
which may have perceptions, a memory, and even a moral
character, of its own. . . . Consequently, the limits of our
personal and conscious memory are no more absolute limits
than are those of our present consciousness. Beyond these
lines there are memories, just as there are perceptions and
reasoning processes, and what we know about ourselves is but
a part, perhaps a very small part, of what we are.

(Binet 1892: 243)

Ribot published a book in 1895 which explicitly denied the
existence of a superordinate self and postulated the existence of
multiple selves.

In 1897 J. M. Baldwin published the first social psychology text,
and in it gave some credence to the possibility of multiple selves,
based on social conditioning. In the field of philosophy, too, there
was an interest at this time, and one of the most eloquent
statements was made by the British Hegelian William Wallace,
when he said: 'We have hardly formed our resolve when we regret
it: the voices of our other selves, of that manifold pack of half-
formed personalities within us, none of which we dare honestly
disown, are raised in protest against the usurping monarchy of our
overt resolve' (Wallace 1898: 109).

And so we come into the early years of the present century.
In 1904 Sidis and Goodhart came out as saying the multiple

personality was just an exaggerated expression of something which was actually quite normal in the human personality. Different selves are elicited by different situations.

H. F. Ellenberger (1970), in his book *The Discovery of the Unconscious*, draws attention to the upsurge during the early part of this century of a literature concerned with subtler descriptions of the many facets of human personality, and their interplay. He quotes in particular Marcel Proust, who maintained that the personality can be 'composed of many little egos, distinct though side by side'. Ellenberger feels that hypnotism provided the first model of the human mind as a double ego, and in discussing the multiple personality he recommends the notion that the personality is 'like a matrix from which whole sets of sub-personalities could emerge and differentiate themselves'. He discusses also the important question of what can happen once we give names to certain phenomena; subpersonalities may develop spontaneously, but they may also be influenced by suggestion, exaggerated by investigators and established more firmly through personification. Ellenberger quotes Janet's observation that 'once baptized the unconscious personality is more clear and definite; it shows its psychological traits more clearly'.

Similarly, Decker (1986) makes the point about Proust and others of this time:

> These authors [Pirandello, Proust, Joyce, Woolf] share an interest in the unconscious in its many manifestations, no longer primarily emphasizing the obvious aspects of unconscious phenomena as seen in hypnotism and dual personality. They have left the stark dichotomies of awake vs. hypnotized, or personality A vs. personality B. They are dealing with *multiplicity* in personality rather than the flagrant *multiple* personality, yet with a recognition that illness and bizarreness can be present in the more muted manifestation. Proust, for instance, mentions only one clear-cut case of dual personality. He was interested instead in the many facets of personality in all of us. Personality changes from moment to moment, depending on place, time, and our companions. There is no one 'real' ego, but rather a succession of egos, or the alternating dominance of different aspects of the ego.

17

Virginia Woolf in The Waves (1931) has her character
Bernard say: 'I am not one person: I am many people.'
(Decker 1986: 35)

These literary pursuits were paralleled by work in psychology and
psychiatry. Jung was talking about the complexes as early as 1908,
and had much more to say about them from his experiments with
word association. Freud was very interested in this work, but did
not come up with his division into the it, the I, and the over-I until
the 1920s. I would describe the over-I (superego) as a complex,
and as a typical subpersonality.

In 1924 the concept had been taken into psychiatry by Bleuler,
who said in his *Textbook of Psychiatry:* 'the complexes can actually
acquire sub-personalities with some sort of independence of the
psyche'. But psychiatry apparently did not retain this insight, and
in today's texts no such admission is found.

In 1936 Kurt Lewin published his book *Topological Psychology*, in
which he described how regions of the personality could become
relatively independent. He said:

The degree of dynamical connectedness of the different parts
of the person can be nearly equal within the whole region of
the person, or certain regions can separate themselves to an
especially high degree from the others and develop relatively
independently. This can be observed in the normal person
and it seems to be important for certain mental diseases.

This is a most important insight, but it was never followed up in
psychology generally, in spite of the great respect in which Lewin
was held.

In the 1940s Melanie Klein started talking about internal
objects as being highly important in the understanding of infantile
fantasies. And this led on to the distinction which the object
relations school developed between the real or true self, and the
false self or selves. We shall be taking this most seriously in Chapter
7.

Since then there has been a burgeoning quantity of different
applications of this general idea, all of which are dealt with in
detail in later pages. All we wanted to do here was to outline in a
brief way the early steps in the process.

POLITICAL IMPLICATIONS

Not only is a theory of subpersonalities a concept which is important for psychology and psychotherapy: it is also one which is crucial for political theory. Many theories of politics, both conservative and radical, say that the person is conditioned early into conformity with society. The pressures of society are so great, they say, that the person is bludgeoned willy-nilly into being the kind of personality which a particular society needs. It is difficult, with all such theories, to see any place for radical social change.

But if there are subpersonalities, it may be the case that some of them are conditioned by society, and some are resistant to such conditioning; just as in a family three children may be conformists, and the fourth may be a rebel. The less conditioned, or differently conditioned, subpersonalities may lie beneath the surface waiting, as it were, for their chance; and when the situation changes, these other subpersonalities may come to the surface and take over.

This would parallel the situation in biology where geneticists say that there are dominant genes and recessive genes. The dominant genes have their way in normal circumstances; but if the environment changes substantially, the recessive genes may come into play and take their turn on stage. This is the concept of the understudy, the player who comes on in place of the main actor when that body goes sick or absent. We all have egos and we all have understudies – recessive parts of ourselves which are only awaiting a chance to have their way.

This means that in a social revolution people can change radically in a short space of time, adapting to the new circumstances and helping to create them. Without some such concept it is hard to account for the remarkable phenomena of change in emergencies, when a whole different side of people may come out. But with such a concept these things become much easier to understand.

A WARNING

There is one warning which should be given here, however, and that is that I do not believe that subpersonalities should be understood as taking away the responsibility of the social person.

There have been attempts to say that if the idea of subpersonalities holds water, then it could be said that if one subpersonality committed a crime, another subpersonality could not be held responsible. This has actually been tried.

John Watkins is a hypnotherapist with a great interest in subpersonalities, which he calls ego states, and he has described his work in a chapter in Corsini (1981), as well as in an excellent book called *The Therapeutic Self* (1978). He is often used as an expert in legal cases where there is a defence of diminished responsibility due to the presence of a 'second personality' or something of that kind. (There was a case like this in the newspaper at the time this chapter was being written, about a man on a Greek island who the local police said had a Jekyll and Hyde personality.) In one paper (Watkins 1976) he goes into the Patty Hearst case; in another (Watkins 1978a) he goes into the case of 'Patricia W'; and in a third (Watkins 1984) he deals with the case of the Los Angeles 'Hillside Strangler'. In each case the defence lawyers tried to argue that the person in the dock was in effect not the person who committed the crime – even if they happened to share the same physical body. And in each case Watkins argued that there were in effect two different personalities involved, one guilty and one innocent; and that the one in the dock was the innocent one. There would be no way of punishing the guilty one without, by the same token and at the same time, punishing the innocent one. But in each case the court refused to accept this argument.

There is of course an important difference between subpersonalities and multiple personality, based on the substantially higher barriers and divisions present in the latter – a qualitative difference of dissociation. But even in cases of true multiple personality, it seems to me that it would be wrong to diminish the responsibility of the social person who is visible to all, or the legal person who signs cheques, owns property, enters into contracts, and so forth. In that sense the courts were right.

So the warning is: don't run away with the idea that the concept of subpersonalities can be used to diminish any of our human responsibility for all of our actions, no matter how partial or one-sided or inadequate the impulse behind it may be.

ORIGINS

This is a book which goes into the whole story of subpersonalities, defined as permanent or semi-permanent autonomous or semi-autonomous regions of the personality: it tells of where they come from, how they work, how they can be dealt with and transformed, and how ultimately they can be transcended.

On the question of where they come from, this seems a good place to outline the whole set of sources which we shall be looking at in the rest of the book. There are at least these six of these.

Roles Different roles bring out different subpersonalities, as William James (1890) urged long ago. So do different social frames, as Goffman (1959) has outlined. Even children can play different roles at home and at school, for example. This is probably the aspect which needs least arguing: it is quite obvious in the work of Lewin (1936) and Allport (1937) and of psychologists and sociologists before and since. Merton (1957) has written very well about the social deformation which roles impose on the person, and how 'trained incapacity' can be positively crippling. McCall and Simmons (1966) show how role-identities can cluster into subpatterns and that 'these clusters may themselves be linked more or less closely with other clusters or may be quite rigidly "compartmentalized" or dissociated from others'.

Internal conflicts Two or more sides arguing within us (on the one hand I want to – but on the other hand . . .) may become repetitive enough and frequent and vivid enough to require an identity each before they can be worked out. Gestalt therapy (Fagan and Shepherd 1970) and psychodrama (Greenberg 1974) are full of this. Most of the people who have written about subpersonalities under various names and titles make use of this category. Many examples are collected together in the excellent little book by O'Connor (1971), and McKellar (1979) has a good discussion of Jekyll and Hyde. This again is familiar to us all. Also under this heading come those times when our bodies, or parts of our bodies, seem to act as if they were our antagonists. They, too, can be regarded as subpersonalities with motives of their own, as we shall see in more detail later.

Fantasy images We may identify with a hero or heroine, or with an admired group, and take on their characteristics. For example, in the 1970s I frequently came across hippie and revolutionary subpersonalities in the people I was working with. Klapp (1969) has an excellent discussion of how heroes and celebrities are used in a search for identity. These fantasy images may come from the past or future, as well as from the present. Markus and Nurius (1987) have shown that the idea of 'possible selves' can actually help us in the practical question of understanding and explaining people's motivations and orientations toward the future. Watkins (1978) has shown how the psychotherapist can deliberately set up within himself or herself a fantasy image of the client, so as to be able to tune in to the client better; this is the deliberate setting up of a subpersonality for the purpose of developing resonance with the client. Mahrer (1983) suggests something similar. Actors of the 'method' school work by setting up within themselves a subpersonality corresponding to the character they are playing. Most of the time, of course, it is not done in this deliberate way, but rather as an attempt to live up to some ideal, which in this case takes the form of an individual.

The personal unconscious The complexes described by Jung (Frey-Rohn 1974) can be worked with through the Jungian technique of 'active imagination', as has been well described by Johnson (1986). The internal objects described by Guntrip, Fairbairn, Winnicott, and others come out as subpersonalities, as well as Berne's Parent, Adult, and Child ego states in Transactional Analysis. Fritz Perls introduced his ideas of split polarities within the person, and his very free use of the empty chair to work with such entities. The Voice Dialogue approach of Stone and Winkelman (1985) has taken this further. All these seem to derive from early experiences in the family, although as Grof (1985), Lake (1966), and Laing (1982) have pointed out, some of the traumas which can lead to the violent defence of splitting can happen at or before birth. Janov and Holden (1977) have tried to give a theoretical account of this linked to physiology.

The cultural unconscious This is where the Patripsych comes from, as Southgate and Randall (1978) have described – the 'internal constellation of patriarchal patterns'. They go on to explain that 'By this we mean all the attitudes, ideas and feelings, usually compulsive and unconscious, that develop in relation to authority and control . . . . In general, men tend to internalise mastery and control. In general, women tend to internalise self-effacement and morbid dependency.' This is similar to what Steiner *et al.* (1975)

have called the Pig Parent – an internalized form of cultural oppression. It is the voice within us which says that hierarchy is the only right way of organizing, and patriarchy the truest form of hierarchy. It has not been much written about, but I believe it is most important, and requires a great deal more attention, particularly in relation to the political scene.

The collective unconscious If Jung (1968) is right, this is where the archetypes come from, and the Shadow often seems to emerge as one of the subpersonalities. Anima figures are also quite common. So it seems that we should allow this as one of the sources. The Jungians, in fact, turn out to provide some of the most fertile soil for the study of subpersonalities, and have tilled it more than most. Another important group who have worked in this area have been the practitioners of psychosynthesis (Whitmore and Hardy 1988), from whom I first heard the idea of subpersonalities.

So this book tries to give the origins in this way, and also to cover many other areas of work. It shows how in literature and life we are already familiar with this notion, how important it is for personality theory, and how all the great classic psychotherapists have had perforce to resort to some such construct.

AN EXAMPLE

Carl Rogers was known as a great psychotherapist who employed no techniques, and who had very little in the way of theory about internal dynamics. But right at the end of his life even he was forced, by the sheer logic of his own work, to adopt the use of subpersonalities. In a session for which we have the complete audio transcript, because it was done as a public demonstration at a conference, he talked with a thirty-five-year-old woman about her fear of marriage and children, and her fears about ageing. At one point in the interview, she talks about amateur dramatics, and how she loves playing the naughty little girl. 'And whenever I want to get away with something or I want something, I would play that naughty little girl.' The interview then goes on to other things, including a feeling, over the past eighteen months, of walking into darkness; about her feelings of loneliness, and the need to relate to someone. And then this happens:

CARL: Somebody you can relate to. And I guess that – this may seem like a silly idea, but – I wish that one of those friends could be that naughty little girl. I don't know whether that makes any sense to you or not, but if that kind of sprightly, naughty little girl that lives inside could accompany you from the light into the dark – as I say, that may not make any sense to you at all.

JAN: [*in a puzzled voice*] Can you elaborate on that a little more for me?

CARL: Simply that maybe one of your best friends is the you that you hide inside, the fearful little girl, the naughty little girl, the real you that doesn't come out very much in the open.

JAN: [*Pause*] And I must admit – what you have just said, and looking at it in retrospect – I've lost a lot of that naughty little girl. In fact, over the last eighteen months, that naughty little girl has disappeared.

At this point something shifted in the interview, and it was as if both parties felt an enormous sense of relief. This was a good moment in therapy – one of those rare good moments which mean such a lot and make such a difference. A minute or two later, after some exchanges involving a good deal of laughter, we get this:

CARL: I think that's a very significant question you're asking yourself. If you were a better friend of the little girl inside you, would that make you less fearful of the risk of marriage? I feel badly that she's been missing for the last eighteen months, I really do.

JAN: [*Pause*] You're so right. You've really hit the nail on the head.

The interview ends soon after that, and Rogers makes some theoretical comments on his way of working, which he says has become more intuitive, and open to the possibility of altered states of consciousness. Right at the end of the chapter, he says this:

The next morning Jan told me that the interchange about the 'naughty little girl' had initiated a self-searching. She realized that not only was the naughty little girl missing, but several other parts of her self had also disappeared during the past eighteen months. 'I realize that to face life as a whole person, I need to find those missing parts of me.' She said that for her the interview had proved to be a 'soul-shaking experience'. The process that started in the interview appears to be continuing in her.

(Rogers 1986: 208)

This is a good example of how the notion of subpersonalities can be continually rediscovered, even by therapists who have no such concept in their theoretical system. In this book we shall be examining many aspects of this matter, and we shall go deeply into the psychotherapeutic use of the idea, and deal with all the practical advantages and difficulties involved in using it when helping people change. And we shall go on to show how we go beyond subpersonalities and the false self, to the real self, the higher self and the soul.

Chapter Two

SUBPERSONALITIES IN EVERYDAY LIFE

It is a common experience to find that a child is an angel at home and a devil at school, or a devil at home and an angel at school. Even at such early ages, it is possible for one role to be so distinct from another that the two become contrasted, even opposite.

It is a common experience for a man to be a bully at work and meek at home, or meek at work and a bully at home. The roles again are different, and call forth different and perhaps contrasting qualities within the person.

Few of us are the same when talking to our bank manager and when talking to our children.

It is a common experience to hear someone talking over the telephone in a certain voice, and when coming off the phone to talk to someone in the room in a quite different voice. Some people actually have a 'telephone voice' which they cultivate; others do it without thinking, quite without any intention of changing their voice at all.

It is well known that people often become much more aggressive when they are behind the wheel of a car. The role, very masculine as it normally is, brings out the inner aggression which might normally be hidden or suppressed or diverted.

In novels, we are given many ordinary experiences in the form of fiction, as for example in *Les Liaisons Dangereuses* by Choderlos de Laclos, published in 1782:

> After supper, by turns childish and sensible, crazy and serious, sometimes as sexy as I pleased, I enjoyed thinking of him as a sultan in the middle of his harem, where I was by turns each of his different favourites. In fact, his repeated overtures,

although always sent to the same woman, seemed each time to be received by a new mistress.

This playful sense of being able to move from one personality to another is not uncommon in our experience. But of course it can be much more serious than that.

CONFLICTS

All these things are regularly discovered and rediscovered, as for example this experience suggests:

> It was during a time of painful conflict that I first began to experience myself as more than one. It was as though I sat in the midst of many selves. Some urged me down one path and some another. Each presented a different claim and no self gave another self an opportunity to be fully heard. In quiet meeting with friends I would often be made aware of the conflicting voices within. When it was my turn to join in the talk or initiate conversation, I would miss the opportunity. I would think, 'I will say this,' and another self would intrude and have a very different subject for which it demanded attention. And when I assented to speak for it there pushed to the fore still another self with another claim. While I listened to one and then the other, the conversation outside me went on to other things, and none of my selves found a spokesman in me. To others I seemed sometimes far removed, and it was true. I had been called away to attend to an inner clamour – the voices of my own many selves.
>
> (O'Connor 1971: 3)

This is the testimony of an ordinary person. And we are talking here of something very simple and basic, which children are quite capable of understanding and carrying out. A good example is given by the following extract:

> Though the nine-year-old girl may be queen of a planet in the distant future of space travel, this space-queen's problems are, to the observing adult, remarkably like those of the 'English queen' of a month ago, and all these royal problems are, in

27

turn, remarkably reminiscent of the child's present tensions and problems, the dynamic conflicts which dominate her present family life and 'real' social life. There is a remarkable ability – which we tend to take for granted until we recall the case of the psychotic – to keep a variety of conscious and closely interrelated lives entirely unconfused.

(Fingarette 1963: 191)

A psychologist worthy of the name may say something very similar from his own point of view, as we see in the example which follows:

> Perhaps it is easiest to introduce the idea of 'self as a community of selves' by referring to the smallest form of community, namely a community of two persons. Most of us have probably, at some time, found ourselves talking or acting as if we were two people rather than one. We talk sometimes of being in 'two minds' about something, part of you wanting to do one thing and part wanting to do something else. Quite often we hear people talk of having to 'battle' with themselves, as if one aspect of themselves was in conflict with another.

(Mair 1977: 130)

Miller Mair goes on to speak of how this sort of thing can be used in psychotherapy, and we shall be coming to that in later chapters. But he adds in the everyday terms which are occupying us here:

> The notion of oneself as a 'community of selves' can readily be elaborated further by some people to incorporate three, four or any other number of 'selves'. Some of these 'selves' will be found to persist and others may be more transitory, some will be 'isolates' and others will work in 'teams', some will 'appear' in many circumstances and others only on a few special kinds of occasions, some will be 'more powerful' and others will give way to them. Sometimes, people can offer and use quite elaborated accounts of their 'community of selves'.

(Mair 1977: 131)

This immediately gives us a common-sense perspective for looking at these matters. But how practical are they?

28

SOCIAL ROLES

Such examples have been studied in role theory. A classic here was the investigation by Lieberman (1956), where attitudes towards union and management were obtained from 2,354 rank-and-file workers in a factory. During the ensuing year, many workers changed roles, some becoming foremen and some becoming shop stewards for the union. The new foremen changed their attitudes so as to become more favourable towards management and more critical of the union; the new shop stewards changed their attitudes also, so as to become more favourable towards the union and more critical of management. These attitude changes occurred soon after the role changes, and within three years the two groups of men had developed almost diametrically opposite attitudes. It happened, two years later, that fewer foremen were needed in the plant, so that eight of them were demoted to their former positions. These eight were therefore compared with twelve other foremen who continued in that role, and it was found that their attitudes had changed back to what they were originally. It is quite clear that attitudes followed role enactment in just the way in which role theory would predict.

What we are saying, then, is that we are all very familiar with the idea that people can behave very differently in different circumstances. This has been shown more objectively in the work of Kenneth Gergen, who reported some of his research in *Psychology Today* for May 1972. His experiments show very clearly that we do modify our self-presentation, and also the way we actually see and experience ourselves, with different people in different situations. We are often quite unaware of what we are doing, and it feels to us as though we are being sincere and retaining our integrity all the way through. But as Gergen (1972) concludes: 'The individual has many potential selves. He carries with him the capacity to define himself as warm or cold, dominant or submissive, sexy or plain. The social conditions around him help determine which of these options are evoked.'

This has also been brought out in the work of Goffman (1959) on impression management. He shows with a wealth of example how we all create impressions of ourselves, and also try to create different impressions on different people.

A specific illustration may be cited from Shetland Isle. When a neighbour dropped in to have a cup of tea, he would ordinarily wear at least a hint of an expectant warm smile as he passed through the door into the cottage. Since lack of physical obstructions outside the cottage and lack of light within it usually made it possible to observe the visitor unobserved as he approached the house, islanders sometimes took pleasure in watching the visitor drop whatever expression he was manifesting and replace it with a sociable one just before reaching the door. However, some visitors, in appreciating that this examination was occurring, would blindly adopt a social face a long distance from the house, thus ensuring the projection of a constant image.

(Goffman 1959: 8)

These social faces are of course very common and may be quite transient. What interests us more, in this book, is the more long-lasting face which we may take into numerous situations. Such subpersonalities can sometimes be extraordinarily powerful. In the case of transvestites, for example, the contrasex personality is often very different from the original personality, and the fact that each has a different name helps in the process of differentiation.

Also very powerful, however, may be the absence of a necessary subpersonality at the right time. Lack of an appropriate sub-personality or being unable to get out of an unsuitable subpersonality can be very serious at times.

There are cases, particularly in England, where people have burned to death in their homes, even though they could have escaped. Their bodies were found just inside the unlocked front door. But they were naked. Decent people never appear naked in front of anyone but their closest intimates, much less strangers like firefighters or crowds. 'Better to hope for rescue, even against all evidence of your senses, than be shamed!' seem to have been the philosophy of whatever identity states last inhabited their bodies. Identity states can kill.

(Tart 1986: 128)

As mentioned in the last chapter, identity states are what we would call subpersonalities. It can be fatal to get locked into the wrong identity state and be unable to escape from it.

IDENTITY PROBLEMS

One of the most commonly noticeable aspects of subpersonalities has been well described by Middlebrook (1974), who quotes the comments of a student she calls Anne:

> There are many facets and sides of Anne. In fact, there are many Annes that different people interacting with her encounter. She is a hippie chick, a conscientious student, a snotty spoiled brat, an insecure little girl, and so on. 'There are so many different me's that I am confused about who I really am. It seems that I change according to who I'm with: My parents think I'm really hard-working and dedicated to getting good grades and doing well. My friends think I'm a real party girl. And I don't know who I think I am.'

This again is a common enough experience. We can all put it down to adolescent identity problems. Of course, adolescence is a vague period of time – it is hard to know when it has finally ended; maybe it doesn't end at all for some people.

Consider, for example, this quotation from a marvellous book by Carl Rogers and Barry Stevens (1967). Barry Stevens is talking:

> In the beginning, I was one person, knowing nothing but my own experience. Then I was told things, and I became two people: the little girl who said how terrible it was that the boys had a fire going in the lot next door where they were roasting apples (which was what the women said) – and the little girl who, when the boys were called by their mothers to go to the store, ran out and tended the fire and the apples and loved doing it. So then there were two of I. One I always doing something that the other I disapproved of. Or other I said what I disapproved of. All this argument in me so much ...
> The most important thing is to have a career. The most important thing is to get married. The hell with everyone. Be nice to everyone. The most important thing is sex. The most important thing is to have money in the bank. The most

31

important thing is to have everyone like you. The most important thing is to dress well. The most important thing is to be sophisticated and say what you don't mean and don't let anyone know what you feel. The most important thing is to be ahead of everyone else. The most important thing is a black seal coat and china and silver. The most important thing is to be clean. The most important thing is to pay your debts. The most important thing is not to be taken in by anyone else. The most important thing is to love your parents . . . Suddenly: 'What am I doing?' 'Am I to go through life playing the clown?' 'What am I doing, going to parties that I don't enjoy?' 'What am I doing, being with people who bore me?' 'Why am I so hollow and the hollowness filled with emptiness?' A shell. How has this shell grown around me? . . . I refuses to play the clown any more. Which I is that? 'She used to be fun, but now she thinks too much about herself.' I lets friends drop away. Which I is that? 'She's being too much by herself. That's bad. She's losing her mind.' Which mind?

Is this still the voice of the adolescent? Or is is not rather the voice of someone seriously and touchingly concerned by the manyness of the I, and by the falseness of the I, in a much more adult and existential way?

So we are not speaking here merely of different roles which we may take up; we are also talking of internal conflicts which are giving us trouble in one way or another. One woman in a research group I led found that she had two subpersonalities called Can't Cope and Bill the Gaoler. Can't Cope wouldn't let her wash up the dishes, and Bill the Gaoler wouldn't let her go out of the house without washing up the dishes. So she wandered around the house, not being able to wash up the dishes and not being able to go out either.

DREAM CHARACTERS

The characters who appear in our dreams (and the things too, as Gestalt therapy shows, but let us not bother with that at the moment) are of the nature of subpersonalities. We create them, and they perform on our stage. The realization that they belong to us in this way goes back a long time. At the beginning of the nineteenth century the German writer Johann Christian Reil became interested in this question:

> Reil . . . quotes among others a dream reported by Lichtenberg, a German writer, who dreamed that he was relating a sad but true story to someone when a third person interrupted him to remind him of an important point, which he, Lichtenberg, had forgotten. 'Why did his fantasy', asked Reil, 'create a third person who surprised him and made him feel ashamed, how can the ego divide itself into persons who, out of himself, produce things of which he is not aware that they were in him, and surprise him as outside wisdom?'.
>
> (Ellenberger 1970: 127-8)

This early questioning was followed up in the rest of the century by the magnetizers and hypnotists, as Ellenberger has expounded at length, and today it is widely accepted. Sometimes the importance of these dream characters is more obvious to other people than it is to us ourselves. Ann Faraday (1974), in reporting her work on dreams in therapeutic settings, also, as in the example above, uses a method of actually naming the subpersonalities:

> Bonime also talks about the advantages of collecting a personal glossary for each patient, which is a kind of shorthand language for describing personality units in symbolic form . . . . For instance, whenever Joseph's wife finds her husband procrastinating over a decision, she asks, 'Is it really a difficult decision requiring lots of thought, or is it old "Slowcoach" up to his tricks again?' . . . . In my own case, when I refuse help with some task or criticise people for not standing on their own two feet, I often get asked, 'is that Ann or the "Ray of White Light" talking?', a question which has often brought me to my senses and put me in touch with my real feelings.

Once a subpersonality has been named, it becomes easier to use it in this kind of way, as a method of raising awareness of what is going on internally.

RELATIONSHIPS

Recognizing subpersonalities is also very useful in our interactions with other people. For example, when we criticize someone, they very often find it hard to take, because they take it personally. But once we think and speak in terms of subpersonalities, the process is much easier. 'I think your martyr is trying to make me feel guilty. Do you agree?' We have stopped saying that the whole person is bad – now we are drawing attention to a problem for us that may also turn out to be a problem for the person themselves. It is more straight and more accurate to speak in this way.

> We are responsible for our subpersonalities, just as we're responsible for our children, our pets and our car. We certainly need to see that they don't cause trouble to ourselves or to others. But we are not them. People can use the concept of subpersonalities very effectively when they're dealing with problems in interpersonal relationships – especially in couples.
>
> (Vargiu 1974)

This latter point has been taken up by others, and especially by Elizabeth O'Connor..She has a great deal to say about how the idea of subpersonalities (which she calls 'selves' or 'I's') can help us in every relationship we may have in our lives:

> If I say, 'I am jealous', it describes the whole of me, and I am overwhelmed by its implications. The completeness of the statement makes me feel contemptuous of myself. It is little wonder that I fear letting another know when my own identity with the feeling is such that it describes the totality of who I am. But suppose that each of us understood the multiplicity of his life. What if it were such common knowledge that only an ignorant person would ever be heard to say, 'Well, if he is that way, I want nothing to do with him,' as though the 'way' of a person could be known just because one of his selves was glimpsed for a moment.
> If I respect the plurality in myself, and no longer see my jealous self as the whole of me, then I have gained the distance I need to observe it, listen to it, and let it acquaint

me with a piece of my own lost history. In this way I come into possession of more of myself and extend my own inner kingdom.

(O'Connor 1971)

This seems extremely useful as a general strategy, and it gives a much better handle by which to grasp many social situations. If I can say, 'Yes, part of me does feel that, but only part of me', that does justice to the fact that I do feel it, but does not overwhelm me by suggesting that that is *all* that I feel.

MATURITY

And this bespeaks maturity. Jane Loevinger (1976) has done a long and hard series of investigations into the maturing of the ego, and has found that at the highest levels of development there arises the ability to recognize and face one's own internal conflicts. To deny any internal conflicts bespeaks a lower level of maturity.

Mary Watkins (1986) has developed this idea further, as we shall see in Chapter 5. Most psychologists assume that, no matter how many subpersonalities we find, ultimately all has to be reduced to one. This is the most general conception of mental health. But Watkins, and her mentor James Hillman, ask the question 'Why?' Would it not make more sense to live with multiplicity, to recognize more than one centre within ourselves? Hillman suggests that this quarrel is rather like the quarrel between monotheism and polytheism. Psychology, he says, is secretly monotheistic, and wants everything to be neatly hierarchical or bureaucratic. But could we not envisage a polytheistic psychology, which admitted that there could be many gods and goddesses, many egos, many identities, many selves

We conceive our psychological nature to be naturally divided into portions and phases, a composition of earlier and later historical levels, various zones and developmental strata, many complexes and archetypal persons. We are no longer single beings in the image of a single God, but are always constituted of multiple parts: impish child, hero or heroine, supervising authority, asocial psychopath, and so on. Because we have come to realize that each of us is normally a flux of figures, we

35

no longer need be menaced by the notion of multiple personality. I may see visions and hear voices; I may talk with them and they with each other without at all being insane.

(Hillman 1975: 24)

And in terms of everyday life, this is a reassuring thought for many of us. How often have people said, 'Talking to yourself – first sign of insanity', and put someone into a panic? It is true that at certain stages of senile dementia, talking to oneself may be the first sign of insanity, but for most of us it is a normal daily occurrence.

Nor need it be threatening to those of a monotheistic disposition. Hillman said in a later piece, to those who had criticized him for suggesting that there could be something like six characters in search of an author,

So I preferred Lopez [Pedraza's] formulation: 'The many contains the unity of the one without losing the possibilities of the many' . . . Here the one is not something apart and opposed to the many, leaving them as inchoate fragmented bits, but it appears as the unity of each thing, that it is as it is, with a name and a face.

(Hillman 1981: 131)

We shall return to this question of the one and the many in Chapter 10, where we shall go into it much more deeply. All we are trying to do here is to show that our everyday experience is very much concerned with subpersonalities already; it is just a matter of recognizing and allowing this fact.

ALTERED STATES OF CONSCIOUSNESS

This may be a good place to discuss the idea of altered states of consciousness. Usually these do not come within our scope, because they are too transient, but some of them may become so regular that they virtually bring into being a specific sub-personality. It was apparently the custom of the ancient Teutons to make any important decision twice, once drunk and once sober, thus getting the benefit of two different angles on the problem. This again suggests a regular and dependable contrast between the two states of consciousness.

36

More academically, Charles Tart (1975) has suggested that almost everyone has at least two altered states of consciousness – the dreaming state and the state between waking and sleeping. This latter has recently been dealt with very fully by Andreas Mavromatis (1987) who suggests at one point that it is a state in which it is particularly easy to work with extra-sensory perception and other activities connected with the paranormal. But in this kind of work, he suggests, it is a subpersonality which has the psychic ability, and which simply co-operates and communicates with the mental ego. He quotes LeShan (1973) as saying, 'The apparent triviality, tangentiality and superficiality of much of the sensitives' production is due to the data being translated from one system to another.'

In addition, many of us have experienced alcoholic intoxication, marijuana intoxication, and other drug states. Less common, but still quite frequent, experiences are those of meditation, so-called spirit possession, and hypnotic states. Tart argues that scientists studying meditation and similar topics may have to go into an altered state of consciousness themselves in order to get on the right wave-length, so to speak, to do the work adequately. He says:

A state-specific scientist, one able to enter a particular state of consciousness and carry out scientific work there, might find his own work somewhat incomprehensible when he is back in his ordinary state, or some other altered state, because of the phenomenon, for which experimental work is now accumulating, of state-specific memory. That is, not enough of his work would transfer to his ordinary state of consciousness to make it comprehensible to him in that state, even though it would make perfect sense when he was again in the altered state of consciousness in which he did his scientific work. To put it humorously, when the scientist returned home his wife might ask, 'What did you do in the laboratory today?' and he would honestly reply that he had no clear idea at all, but when he was there he knew that his work was progressing nicely!

(Tart 1975: 29)

This certainly suggests a laboratory subpersonality which has become distinct from the home subpersonality, not as a question of role but as a question of a specific state of consciousness.

What we have seen so far in this chapter is that we are talking about things which are in the experience of many, perhaps most of us. We are not talking about anything abnormal or unusual. This is the fascination of subpersonalities – we can see them every day, in various different circumstances, and once we are aware of them we can see them everywhere.

SUBPERSONALITIES IN THE MEDIA

Here we have a brief examination of the way in which the idea of subpersonalities has been used in literature, the cinema, and so on. It is such a familiar idea, and has been used so often, and goes so far back, that we are all quite conversant with how it has been spoken of and dealt with.

There is a long history of subpersonalities in literature, but it was not until the eighteenth century, as we saw in Chapter 1, that the idea of the unconscious really caught on and started to be understood. This was the first essential step, because until the division is made between conscious and unconscious, there is no place, as it were, for the subpersonalities to be located.

At first the fascination was with dual personalities, but as the nineteenth century went on, the emphasis changed more towards what we would call more normal subpersonalities. There is a very interesting discussion of all this in Decker (1986), whose view of Proust, Pirandello, Joyce, and Woolf we noticed in Chapter 1.

This whole area of the work of the novelist is of course very much open to examination from the point of view of subpersonalities. As soon as it is pointed out, this becomes obvious. In the nineteenth century this became part of the polypsychic view of the human personality:

Since the human mind is a cluster of subpersonalities, one can imagine that a great novelist, say Balzac, is able to give to many of them an identity, an occupation, personality traits, and to let them slowly develop in their own way. Speaking of the multitude of well-differentiated characters in Balzac's novels, Jules Romains (1958) supposed that every one of them was one of the writer's 'embryonic personalities', that is, they

38

were not unconscious or repressed personalities, but 'complete psychological systems, organic and individualized, each one having in itself all that is necessary to supply, at the contact of vital occurrences and social conditioning, a complete destiny of man or woman'. Jean Delay (1957) also thinks that the novelist has this power of developing latent subpersonalities in himself and of transforming them into literary characters. He also emphasized the process of the 'creation of a double': anyone keeping a personal diary tends to develop a dual personality that gradually emerges in that diary, so that a peculiar interpersonal relationship develops between the diarist and his fictitious second self. This second self may then at a given point come to life, so to speak, in the form of a literary character in whom the writer will bring out his secret problems, his 'poisons' (as did Goethe with *The Sorrows of Werther*, and André Gide with *André Walter*).

(Ellenberger 1970: 169-70)

Of course, things are not always so subtle. The media have always been more prone to use the more dramatic dual or multiple personality, which are clearly pathological states. Who has not heard of Jekyll and Hyde? There is a powerful image here, which has made such an impression on the public mind that one can refer to it with all kinds of people and be understood. Yet there a drug was involved – one of those magic drugs, to be sure, which are common in literature to help us to go along with the story – and we may feel immune from such things because no such drug has been given to us.

However, there is one drug with which many of us are familiar, and this can sometimes have strange effects. For example, in the film *City Lights*, Charlie Chaplin is befriended by a drunken millionaire, who takes him home and gives him the run of the house. In the morning, the millionaire wakes up, sees this dirty tramp spoiling his nice house, and kicks him out. Quite bemused, Charlie mooches off back to his usual haunts. That evening the millionaire is drunk again, sees Charlie, recognizes him as his pal, and takes him back again. In the morning, sober again, he rejects him again, and so on. In other words, there are two personalities involved here: the drunken millionaire, who treats Charlie in one way, and the sober millionaire who treats him quite differently. In one state of consciousness Charlie is a friend, in the other he is a nuisance. These repeated states of consciousness, with their consistency over time, certainly approach our definition of subpersonalities.

Similarly, in *The Moonstone*, by Wilkie Collins, the whole plot depends on the way in which a man behaves quite differently, but consistently so, when under the influence of a drug in this case, laudanum. This is an example of the phenomenon of state dependency, which we shall come back to again in the next chapter.

There are more subtle examples in drama. In *The Wild Duck*, by Henrik Ibsen, the character Dr Relling brings out the way in which unconscious malice can underlie the activities of someone who appears to others, and to himself, as a sentimentalist. In the powerful play *Brand*, Ibsen uses a rather similar character to bring out the way in which the apparent purity and single-mindedness of Pastor Brand (with his slogan of 'All or nothing!') conceals a real destructiveness which ultimately kills everyone he loves.

In the novel, the work of Dostoevsky shows us how powerful the idea of subpersonalities can be, when in *The Brothers Karamazov* the conflict between the good self and the evil self in Ivan Karamazov is brought out with stunning effect.

STEPPENWOLF

The best example for our purpose here is the novel *Steppenwolf*, where Hermann Hesse takes time off from his main narrative to write a complete 'Treatise on the Steppenwolf', and this was published separately in 1975 with some remarkable paintings by Jaroslav Bradac, based on his work for the film of *Steppenwolf*, which came out in 1975, directed by Fred Haines. In this treatise, Hesse explains that his hero Harry Haller, as well as being a human being, was also a wolf of the steppes.

> Clever men might argue the point whether he truly was a wolf, whether he had been changed, before birth perhaps, from a wolf into a human being, or had been given the soul of a wolf though born as a human being; or whether, on the other hand, this belief that he was a wolf was no more than fancy or a disease of his. It might, for example, be possible that in his

childhood he was wild or disobedient and disorderly, and that those who brought him up had declared a war of extinction against the beast in him.

Hesse is here playing with an idea which we shall be dealing with seriously in Chapter 7 – that perhaps the wolf is a defence, a result of some events in childhood which have resulted in this way of dealing with the world. He goes on to say that perhaps such internal animals are not uncommon, and that sometimes they may be benign rather than a constant problem. But for Harry this is not so.

> In him the man and the wolf did not not go the same way together, they did not help each other, but were in continual and deadly enmity. The one existed simply and solely to harm the other.

So far we are on rather similar ground to the other literary examples we have quoted, where for the most part the internal characters are malevolent and dangerous. Hesse goes on to say that when one did any action in the world, the other would criticize and laugh, or criticize and weep, and see through it. Any good action would be weakened and its enjoyment lost; any bad action would be wished away before it could be savoured. We shall see in Chapters 4 to 6 how common are these internal critics and saboteurs, and how they are dealt with in therapy. Hesse brings out how these internal characters actually do become visible to those outside. Speaking of Harry's friends, he says:

> Many loved him as a refined and clever and interesting man, and were horrified and disappointed when they had come upon the wolf in him. . . . There were those, however, who loved precisely the wolf in him, the free, the savage, the untamable, the dangerous and strong, and these found it peculiarly disappointing and deplorable when suddenly the wild and wicked wolf was also a man, and had hankerings after goodness and refinement, and wanted to hear Mozart, to read poetry and to cherish human ideals.

In spite of all this, there were times when Harry was quite happy with his two sides, and could manage them well enough. He could even sometimes combine the two, and get something quite special from their combination. But at other times he felt quite alone, as if his freedom was a death. He dreamed of suicide. Sometimes he thought that his fiftieth birthday would be the best time to do this.

But now Hesse becomes rather more sophisticated than the other writers we have mentioned so far: he says that the Steppenwolf Harry is still better off than the bourgeois who has no such conflict, but keeps to the middle way all the time. He does at least have some conception of the heights and the depths, the extremes of life. And he does have a sense of humour. But the only way to make all of this work for him instead of against him is to know himself better. ·

> To make all this come true, or perhaps to be able at last to dare the leap into the unknown, a Steppenwolf must once have a good look at himself. He must look deeply into the chaos of his own soul and plumb its depths . . . . Man and wolf would then be compelled to recognise one another without the masks of false feeling and to look one another straight in the eye.

This is much more the kind of approach we are using in this book, where we are arguing that the subpersonalities need to know one another in order that the whole person can develop.

But then Hesse makes his masterstroke. He shows how this story of a man and a wolf is a convenient fiction, a way of simplifying and making understandable what in reality is far from simple and not at all understandable. For in reality there is not a single human being, not the simplest or most primitive, who is so obvious as to be explained as the sum of two or three principal elements.

> Harry consists of a hundred or a thousand selves, not of two. His life oscillates, as everyone's does, not merely between two poles, such as the body and the spirit, the saint and the sinner, but between thousands, between innumerable poles.

Man, says, Hesse, is not capable of thought in any high degree, and even the most cultivated of men use absurd simplifications in their thought and understanding. People will do anything to make their life easier. And the idea that there is just one simple, single self is the crudest and most oversimplified assumption of all. Here Hesse is anticipating our argument (and that of James Hillman, who has also thought a great deal about these matters) later in this book that psychologists have for the most part been guilty of just such an oversimplification. He goes on to say:

> For it appears to be an inborn and imperative need for all men to regard the self as a unit. However often and however grievously this illusion is shattered, it always mends again.

This is an argument we shall meet and deal with in Chapter 10, when we have seen more of the many lines of evidence which all point in the direction of multiplicity. Hesse points to the reason for the more usual emphasis on unity, saying that bourgeois society regards this as so important, so needful, that it punishes any departure from it. There is such a need for order, for predictability, for reliable conduct, that anything else cannot be admitted or acknowledged.

> And if ever the suspicion of their manifold being dawns upon men of unusual power and of unusually delicate perceptions, so that, as all genius must, they break through the illusion of the unity of the personality and perceive that the self is made up of a bundle of selves, they have only to say so and at once the majority puts them under lock and key, calls science to aid, establishes schizophrenia and protects humanity from the necessity of hearing the cry of truth from the lips of these unfortunate persons.

Like many other people, Hesse here confuses schizophrenia with the quite different phenomenon of dissociated personality, which is much more likely to be the diagnosis here, but let that pass. Hesse goes on to say that in a drama or a novel it is the whole group or cast of characters which constitute the representation of a single human soul, not any one of them. When Faust says, 'Two souls, alas, dwell in my breast!' he has forgotten Mephisto and a whole crowd of other souls that he also has in his breast. The trouble with Harry is that he thinks that two is too many: in reality the problem is much more that two are not enough. Two can tear you apart;

many can enrich and sustain you. This again links with the argument which we shall try to sustain in later chapters.

> Imagine a garden with a hundred kinds of trees, a thousand kinds of flowers, a hundred kinds of fruit and vegetables. Suppose, then, the gardener of this garden knew no other distinction than between edible and inedible, nine-tenths of this garden would be useless to him. He would pull up the most enchanting flowers and hew down the noblest trees and even regard them with a loathing and envious eye. This is what the Steppenwolf does with the thousand flowers of his soul.

This treatise ends here, with a smile of forgiveness for the poor old Steppenwolf, who had to put up with all this analysis.

This is a very fine and sophisticated view of subpersonalities, and we can go along with most of it. If someone were to claim several different personalities, what might happen in medical terminology, as we mentioned earlier, is that they might get classified as 'multiple personality' or 'dissociated state'. But this would only be the case if the various personalities did not know about one another, and systematically had ways of hiding from one another. The Steppenwolf is not like this at all: the man knows about the wolf, and the wolf knows about the man, and there is no cut-off or hiding at all. This is the normal state with sub-personalities: they are or can be perfectly well aware of one another, though sometimes they may not care about one another enough to bother.

So with those misunderstandings out of the way, we can go along with Hesse's ideas pretty well intact. It is important not to dismiss this as merely fiction. Shorr gives this example:

> I once asked a patient to imagine a person other than himself if he were to look in a mirror. He answered that he saw a werewolf. As he continued, he realised the meaning of what he imagined seeing: the werewolf was the despised image that he didn't want the world to know about.
>
> (Shorr 1983: 265)

There is much more in literature, as McKellar (1979) makes clear,

44

referring to stories by Melville, Poe, and others. Many more examples are given in Hawthorn (1983) and in the unreadable *Doubles* by Karl Miller (1987).

Chapter Three

BEGINNING TO INVESTIGATE

For about three years in the early 1970s I was exploring, in a rather on-and-off manner, my own subpersonalities. It started off from two or three experiences in Gestalt therapy, and some research work I was doing on roles, reference groups, situations, and social frames. And my first step was to write down, over a period of two or three months, all the separate aspects of myself I could discover. For example, No. 1 was 'Enthusiastic project-doer; intense absorption for short period. Very sensitive in this phase, but very selectively.'

After a certain point, I didn't seem to be adding any more. And one day it suddenly occurred to me that these were aspects, rather than personalities. Some of them could be grouped together to make personalities. At first I grouped them together into five personalities, and then one of them seemed to split more naturally into two, to make six in all. I gave each one of them a name, which at first was quite arbitrary, having to do with how they had appeared; but later I gave each one a more explicit name, making it clearer to me what function it was performing.

Then I took an LSD trip (perhaps more common then than now, but in any case something familiar to me – I regarded myself as something of an astronaut of inner space), with the explicit object of getting into each of these personalities in turn, and asking the same eleven questions of each of them. This was an extremely useful exercise, which made a number of things very much clearer to me, and made me feel that here was something quite powerful, which could be pushed quite a long way in terms of self-understanding and self-acceptance.

MY OWN RESEARCH

The next step was to ask the question, if this works for me, does it work for anyone else? So in 1974 I got together fourteen people who wanted to explore this thing with me, and we held six meetings (four evenings and two whole days) for the purpose. I was already using the new-paradigm model of research, which was later worked out much more fully (Reason and Rowan 1981). At the first meeting, the mean number of subpersonalities reported was 6.5, with a range from zero to 18. I am inclined at the moment to feel that from 4 to 8 is the normal range, and that anything outside this bears traces of insufficient coverage at one end, or of duplication at the other. But it seems also that some people have a different character structure, which does not lend itself to talking in terms of subpersonalities. The people taking part were a mixture of sexes and ages, but all had in common that they had done a certain amount of group work involving self-examination and the acknowledgement of unconscious aspects of themselves.

At the second meeting, certain difficulties were reported, which seem worth mentioning. First, giving names to the sub-personalities aroused some kind of resistance; it seemed to some people a little too much like playing party games. There was something rather frivolous about it.

Second, for some people there did not seem to be any limit to possible personalities. There just seemed to be a proliferation of them. As Vargiu (1974) noted:

> When people are first acquainted with the idea of working
> with subpersonalities, they often tend to do just that,
> becoming so fascinated with uncovering a teeming cast of
> thousands that the more fruitful work, of understanding and
> integrating the central ones, is neglected.

One way out of this may to regard 'aspects' as different from 'personalities', and to say that each subpersonality may have two or more aspects. But it has to be admitted that this will not do for all cases, and that therefore the notion of subpersonalities may not be the optimal way of therapy for some people, and as a theory of personality it may need to be supplemented from elsewhere. This whole book is an attempt to explore such questions.

47

Third, some of the subpersonalities mentioned or discovered seemed to be old ones, which could still be remembered, but which were fading or quite unimportant now. This does not seem to be a great problem.

During the second meeting the lists of subpersonalities were revised after discussion, and the mean number of subpersonalities now went up to 7.2, the median and the mode both being 6.

Little Wilhelmina

At the third meeting, we tried to find out more about a subpersonality mentioned by one of the group members, a woman of about thirty-five. Her total list of subpersonalities was as follows:

Carmen Miranda: Black, beautiful, dramatic, sensual, bitchy.

Earthy Mangold: Has children, animals, grows things, intuitive, compassionate. Can also be gossipy, dirty, lazy, sluttish.

Good son: Very brave, never cries, tough, male.

Little Wilhelmina: Very suppressed, needs taking care of, doesn't like imposing on people. Needs to ask for love.

Apple juice: Ascetic, meditates, wrapped up in mysticism, vegetarian. Wants to be balanced.

Mostly Me: Strong, independent, rather impatient, easily hurt, expects rejection and criticism. Can also be stiff-necked, proud, not to be comforted.

The subpersonality we investigated was Little Wilhelmina. First of all we made the subpersonality more concrete and explicit by asking her questions. (A list of such questions is to be found on p. 198.) From these it emerged that this subpersonality was strongly related to rejection by a male figure, originally the father. The thought then occurred of asking all the male subpersonalities in the room how they would relate to Little Wilhelmina. It turned out, however, that the only subpersonality who supported Little Wilhelmina was in fact one of the female subpersonalities of one of the men. All the male subpersonalities put her down in various ways. This woman then came to the conclusion that Little Wilhelmina was right not to come out more with men, but that perhaps she could afford to come out more with women. On the whole, she was a bit dismayed by what she had found.

In a discussion of this episode, one of the women in the group said that in the first stages of a sexual partnership she would be attracted by the stronger subpersonalities of a man. One of the men replied that he often responded as a stronger subpersonality in such situations, but that at a certain point his 'Weeny Willy' equivalent would appear. Another woman said that it was sad that just at the point when her 'Weeny Willy' appeared, the other person's 'Weeny Willy' would come to the surface too, so that neither could get what they really wanted or needed. It seems, then, that this 'Weeny Willy' character is found in both men and women, and tends to be held back as not attractive. So when it does come out, it tends to come out as a surprise, and not bargained for. This was the first indication that some of the subpersonalities might be held in common, and not just be purely individual things. We have seen elsewhere in this book that this is indeed the case, and that some subpersonalities are frequent and popular, while others are more idiosyncratic.

Freem

At the fourth meeting, another character was worked with, this time coming from a woman of about twenty-five who was significantly overweight, though not extremely so. Her total subpersonalities were as follows:

Freem:	Monster, enormous, fat, lazy, apathetic, self-destructive. (Freem was originally very beautiful.)
Madman:	(Compound of man and madam.) Parent, moral, critical, demanding, ambitious, competitive, mocking.
Child:	Very dependent, demanding, intense, desperate at times. (Forms torture pattern with Madman and Freem.)
Professor:	Tall, intellectual, interested in everything.
Creative:	A creative self, able to invent and solve problems.

Ruth:	Stable, understanding, sensitive. (Used as front.)
Gina:	Attractive, happy-go-lucky.
Bulldog:	Aggressive, rebels against Madman and everyone else.

Again a questioning procedure was used to make concrete and explicit the subpersonality in question, which in this case was Freem. It turned out that Freem saw itself as being from some outside space, a kind of limbo. It had seen this girl as a suitable victim, and invaded her at about the age of fourteen. It grows in strength whenever she is offered conditional love. She says, 'Don't make me pay for what I get!' But whenever she does have to pay, by conforming to some standard, Freem uses the opportunity to take over. It seems that if this woman could get a regular supply of unconditional love, Freem would find it hard to get any kind of foothold.

In the course of the long chase after Freem, almost everyone in the group, it seemed, was deeply involved, either with their own Freem equivalents, or with their own relationships with some Freem-type figure. There was a lot of energy in Freem, which appeared to be locked up by the extreme disapproval in which Freem was held, and seemed destructive when it came out. By the end, it seemed that most people in the group were convinced that this energy could be transformed rather than needing to be locked away so firmly. This is a typical example of what Mahrer refers to as a disintegrative relationship with a deeper potential, which in the research group was examined and questioned.

Six months after the group had met, this woman wrote to me a letter in which the following paragraph appeared:

> I have always been aware of a very self-destructive critical aspect of myself (Freem) which up until our investigation was always strongly disapproved of. Now I am more able to conceive of Freem possibly having positive attributes! I am now about two stone lighter than I was when I last saw you! I hope I remain so!

It seems from this that the uncovering of subpersonalities can be a useful means of dealing with self-destruction in at least some of its

50

forms. It is also interesting that this worked even though there was no cathartic experience on the part of the woman involved – though it has to be said that the event was highly emotional for all concerned. One of the big disagreements among therapists of different schools is as to whether catharsis is really necessary or not, and I believe the consensus is now coming round to the view that it is not always necessary.

Real Self

In the fifth meeting, we tried to adapt a technique from psychosynthesis, and had one of the men in the group go on a fantasy trip to the top of a mountain, where he was to meet his Real Self. Accompanied by his Real Self, he was then to go down the various layers and levels inside the mountain until he reached some natural terminus. This worked very well, and a number of very useful insights were obtained on the way; unfortunately, however, no terminus was reached, except the exhaustion of all concerned after something like the eighteenth level had been described and dealt with. It was interesting that while at first there had been a large difference between Real Self and Confused Self, as the latter levels were reached the gap between them seemed to close. This gives a quantity of food for thought and further work. It was never, in fact, followed up, however, and remains as an isolated curiosity.

Achille and Green Elf

Also in this meeting two new characters appeared for one of the women, who were able to inspire her to take up writing again after a two-year block. These were both subpersonalities from her immediately pre-pubertal years, very lively and full of energy. One was called Achille, and was a boy who ran about waving a steel ruler around his head; he had a lot of energy, and she liked him. She had thought he was dead, and it was very moving to find that he was still alive, and still there. The other was called Green Elf, and again was a very lively child figure. She felt more complete to have found this character after all these years. This again was very suggestive. There is plenty of research to show that the very creative and fresh art of childhood gets lost during the years of secondary schooling – what if that subpersonality were still there, ready to spring to life again if one could only believe in her or him?

51

This effect has turned up spontaneously in my work since that time, and it seems quite an important finding.

Tiger

In the sixth meeting we again worked with existing subpersonalities, in this case those of one of the men in the group, aged about thirty. His subpersonalities were as follows:

Little Me:	Unsure, unconfident. Finds English society threatening.
Major Wheat:	Schoolmaster, rather precise, definite, somewhat aloof. Covers up for Little Me.
Clinger:	Wants to be needed, wants women to like him and take the initiative. To do with German mother. Wants love from parents but can't get it if they are unhappy.
Hurt Me:	Masochistic, likes difficult, painful situations, but quite positive.
Tiger:	Black with orange stripes, very bad, dangerous, insensitive. Jungle dark.
Ha Ha:	Very pleased when other people's big plans come to nothing. Motivated by fear.
Atlas:	Has to hold everything up. Ultimately responsible. It's his fault. Split from Little Me, whom he denies.
Jesus Christ:	Sacrifices himself to resolve antagonisms. Like Atlas but nicer. Non-sexual. Lets things happen.
The Intellectual:	Analyses well, uses mind skilfully.

This man worked as a professional, and when clients came to him for advice, he found himself too often slipping into the role of Little Me. So we worked on Little Me, and found that this character was very much one of those caught in the double bind of parental approval/disapproval. He was encouraged to break through this by repeated role-playing, and then re-enacted his professional role with one of the group members. The difference was positive and very striking. And when asked which of his subpersonalities was now coming into play, this man replied, 'Tiger'.

So again it turned out that a character who had been dismissed as very bad and dangerous had turned out in the end to be not always so dangerous and unruly as had been assumed, and could be very valuable in giving a greater feeling of life and spontaneity.

MY OWN SUBPERSONALITIES

In my own case, since these first six group meetings, I have done quite a number of workshops on subpersonalities, in which I have discovered many more things about my own and other people's possibilities in this area. One workshop in Altrincham seemed to be full of Hopeless characters, who at some point had made the decision that they could not get what they wanted in any way – this of course led very directly into Primal work. Another workshop in York was remarkable for the way in which one person discovered her Real Self and another person discovered her Transpersonal Self; this was very powerful, and made me feel very good about the process.

My own characters have changed as time has gone on. It may be interesting to detail something about this, just to show that there is nothing fixed about the subpersonalities, and that to study them does not introduce unnecessary rigidities into the growth process:

Big Eggo:	This was the main executive personality, corresponding very much to Jung's Persona. He has appeared as Old Reliable, as Magician, and as Clown. From being over-dominant, he is now more of a gatekeeper, or commissionaire, useful on occasion; also now much less of a male stereotype.
Jean Starry:	This arose as an amalgam of two other characters, Brown Cow (a natural, sensual woman who could let things happen and lead groups, a bit like Barry Stevens but younger) and Mr Commitment (a progressive, militant character, sometimes like a wooden soldier and sometimes like Jesus). Has appeared as a French Existential Androgyne, as Queen Christina and as a Giant Fairy.
Black Dwarf:	Also known as Mr Putdown. Very much like Jung's Shadow – purely destructive and hateful. Has also appeared as a Black Dog. Also

very witty. Used to be very powerful, till I gave up trying to destroy my mother – that was his main purpose in life. This represented a very important breakthrough in my therapy.

Behemoth: Creative self. Hasn't changed much, except that I later saw it as an appreciator of discovery, as well as a discoverer. Very changeable, unreliable, brilliant. Later still became integrated into other characters.

Babette: A very lovable girl child. Also appeared as a Fairy, and a Magical Child. Attractive, dimpled, feminine. Used to be the only lovable one (just as Mr Commitment was the only one who was allowed to be angry) but not really needed now that others are allowed to be lovable.

Lilith: A slim dark woman in a shiny dress. Reminds me of my mother when she was young. Maybe Jung's Anima, because she now seems to be very much a permanent part of me, very attractive, sophisticated, positive.

Father: Just like Jung's Father Complex. Has appeared as Bishop Makarios, as a Door and as a Big Darkie. Didn't deal with him until after the research project was completed, but was very important when I did. Fully absorbed now, and not an issue any more.

Just Me: Seems to have links with Loving Me, Centred Me, and Real Self, but there may be more here to sort out in more detail. Later linked up with the archetype of the Horned God (Rowan 1987).

The Dome: My Transpersonal Self. After the first occasion when I got in touch with it (Rowan 1975), it gradually became more and more accessible, until now I can get in touch with it at any time. Made a very important difference to my whole way of seeing the world.

Little Lady: A kind of grandmother figure – appeared once as a pair of elderly sisters – very precise,

> full of knowledge of various things, very
> patient, very good with their fingers. Now
> fully integrated, not separate.

I hope this makes it clear that in my version of subpersonality work
there is no desire whatsoever to limit the subpersonalities to one
type or one number, or one way of developing, changing, fading,
appearing or disappearing.

SCHWARTZ

More recently, I have come across the approach of Richard
Schwartz, whose work I find very similar to my own. He came to the
idea in quite a different way, however. He was working with a
family, in a fairly normal family-therapy kind of way, where the
twenty-three-year-old daughter was suffering from bulimia. At a
certain point he became dissatisfied with the progress so far, and
decided to see the daughter on her own:

> I began discussing with Sally what her internal experience was
> just before she went on a binge and vomit spree. She
> described a confusing cacophony of voices that seemed to
> carry on conversations inside her head. When I pressed her to
> differentiate the voices, she found, to her own and my
> surprise, that with relative ease she could identify several
> voices that regularly participated in heated conversations with
> each other. One voice was highly critical of everything about
> her, especially her appearance. Another defended her against
> this criticism and blamed her parents for her problems.
> Another voice made her feel sad, hopeless, and helpless; and
> still another kept directing her to binge. I found her inner life
> fascinating, both because her report was so similar to the
> reports of other bulimics I had treated, and because, as I
> listened to her, I became aware of somewhat similar voices
> within me.
>
> (Schwartz 1987: 26)

As he went on dealing with Sally and also with other patients of a
similar type, he began to realize that dealing with these inner
voices of one person was rather like family therapy itself. It was as
if there were a whole family within the person. 'It seemed that each

voice had a distinct character, complete with idiosyncratic desires, styles of communication, and temperaments.'

He then discovered Gazzaniga (1985) and Ornstein (1986) and Hofstadter (1985), and was much encouraged to realize that his own findings had some kind of backing. He started to use the word 'parts' to refer to the inner characters he was discovering, because that was the word which came most easily to his clients. And he arrived at this definition:

> By 'part' I mean not just a temporary emotional state or habitual thought pattern. Instead, it is a discrete and autonomous mental system that has an idiosyncratic range of emotion, style of expression, and set of abilities, intentions, or functions.
>
> (Schwartz 1987: 27)

This is very close to my own definition, laid down in Chapter 1. Schwartz also quotes another worker in the field of family therapy (Watanabe 1986) as having made similar discoveries. But the contribution of Schwartz is to point out how limiting is the idea of what he calls 'the monolithic self'. It actually prevents us from thinking creatively about situations. For example, take this description from a typical case conference: 'Johnny is a needy, dependent child who is trying to protect his parents' marriage. His mother is enmeshed with him, and afraid to let him grow up. Father is overly rational and afraid to deal with his wife's feelings.' Not an uncommon way of seeing such a pattern of family relationships. But see what happens when we put it in terms of subpersonalities:

> There is a part of Johnny that, when extreme, worries about being deserted and tells him to protect his parents' marriage. There are other parts of him that feel strong or competent but get overridden when that scared part is activated. There is a part of his mother that can take over and make her feel helpless and fearful, but there are other parts of her too. The father relies on a part of himself that is afraid of emotions and makes him very rational, but it is only one of his many parts.
>
> (Schwartz 1987: 28)

This immediately makes for a much more flexible and hopeful approach, and good family therapists like Virginia Satir (Satir and Baldwin 1983) seem to use this approach almost instinctively, seeing new possibilities and reframing the situation in terms of these new visions.

Schwartz sees the contribution of the object relations school as both positive and negative. It is positive because it does recognize the possibility that someone might have internal objects and part-objects which play an important part in their unconscious lives, and particularly in their fantasy lives. (Or phantasy lives, as they would say.) But it is negative because it does not really do justice to the complexity of these internal objects, which are much more in reality than internalized mothers, o good or bad breasts:

> Just as a therapist gets a very different, usually less sinister,
> impression of a client's family when the family members
> actually come to a session, an individual's 'inner family' looks
> very different when its various members get a chance to show
> up in an interview.
>
> (Schwartz 1987: 29)

So he works directly with the subpersonalities, in the manner described by the Gestalt people, the psychosynthesis people, the Voice Dialogue people, the Johnson approach, and so on. And he, like others, finds the external observer, the fair witness, a useful character to bring on sometimes.

It is good to know that others are spontaneously discovering the very same things that we are all talking about here, because it shows how the idea of subpersonalities is something very natural, which emerges very easily, rather than something belonging to a system which owns it and has developed a jargon for dealing with it.

Part Two

FUNCTIONS AND USES
OF SUBPERSONALITIES

Chapter Four

SUBPERSONALITIES IN PSYCHOTHERAPY: THE EARLY YEARS

It may have been Janet and Charcot and their colleagues who practised hypnotism and contemporaries in the nineteenth century who first really outlined the idea of autonomous or semi-autonomous parts of the person, but using this idea as an adjunct to normal psychotherapy is another matter. Let us now look at this whole business of how the idea of using subpersonalities developed in the therapy setting.

FREUD

It has often been pointed out how dramatic is Freud's whole conception of psychodynamics. The interactions between id, ego, and superego are dramatic dialogues in which there is threat, counter-threat, domination, submission, wheedling, manip-ulating, attacking, defending, and so forth. Don Bannister, in a paper which I cannot now locate, once said that it was like a fight between a gorilla and a severe schoolmistress in a dark cellar, supervised by a rather nervous bank clerk. More seriously, we can look at what Bruner (1956) says about it:

> Freud's is a theory or a proto-theory peopled with actors. The characters are from life: the blind, energetic, pleasure-seeking id; the priggish and punitive superego; the ego, battling for its being by diverting the energy of others to its own use. The drama has an economy and a terseness. The ego develops canny mechanisms for dealing with the threat of id impulses; denial, projection, and the rest. Balances are struck between the actors, and in the balance is character and neurosis. Freud

61

was using the dramatic technique of decomposition, the play
whose actors are parts of a single life.

(Bruner 1956: 343)

It is interesting to see exactly what Freud says about the superego.
And when we read about the nature of the superego, we find that
it again answers very precisely to our description of a
subpersonality. Freud (Collected Works Vol.23) says, in explaining
the origin of the superego:

A portion of the external world has, at least partially, been
abandoned as an object and has instead, by identification,
been taken into the ego and thus become an integral part of
the internal world. This new psychical agency continues to
carry on the functions which have hitherto been performed
by people in the external world.

(Freud 1938: 203)

In other words, we have taken inside us a voice from our external
world, and internalized it. This is the process known in
psychoanalysis as introjection, a term originated by Ferenczi
(1909) to describe the way in which external people, together with
the feelings associated with them, can become internal objects of
fantasy. The purpose of introjection is to keep in contact with
important people when separated from them.

An important point, however, is that the term 'introjection' is
often regarded in rather too simple a way. Some correction may be
needed:

The term introjection is a question-begging one in that it
assumes that one is incorporating into the personality
something that is outside the personality, or incorporating
into the 'myself' something that is originally experienced as
'not-myself'. For example, I may say that the infant tends to
'introject' the mother's affirming and rejecting attitudes
respectively towards different behaviours (termed 'good' and
'bad' respectively by the mother). But the infant can only
incorporate the mother's attitudes in so far as it is capable of
having these attitudes. It will incorporate his own version or
his own experience of these attitudes, and what he

'incorporates' will be essentially what he himself is and what he is 'projecting' on to the mother.

(Redfearn 1985: 10)

Redfearn is an interesting theorist in this area, and has much to say about the origins and dynamics of subpersonalities. He believes that not only the superego, but also the ego and the id, should be regarded as subpersonalities.

Freud's 'sub-personalities' (my term), his ego, id and super-ego all behave as though they are integrative, organizing centres of our personalities, almost as if they are people or daemons within us, partly conscious, largely rooted in the unconscious, first one taking charge of the 'I', or of behaviour or both, then the other.

Jung's sub-personalties, the ego, the persona, the shadow, the anima, the wise man, the wise woman, the self etc., as well as the complexes, behave as organizing centres and each may take charge in turn of the feelings of 'I' and of behaviour. They all have an innate basis and yet all are influenced by experience and they all differentiate through experience.

(Redfearn 1985: 10)

But whereas Freud never took it much further, and transferred his attention to the Oedipal drama, others did more more to exploit the idea of different parts of the person coming into conflict.

JUNG

One of the great pioneers in this field was Jung. Some of his first work, in the first ten years of this century, was with association tests, where the experimenter says a word and the subject comes back with the first word which comes into his or her head. Through the use of this device, Jung became convinced that within the person there were semi-autonomous systems which he called at first the 'feeling-toned complexes.' His first thought was that the complex was like a theme or leitmotiv in music, which came back in various forms in different circumstances, but later he saw it more as a subpersonality.

> As the association experiments prove, complexes interfere
> with the intentions of the will and disturb the conscious
> performance; they produce disturbances of memory and
> blockages in the flow of associations; they appear and
> disappear according to their own laws; they can temporarily
> obsess consciousness, or influence speech and action in an
> unconscious way. In a word, complexes behave like
> independent beings.
>
> (Jung 1936)

As Frey-Rohn (1974) says, Jung's interpretation of these findings
was influenced by the work of Janet and Charcot and his French
co-workers on the phenomena of 'double consciousness' and
'second existences' which they had discovered in their work on
hysteria. Jung came to agree that the split-off, unconscious
complex formed a miniature self-contained psyche. But it was
important to keep distinct the difference between the phenomena
found in quite normal and well-adjusted people and those found
in extremely dissociated personalities.

> The tendency to split means that parts of the psyche detach
> themselves from consciousness to such an extent that they not
> only appear foreign but lead an autonomous life of their own.
> It need not be a question of a hysterical multiple personality,
> or schizophrenic alterations of personality, but merely of
> so-called 'complexes' that come entirely within the scope of
> the normal.
>
> (Jung 1936)

But Jung went further. And this is a strand of his work which has
been taken up in recent years by followers such as James Hillman
and Mary Watkins. Not only are complexes a result of problems
(usually traumatic, in Jung's opinion) and a cause of problems
(such as lack of control over one's daily actions), but they can also
be an important and healthy feature of the total person in
themselves. In other words, the job of the psychotherapist is not
just to get rid of complexes or tinker with complexes, but also to
respect, and encourage the client to respect, those complexes.

Complexes obviously represent a kind of inferiority in the broadest sense – a statement I must at once qualify by saying that to have complexes does not necessarily indicate inferiority. It only means that something discordant, unassimilated and antagonistic exists, perhaps as an obstacle, but also as an incentive to greater effort, and so, perhaps, to new possibilities of achievement. In this sense, therefore, complexes are focal or nodal points of psychic life which we would not wish to do without; indeed, they should not be missing, for otherwise psychic activity would come to a fatal standstill.

(Jung 1928)

This notion, that the complexes are good and to be taken seriously as necessary parts of human development and functioning, has been taken further by James Hillman. Hillman is a modern Jungian who has taken particularly seriously the whole question of the imaginal life – the deep life of the psyche beneath the surface. He sees this as 'no longer single-centred but polycentric'. 'We are no longer single beings in the image of a single God, but are always constituted of multiple parts: impish child, hero or heroine, supervising authority, asocial psychopath, and so on' (Hillman 1975). If we take this as our basis, he says, we can then do all sorts of good work in psychotherapy. All we have to do is to allow and encourage these semi-autonomous parts to speak their minds, to interact with each other, to change, merge, separate, integrate, and differentiate, to transform. And to do all this the first step is to personify the complex. It is as if we had to admit that the ego were not the whole story of who we might be at any given time, and that even the self were not the whole story. 'For the ego is not the whole psyche, only one member of a commune.'

Personifying, says Hillman, helps place subjective experiences 'out there'. It then becomes much easier to have relations with them. And it then becomes easier to own them, to own up to them. One of Jung's great interests was in ancient alchemy, seen as a way of talking about the psyche and its processes of transformation in symbolic form. And in alchemy there is a process called the separatio, where the different ingredients are set side by side. 'Only separated things can unite', said the alchemists. And essential to this separation, says Hillman, is naming the subpersonalities, who often appear to us in dreams and visions.

> We sense these other persons and call them 'roles' – mother,
> mistress, daughter, witch, crone, nurse, wife, child, nymph,
> innkeeper, slave, queen, whore, dancer, sibyl, muse. But can
> there be roles without persons to play them? To call them
> roles and games is itself a game by which Number One may
> deny the autonomy of these persons and keep them all under
> his control.
>
> (Hillman 1975)

This process of naming is very important. We must not fall into the
trap of going immediately into theory and saying that the person
who arises in our dream must be one of the Jungian archetypes
already discovered and named by Jung or someone else.

Another Jungian who, like Hillman, has paid attention to this
matter, is William Johnson. But whereas Hillman says nothing
about how to go about working with the subpersonalities, Johnson
does. He warns us that

> It is a mistake to jump to conclusions and to call your inner
> person anima or shadow or one of those terms if you are not
> really sure. For every dream-person who fits clearly within one
> of the archetypes, there are many others who don't: They are
> just persons in your dream. In that case, don't force them into
> a mould. Let them be who they are.
>
> (Johnson 1986)

He, too, thinks it very important to name the persons who emerge
as subpersonalities. This is particularly the case, of course, if the
same person can be identified in several dreams, visions, or other
aspects of what Jung calls 'active imagination'.

ACTIVE IMAGINATION

So this activity is called in Jungian analysis the use of active
imagination. It was in 1935 (*Collected Works*, vol. 6) that Jung first
used the concept of 'active imagination'. In active imagination we
fix upon a particular point, mood, picture, or event, and then
allow a fantasy to develop in which certain images become

personified. Thereafter the images have a life of their own and develop according to their own logic.

A classic in this area came from Barbara Hannah, who worked with Jung, and then taught at the C. G. Jung Institute in Zurich. She says that this method enables conversations to take place with contents of the unconscious that appear personified. It does not matter how the image may come, but the essential thing is to hang on to it and not let it go until it has revealed its message through dialogue. She emphasizes over and over again the distinction between passive imagination, where we merely experience a scene as if looking at it on a screen, and active imagination, where we enter into an interactive discourse which goes back and forth between the personified image and ourselves. Barbara Hannah says one surprising thing – that she could never do anything along the lines of active imagination in this sense with someone else in the room – she would have to be quite private to do it. This idea is also put forward by Marie-Louise von Franz, in her introduction to the book: 'In contrast to the numerous existing techniques of passive imagination, active imagination is done alone, to which most people must overcome considerable resistance. It is a form of play, but a bloody serious one' (Hannah 1981: 2).

This is, as it were, the original and traditional way of using active imagination, but because of its solitary nature, it does seem to be very hard and quite rare. But in recent years the technique of active imagination has been developed by people like Johnson. He goes a considerable way beyond the older tradition represented by Hannah, and says:

> A good way to connect to the inner parts of yourself is to
> think of each dream figure as an actual person living inside
> you. Think of each person in your dream as one of the
> autonomous personalities that coexist within your psyche and
> combine to make up your total self.
>
> (Johnson 1986)

This way of personifying the complexes and archetypes must have originally been developed by Jung, but we do not know exactly when. Hannah seems to have been doing this work mainly during the 1950s and after. But Johnson gives details about how to do this which are not found in Hannah at all. He says:

I am convinced that it is nearly impossible to produce anything in the imagination that is not an authentic representation of something in the unconscious. The whole function of the imagination is to draw up the material from the unconscious, clothe it in images, and transmit it to the conscious mind.

(Johnson 1986)

So what one has to do is to carry on a dialogue with the image which has been produced spontaneously. Of course there is no one but oneself to play the other role, so it becomes a question of going back and forth between the two or more roles, just as we shall see shortly in so many other contexts.

One can usually tell whether a person is doing real Active Imagination by the feeling responses that come out. If the normal human reaction to the situation in the imagination would be anger, fear, or intense joy, but none of these feelings are present, then I know the person is detached from the proceedings, just watching from a distance, not really participating, not taking it seriously.

(Johnson 1986)

What we can see here is that the client is doing this in the presence of the therapist, and not alone as before. An important warning comes here, however. And this is a warning that applies to all uses of subpersonalities, whatever discipline it may be within, and whatever terminology may be used.

We must participate completely. There is, however, one line that should not be crossed. We must not stray from the zone of participation into the zone of *control.* In Active Imagination we cannot exert control over the inner persons or over what is happening. We have to let the imagination flow where it will, let the experience develop, without trying to determine in advance what is going to happen, what is going to be said, what is going to be done.

(Johnson 1986)

The point is that one must be willing to engage in real dialogue with the subpersonality. It is not a question of what we would like to be the case, but of what actually is the case. We have to be genuinely open and listening. But this is sometimes not easy. Sometimes these figures from the unconscious may be very powerful, especially if they come as archetypal images from the collective unconscious. We may feel we are dealing with something which is more than human. But it will still make sense to treat it as if it were human, because this is really the only way in which we can begin to discover its meaning for us. We have to filter whatever comes through our own experience: there is no other way.

> Often your dream gives the person a name. If not, you can invent a name that seems to capture the person's character. Or you can use a descriptive name. If it is a masculine figure, it may be Brave Warrior, Wise Elder, Old Miser, Sneaky Crook, Juvenile Delinquent, Young Prince, Trickster, Tribal Brother. If this is a feminine figure you may find yourself calling her Wise Mother, Tyrant Mother, Earth Mother, Faithful Sister, My Lady Soul, Lady of the Sparkling Eyes. If she fits the mythical role, you may give her a mythical name: Helen, Iseult of the White Hands, Guinevere.
>
> (Johnson 1986)

Hillman seems particularly keen on the Greek gods and goddesses, and tries wherever possible to name the sub-personalities along these lines, and Bolen (1984) and McAdams (1985) do the same thing. Obviously there are advantages in such a move, because the Greek pantheon is very rich and very familiar to most of us, and there is much literature easily available around the subject. And some interesting ideas can come out of this approach, as, for example:

> In ancient Greece there was an understanding that one was required to worship all the Gods and Goddesses. You might have your favourites, but none of the remaining deities could be ignored. The God or Goddess whom you ignored became the one who turned against you and destroyed you. So it was with the Trojan war. So it is with consciousness work. The energy patttern that we disown turns against us.
>
> (Stone and Winkelman 1985)

This is a useful and important insight. There is still a danger, however, that we can become inflated or misled by this emphasis on gods and goddesses. I very seldom find, in my own work, that people spontaneously come up with gods and goddesses, so to impose this would be a kind of interpretation on the part of the therapist which could enhance any narcissistic tendencies on the part of the client. It seems better to me to stick rather close to the client's own experience, and to let the client name the subpersonality as it appears. Where I have found the idea of a goddess to be useful is when encouraging women to see strong aspects of themselves as female rather than male, along the lines suggested by Jean Shinoda Bolen (1984), who suggests that Athena, for example, is very warlike and very intellectual but also totally female. So a warlike and intellectual woman client can be encouraged to see herself in this light, rather than as an imitation man, as the general culture of today would tend to suggest. But William Johnson says that we should have a great humility in the face of our subpersonalities:

> One must be willing to say: 'Who are you? What do you have to say? I will listen to you. You may have the floor for this entire hour if you want; you may use any language you want. I am here to listen.' This requires a formidable realignment of attitude for most of us. If there is something in yourself that you see as a weakness, a defect, a terrible obstruction to a productive life, you nevertheless have to stop approaching that part of yourself as 'the bad guy'. For once, during Active Imagination, you must try to listen to that 'inferior' being as though he or she were the voice of wisdom. If our depressions or weaknesses come to us in personified form, we need to honour those characteristics as part of the total self.
>
> (Johnson 1986)

I think, however, that Stone and Winkelman are right when they say that 'Whatever energy we disown, life brings to us, exactly as we have disowned it.' Each subpersonality is a distinct energy pattern. Each has a distinct facial expression, posture, tone of voice, and each creates a different set of energetic vibrations in its surroundings. It often makes sense to ask a subpersonality, 'How old are you?' or 'What do you look like?'

But what kind of reality are we talking about here? Is all this something which is way outside anything practical or real? Someone who has written very well about this is another Jungian, Mary Watkins. She says this:

> I shall place before you the view that imaginal dialogues do not merely reflect or distort reality, but create reality; that the real is not necessarily antithetical to the imaginal, but can be conceived of more broadly to include the imaginal; and that personifying is not an activity symptomatic of the primitivity of mind, but is expressive of its dramatic and poetic nature.
>
> (Watkins 1986)

She goes along with the view of Franklin (1981), when he says that symbolizing does not merely reflect or communicate what is already known, but is formulative, and creates meaning. So the activity we are engaging in when we have a dialogue with our internal subpersonalities is a healthy and constructive one. Hillman (1975) defines personifying rather formally as 'the spontaneous experiencing, envisioning and speaking of the configurations of existence as psychic presences'.

The word 'spontaneous' is very important in all this. These subpersonalities are not things we invent or choose. Rather, we discover them and work with them as a result of following the normal process of psychotherapy, where we take current incidents and uncover the hidden meanings behind them. The phrase 'configurations of existence' is important too: these are things which exist already, and have a right to exist. As Mary Watkins (1986) puts it so starkly: 'We would not judge a play or novel with one character as necessarily better or worse than another with several characters. So why should we impose this kind of ideal on the richness of our own thought?' After all, in the literature on personality development (Loevinger 1976) it is generally recognized that complexity and the recognition of different sides of the personality side by side with one another is a sign of maturity, of high development. For us to see a person as all good or all bad is regarded as less mature than to see them as partly good and partly bad, and so on. Why not apply the same reasoning to ourselves?

What we have to guard against here is the view that this is

71

somehow unhealthy, or leading away from the main task of psychotherapy. As Mary Watkins says:

> Imaginal dialogues are often looked at askance by clinicians. The suggestion that a person ought to entertain more characters, allow them *greater* autonomy, and enable characterizations to unfold which are *more* vivid and articulated might lead many to believe that we are encouraging hallucination, dissociation or fragmentation of the personality, a dangerous weakening of the ego – and perhaps even that we recommend becoming a 'split personality'.
>
> (Watkins 1986)

But in practice this is not so. I remember one working class woman client of mine whò said in a puzzled voice, 'What I can't understand is how I take myself apart into all these pieces in here, and yet when I go out I feel more whole!'

So this Jungian work is very rich, and has grown over a period of fifty years or so into something which is very sophisticated and well worked out. But more or less of the same vintage is another approach, which is not a million miles distant from it.

PSYCHOSYNTHESIS

One of the first people to have started really making use of subpersonalities for therapy and personal growth was Roberto Assagioli. He introduced his system of psychosynthesis, which in some ways follows Jung and in some ways goes further, in the years after 1910, and opened up his Institute in 1926. So it may have been at any time between then and the publication of his work in English starting in the 1960s that he started working with subpersonalities. Nowadays, of course, psychosynthesis forms one of the main schools working with subpersonalities, actually under that title.

James Vargiu, an eminent American practitioner of psychosynthesis who had worked personally with Assagioli, wrote the first workbook on subpersonalities. In introducing it, he says:

There are in each of us a diversity of these semi-autonomous subpersonalities, striving to express themselves . . . . So one of the easiest and most basic ways to facilitate our growth is to get to know our subpersonalities . . . The Hag, The Mystic, The Materialist, The Idealist, The Claw, The Pillar of Strength, The Sneak, The Religious Fanatic, The Sensitive Listener, The Crusader, The Doubter, The Grabbie, The Frightened Child, The Poisoner, The Struggler, The Tester, The Shining Light, The Bitch Goddess, The Great High Gluck, The Dummy, to name a few.

(Vargiu 1974)

He cautions that it is a mistake to think that they all function at the same level, or that they are predictible in advance. One of the most important mistakes, says psychosynthesis, is to think, as Berne does, that there are just three ego states (with subdivisions) and that everything must be some version of these three.

Subpersonalities exist at various levels of organization, complexity and refinement . . . . No specific cluster or combination of subpersonalities can be considered to be central for everyone, though certain patterns are quite common.

(Vargiu 1974)

He says that in working with subpersonalities it is often found useful to think in terms of a five-phase process. The first phase is simple *recognition* – the subpersonality has to emerge in some way. As we have seen, this may be through the emergence of a conflict within the person, or it may be through a dream or vision or guided fantasy, or it may be through splitting an existing sub-personality into two – however it comes, the therapist enables the client to realize that it is there.

Phase two is *acceptance*. All this means is that the client has to be willing to work with the subpersonality; it does not mean that at this stage the client has to like the subpersonality. Or it may mean the acceptance of one subpersonality by another subpersonality. It may mean a moment of daring where the person takes what may seem the enormous risk of entering into and being the very thing he or she has most hated and feared for many years.

73

This makes possible the third phase, of *co-ordination*. This means the discovery and working through of the relationships between the subpersonalities. If there are interpersonal difficulties between two or more of the subpersonalities some process of conflict resolution or accommodation or time sharing may need to be worked out. This again may sometimes take great daring, but if it carried through, this process may bring about some valuable change on the part of one or more of the subpersonalities.

This then leads on to the fourth phase, of *integration*. Here we go further with the process of resolving conflicts among the subpersonalities and enabling them to work together in a way which now is harmonious rather than fragmented or disjunctive or negative.

The fifth phase is one of synthesis. This is the last phase of the harmonization process, and it leads to the discovery of the Transpersonal Self, and the realization that that is the final truth of the person, not the subpersonalities. This places unity at the end of the road. We shall see later on, as we have briefly already seen in our mention of individuals such as James Hillman and Mary Watkins, that we do not always have to strive for unity, but it is a strong value within psychosynthesis.

Vargiu then goes on to give a case vignette of a session with a woman who discovered within herself three characters: the Hag, the Doubter, and the Idealist. The Hag comes across as being critical and twisted, the Doubter is afraid and mistrusting, and the Idealist has unrealistic ideals, refuses to accept her limitations, and her spirituality is pretentious and desperate. In the course of the session, another character appears, who is not so clear at first, a greater self, a higher self. This higher self looks at the others and sees them very clearly for what they are. The therapist then suggests that the Hag, the Doubter, and the Idealist go for a climb up a mountain, watched by the higher self. When they reach the top of the mountain, the higher self sees them looking at one another and leaning in together and flowing into one. A new person is formed. The client says, 'And she has a bearing that's not puffed up, or on an ego trip, but sure of herself, knowing who she is. She's very, very solid.' The client then goes into this new character and becomes her. There is some further work in this session, and a good deal of consolidation and working through after the session, but that is the main gist of what happens.

Obviously things do not always go as smoothly or easily as this, but it is a good example to show the basic movement which psychosynthesis aims at. Ferrucci (1982) also has a good discussion of the use of subpersonalities within psychosynthesis. He gives the example of Kees, who worked quite a lot with subpersonalities and found them very valuable. One of the major characters he had to work with he called the Golem. This was a very nasty sub-personality, like an animal living underground, and very reluctant to expose itself. Kees says:

> I looked at this sneaky animal, and my whole image of myself as a decent, good person collapsed. It was a filthy creature, with green eyes and a mean disposition. Without a sense of personal centeredness [derived from earlier work] I wouldn't have been able to confront it. I would have been afraid that it was all I was, that it would overpower me, and so on.

But with the therapist's encouragement, Kees went on to bring this character out into the open and have a dialogue with it. As time went on, he began to see The Golem in quite a different light.

> If I didn't possess that personality, I later realized, I would have gotten myself into all kinds of trouble. Though he first emerged as nasty and sneaky, at bottom he was only trying to say 'no' when I was always and automatically inclined to say 'yes' to everyone and everything.

Ferrucci points out that this rightly suggests that there are no good or bad subpersonalities. 'All subpersonalities are expressions of vital elements of our being, however negative they may seem to us at first.' This is a most important truth. Subpersonalities become harmful only when they control us, and this usually happens when we are unaware of them. Kees again has something to say about this:

> One afternoon, some time after I had started my work on subpersonalities, I had an image of myself sitting in the middle of a circle of African huts, and in each of them were living my subpersonalities. Up to then they had been so strong that they could take turns in grabbing at me until one

75

succeeded in holding me prisoner for a while. It might have lasted for ten minutes or ten years. I had no control. But then as I was sitting there, I sensed that this domination was coming to an end. Suddenly, for the first time, I truly felt, 'I can go into this hut or that one, and I can come out. And I don't have to stay there if I choose not to.' And afterwards, this mastery started to take effect not only in an imaginary, static situation, like that of the African huts, but also in the dynamics of life, when I had to respond to various situations.

This is the sort of result which is very acceptable in psycho-synthesis, and it is clearly in line with the aims of most schools of psychotherapy.

PSYCHODRAMA

Another candidate for first use of subpersonalities in therapy is Jacob Moreno. He never used the term, but he did use the approach, very freely and individually. Blatner (1970) mentions the multiple double technique used in psychodrama, and refers to Zerka Moreno's paper, which came out in the journal *Group Psychotherapy* in 1959, and was later reprinted in the book edited by Greenberg (1974). In it she says:

Multiple Double Technique

The patient is on the stage with several doubles of himself. Each portrays part of the patient. One auxiliary ego acts as he is now, while the patient acts himself as he was when he was little, and as he was soon after his father's death, another auxiliary ego how he may be thirty years hence. The masks of the patient are simultaneously present and each acts in turn. With psychotic patients the multiple double technique has been usefully employed when the patient suffered from numerous delusions involving parts of the body; each of the auxiliary egos then represented a different organ, responding to the delusional stimuli produced by the patient.

Now most of Moreno's techniques were developed in the 1920s and 1930s, so it may well be that this method was used as far back as that.

What happens in psychodrama, of course, is that the

protagonist (client, patient) takes all the roles sooner or later, and experiences each of these parts, from the inside, as that person. This is crucial to all that we have seen so far and all the other approaches to come. We have to get to know the subpersonalities from the inside, by playing them, and not from the outside by observing or describing them.

In a way it is absurd to say so little about psychodrama, because in a way psychodrama has a better grasp of how to work with subpersonalities than anyone else, but because psychodramatists do not talk very much in these terms, and prefer to talk so much of the time about actual people, it is perhaps not so surprising in the end.

It is very interesting that recent forms of research in social science have begun to use psychodrama as part of the process of research itself. Hawkins (1988) describes how his research group used psychodrama to explore their own actions. First each researcher sets up a subpersonality of the part of their research with which they have the most trouble, and enter into dialogue with that. Then each person steps back and looks at the dialogue from a third position outside that, thus turning the first protagonist into a second subpersonality. The new observer now starts a dialogue with the original researcher, now a researcher subpersonality. And finally the person steps back to become a transcendental ego, watching and observing the whole thing. This is very sophisticated work, and it is appropriate that it should come from one of the originating disciplines for this kind of work.

Chapter Five

SUBPERSONALITIES IN PSYCHOTHERAPY: THE SIXTIES

In the 1960s there was a great explosion of psychotherapies, and they became used for personal growth, as well as for distressed people, on a scale never known before. The techniques we shall be looking at in this chapter all reached their final form in the 1960s, though of course they had their origins in earlier years.

PERLS

We saw in the last chapter that psychodrama allows many aspects of a person to be represented and to have dialogues. But someone who laid all the stress on the internal conflicts rather than on the external conflicts was the inventor of Gestalt therapy, Fritz Perls. Perls made a general practice of having an empty chair beside him, in individual or group therapy, on which to place the various members of our internal world. This makes it easy for us to talk to them, and let them talk to us, or to one another. Something that often comes out is a *topdog* and an *underdog*.

> The topdog is righteous and authoritarian; he knows best. He is sometimes right, but always righteous . . . . He manipulates with demands and threats of catastrophe . . . . The underdog manipulates with being defensive, apologetic, wheedling, playing the crybaby, and so on . . . . The underdog is the Mickey Mouse. The topdog is the Super Mouse . . . . This is the basis for the famous self-torture game.
>
> (Perls 1969)

The topdog is of course very reminiscent of the Freudian

78

superego, but Perls pointed out that Freud never said anything very much about the equally prevalent and problematic underdog. The self-torture game referred to here is simply the way in which we very often entertain 'shoulds' which we do not really intend to honour. We carry them round with us, and every now and then they beat us over the head with the thought – 'I still haven't written to my grandmother' – or whatever it may be. The reply is something like – 'I will do it, but I haven't got time at the moment'. In Perls's terms this is the topdog and underdog at work. This of course lays the major emphasis on conscious experience, but this view also has a place for earlier and unconscious formations of subpersonalities or ego states, as carriers of unfinished business.

It is interesting that the Gestalt school lays all the stress on polarities as a form of conflict. They seem to see everything in pairs of opposites, rather in the manner of the Personal Construct school in their way, or the Jungian school in another. So there would very seldom be more than two chairs in operation. The fullest statement of this point of view seems to be in Zinker (1978).

GESTALT THERAPY AND THE BODY

So far we have talked mainly in terms of persons, whether male, female, or mythological. Gestalt therapy is more flexible, however, in enabling us to give a voice to the most unlikely candidates. First of all, as in the psychodrama example given above, we can talk to, and talk back as, parts of our own bodies. This is not as odd as it may sound. Even a psychoanalyst like Harold Searles can say this:

> One category includes instances wherein a part of one's own body is, at an unconscious level, not a part of one's body image but is reacted to, instead, as being a separate person to whom one reacts with intense jealousy.
>
> (Searles 1986: 105)

If there is a pain in some part of our body, we may talk to the pain, and talk back as the pain. Usually when this is done, it turns out that the pain, or the part of the body, was actually standing for one of the more important subpersonalities, and was, as it were, its disguise for the day. The reasons why this is possible are spelt out in psychoanalytic terms by Faber (1977) in a paper which discusses in a very sophisticated way the whole question of altered states of consciousness in Castaneda's work:

As for the body image, it is formed by
the deposit of images and symbols of key external figures, internalized by stimuli from without, fusing with sensory perceptions from within . . . . People treat their bodies and themselves much as they react to meaningful persons in their lives.

(Mushatt 1975: 93)

The conclusions are inescapable. The internalized object of infancy and childhood is internalized into our very organs, into our very senses. To truncate the tie to the internalized object is to liberate, or open, the sensorial apparatus, which is rooted in the body. Hence, to receive the world differently is to perceive the world differently, and to perceive the world differently is to experience the body not only in a new way but in a *renewed* way, a way that attests to the restoration of the individual to a sensorial capacity that is no longer expressive of the early internalization of the mother, that no longer belongs to the mother. One's body is, at last, one's own.

In this way subpersonalities are open to all the forms of distortion found in dream symbolism: condensation, displacement, censorship, and so forth. By working with them and bringing out their ramifications, we can begin to understand and to transform them.

This does of course throw a whole different light on the body. It seems to us at first that the person must be single because the body is single. But if the body is itself multiple, that puts another complexion on things. Let us now look at a succinct and persuasive argument on this point:

To proponents of singular self-identity nothing would seem simpler than the human body as clear and irrefutable evidence for locating the structure of subjectivity in persons alone: one self per body. Yet appearances can be deceiving even if, like the peels of an onion, appearances constitute the whole of so-called reality. The body is both complex and ambiguous. Even its apparently obvious unity was less than obvious to the early Greeks. Bruno Snell notes, 'the early Greeks did not, either in their language or in the visual arts, grasp the body as a unit.' Both the use of plurals to refer to the physical nature of the body as well as the crimped joints in the early vase paintings suggest that for the early Greeks, 'the physical body of man was comprehended, not as a unit but as an aggregate.'

(Ogilvy 1977: 108)

The same author goes on to look at the findings of research into the brain and body, and concludes that they all go to show that there is a good basis in the actual way that the body is put together and held together for saying that the body can be seen as multiple just as readily as it can be seen as single: 'Granted the limitations of biological metaphors – physiological patterns neither prove nor cause similar patterns in history – still the body provides living proof that pluralized, multicentered systems of order *can* function' (Ogilvy 1977: 115). This is a very helpful approach, which enables us to escape from the feeling that we are doing something strained or unnatural, or somehow unrelated to the body.

EXTENDING GESTALT THERAPY

Fritz Perls, the originator of Gestalt therapy, was extremely flexible in the entities he was prepared to put on to the empty chair, including such things as: 'your inhibitions'; phoniness; 'your smirk'; 'the old man you saw when you were five and a half'; 'that memory'; 'the dream you didn't have'; the mountain trail; the car number plate; the pillar in the station; the railway station; the water in the vessel; the statue in the lake; the rug on the floor; the two rooms talking to each other; 'your left hand'; Fritz; all these things could be talked to and could talk back. And as they did so, they turned into subpersonalities – sometimes quite familiar subpersonalities and sometimes new and surprising sub-personalities. And as the dialogue progresses, something changes, something moves (Perls 1976).

We saw earlier that Gestalt therapy focuses very much on polarities which naturally emerge in the process of psychotherapy, and that therefore there were seldom more than two chairs in use

81

at any one time. One interesting exception to this is to be found in the work of Patrice Baumgartner. She says this:

> The patient gets stuck in relation to his existence or some aspect of it. He will not move with his feelings and so be a part of his own situation. Have him then see his existential situation outside of himself on the empty chair, expressing to it whatever he is aware of feeling. Sometimes when situational options occur, I like to bring in several chairs, imagining each alternative on a separate chair. The patient can simply let his various alternatives be, get involved with one of them, or explore his conflict by being with or becoming his available situations in turn. Several empty chairs are useful, too, sometimes for the patient's various roles. If he is stuck in one role, his others are then clearly available. Sometimes the patient will feel moved to get involved with another part of himself when he will do nothing with anyone else. Having these other roles 'conspicuously' present helps. I do not remember that Fritz used empty chairs as vehicles for working through stuck points in just this way. The possibility occurred to me one day, and it has seemed to me to offer one more avenue of assistance. Sometimes people who come into the office weekly have special chairs which they designate for their various roles. They seem to use these physical places as emotional correlates especially if they feel stuck in one familiar role. I know something about where they are inside as I see where they sit.
>
> (Baumgartner and Perls 1975: 64-5)

This is one way of varying the two-chair method. The way I like to vary this myself is deliberately to create another subpersonality myself, if the two polarities should get stuck. Sometimes this happens: the two protagonists get into a place where nothing more seems to be happening. Then I may ask the person to get up and stand on a table or chair, and look at the scene from another position. At first I said, 'Be God – what does God say about what is going on here, what does he say to each of those two?' But sometimes all I got when I did this was some kind of rather punitive superego, which was not what I wanted. So now I say, 'Be a fair witness. You are an outside observer, who has seen a good many situations like this in the world. Tell them what you see going on, from your more objective position; give them any hints and tips you may think of value.' This just helps to break up the log-jam and enable something more to happen. It does not prevent us from going back to the first two characters and letting them continue afterwards.

BERNE

Of course it was not only Gestalt therapy which emerged in the 1960s, but also Transactional Analysis, which itself has a number of relatives, all derived from the work of Paul Federn (1952), one of the older generation of psychoanalysts. All these writers and therapists call subpersonalities ego states.

> As we develop greater complexity of living, our own personality separates into myriad functions, related to and isolated from each other, in thousands of ways. We divide our self into patterns of behaviour and experience each of which is appropriate for various situations, and we thrust from activation and awareness reactions that would not be adaptive. Who wants to worry about a mathematics test at a party, or plan one's budget at a football game? We call these patterns of behaviour and experience 'ego states', and they are normally a part of us all. Even as society must separate its merchants from its musicians, its teachers from its builders, etc., so also does the 'society of self' within a single human divide itself into segments for the accomplishing of its various adjustive goals. Thus, ego-state theory holds that normal personalities are characterized by organizational patterns of behaviour and experience that have been partially dissociated from each other for purposes of adaptation and defence.
> (Watkins and Johnson 1982)

One of the most famous examples of this is, of course, the idea of Eric Berne (1961, 1972) that we all have within us a *Parent*, an *Adult* and a *Child*, and that these can sometimes be in conflict with each other. He calls them ego states, but they answer in every way to our description of subpersonalities. Faced with a cream bun, our Parent subpersonality may say 'Put it back!', our Adult may say

'Better not', and our Child may say 'Go on, have it right now!' The conflicts may, of course, be much more serious than that, as we shall see later on.

Berne actually has a very good definition of an ego state, which brings out some important points;

> An ego state may be described phenomenologically as a coherent system of feelings related to a given subject, and operationally as a set of coherent behaviour patterns; or pragmatically, as a system of feelings which motivates a related set of behaviour patterns . . . . Repression of traumatic memories of conflicts is possible in many cases, according to Federn, only through repression of the whole pertinent ego state. Early ego states remain preserved in a latent stage, waiting to be re-cathected.
>
> (Berne 1961)

We would only add to this the point that the whole ego state may not only be repressed, but also split off. This comes out in the way in which an ego state can switch in with great power. Berne later likened it to the way in which a bull stops in mid-arena when the scientist who implanted an electrode in its brain pulls a switch. He actually calls it 'the electrode' because it can be so dramatic and sudden:

> Many people know the instantaneous turn-off in the middle of sexual excitement, and have observed the smile which turns on and then instantaneously off as though someone in the smiler's head had pulled a switch . . . . The electrode got its name from a patient named Norvil who sat very still and very tense during his group sessions, unless he was spoken to. Then he answered instantly with a string of careful clichés . . . after which he crunched up again. It soon became clear that it was a strict Father Parent in his head who controlled him with the 'sit still' turn-off switch, and the 'talk' button that turned him on.
>
> (Berne 1972)

Reasons will be given in Chapter 7 to suppose that this is due not to repression but to splitting.

SHAPIRO

At about the same time Stewart Shapiro was starting to work out his practice of using what he called 'subselves' in therapy. In 1962 he contributed a paper entitled 'A theory of ego pathology and ego therapy' to the *Journal of Psychology*, and followed that up in 1976 with a brief popular book called *The Selves Inside You*. He was one of the first people to discuss the question of how many subpersonalities there were; he said that in his experience there were from four to nine in each person. (This sounds very much like the 'magic number seven, plus or minus two', which the cognitive psychologist George Miller [1956] talked about in a famous paper.) He says: 'In my office are ten chairs, but they're not set up for group therapy; they're for individual work – one chair for each subself . . . . Sometimes I'll use one or two chairs; occasionally three or four; once in a while, all ten' (Shapiro 1976: 13-14) He introduces a new idea which we have met with before, and we shall meet again in the work of Stone and Winkelman. He believes in deliberately creating a Chairman of the Board, who will stand outside the rest of the subpersonalities, and make decisions about how to handle them. But he makes it clear that it is no part of the job of this functionary to exclude or eliminate any of the characters:

> We do not 'kick out of the house' any subself or part of the personality but rather understand and reintegrate its energy and functions back into the self organization. In subself therapy there are no outcasts and no prisons to lock up the deviants.
>
> (Shapiro 1976: 17-18)

Shapiro has his own version of the typology of subselves. This seems to be a regular temptation of people working in this field, to try to classify the subpersonalities in some way. We have just been looking at the way in which Eric Berne handles this. This can actually get very complex, even though at first it seems so simple, and even over-simple. For example, I have found from various sources the following kinds of Child ego state found in Transactional Analysis: the Adapted Child (Compliant Child), the

Natural Child (Free Child), the Little Professor (Mischievous Gamey Little Professor and Creative Inventive Little Professor), Sleepy (a primitive, highly dependent part of the Child), Spooky (that part of the Child concerned with symbolizing), the Adapted Critical Child, the Disturbed Natural Child, the Vengeful Child, and the Self-Protective Child.

Sometimes it is not realized just how intricate the Berne model can get. For Shapiro the structure of ego states is put like this (I have expanded his summary from other places in his own text):

1 *Nurturing Parent Selves.* They're in charge of supporting, giving love, care, attention, praise, and positive reinforcement. [Shapiro's names for this character include Protecting Parent and Guardian Angel.]

2 *Evaluative Parent Selves.* They're often referred to as the Critic, the Pusher, the Voice of Authority, etc., and they usually reflect the norms and values of society. This type of self sets standards and measures you to see if you live up to them, and makes you feel bad if you don't. [Shapiro says that a Pusher and a Critic may work together, or there may be several Critics.] It can be masculine or feminine. [Shapiro also calls this the Prosecuting Attorney, the Slavedriver or the Big Shot.]

3 *Central Organizing Selves.* Examples are the Executive Self, Chairman Self, or Coordinating Self. This Central Self is often in close connection with the Observer, who acts like a trained staff person. In less balanced personalities, the Chairman may be weak, and the power of leadership may be in the hands of the Critic or some other subself. [Shapiro also calls this the Audience subself, or the Other People subself. He likens it to the Freudian Ego.]

4 *Good, Socialized, Adapted Child Subselves.* This is the obedient, conforming Child Self who tries to please authorities. Some of this is necessary for socialization and in cooperative working with others. Too much of this subself inclines the person toward over-conformity, rote obedience, and lack of creativity. [Shapiro also calls this the Performer.]

5 *Natural Child Selves.* These subselves are usually creative, may be nonconforming and rebellious, but carry much of the

spontaneity and playfulness of the Original Child you once were. [Shapiro also calls this the Creative Self.] A sense of humor often comes with this subself.

(Shapiro 1976: 34-5)

It can be seen how similar this is to the Eric Berne schema, and I find this rather disappointing. But unlike Berne, he does have a place for something outside the subpersonalities, and here he comes very close to psychosynthesis, actually using the same disidentification exercise that Assagioli developed:

For example, you may uncover various subpersonalities such as those of the person who found a Clown, a Gorilla or Caveman, a Child, an Earth Mother, and Father Time. The disidentification exercise in this case would be, 'I *have* a Clown but I *am not* a Clown, I *have* a Gorilla, but I *am not* a Gorilla,' etc. After going through all the subselves, the person would say (or think) '*I am I*, a center of pure consciousness.'

(Shapiro 1976: 120)

He also has a place for the Higher or Transcendent Self. He sees the work with subpersonalities as one way of attaining sufficient psychological harmony so that spiritual harmony can follow.

SHORR

Perhaps the most flexible of all the approaches to subpersonalities comes from the psycho-imagination therapy of Joseph Shorr (1983). It is curious that he makes no mention of using different chairs in his work, and he seems to be able to do without all the apparatus the rest of us find so useful. He uses polarities, groups of three, groups of four, and obviously there is no limit to the imagination in his work. I find his approach a continual inspiration and in spite of his frequent superficiality he has much to offer in the understanding of how to work with imaginary persons.

Through his many-sidedness, he makes a suitable bridge between the work of the sixties and the more recent work.

Chapter Six

SUBPERSONALITIES IN PSYCHOTHERAPY: THE RECENT WORK

In the seventies and eighties, there has been a great and important growth in the approaches using subpersonalities. This has involved extension of the older work, and also some quite different and original work.

JOHN WATKINS

Rather similar to the work of Berne and Shapiro but taking off in an interesting direction is the work of the ego-state school, led by John Watkins. This school is prepared to use hypnosis at times in its work, and sees this as legitimate. Like the others, its practioners see the person as a confederation of component segments. The relations between these segments are expressed through the operation of cathexis. 'Cathexis' is an unfamiliar word to most of us, though it is common in psychoanalysis. It means investment; when we are attracted to someone or something, we put energy into getting close to that person or thing, being with that person or thing, getting hold of that person or thing and making him, her, or it our own.

> The theory of ego-states holds that dissociation is not an either–or, but it is rather a matter of degree. When large patterns of personality functioning are relatively withdrawn from 'the me', and when they are not too highly energized, they form the underlying entities in normal people called 'ego-states'. They interact, influence, and emerge (become executive) for normal purposes of adaptation and defence. We behave and experience things differently at different

88

times , but we sense a continuity in the feeling of sameness. Perhaps it makes more sense to assume, as did Federn (1952), that selfness is an energy, an ego energy. When a thought, emotion, motive, or other psychological element is invested with this energy, then it is experienced as 'my' thought, 'my' emotion, 'my' motive, etc. But when the thought, emotion, or motivation is activated by a qualitatively different 'not-self' energy, an 'it' energy, then it is experienced as an object, as a 'not-me', and existing in the world outside the boundaries of personhood.

(Watkins and Johnson 1982)

This seems a very useful formulation. It is as if one of the people in our dream is often given the character of 'me', and the other people and objects in the dream are treated as 'not me'. But this is a decision, and like all decisions it can be changed.

This approach does not seem to have the same emphasis on polarities as does the Gestalt school. They offer a much more general theory, and one which I find more persuasive:

Thus, ego-state theory holds that normal personalities are characterized by organizational patterns of behaviour and experience that have been partially dissociated from each other for purposes of adaptation and defence.

In a sense, each of us is a multiple personality. We exhibit one personality at home, another at the office, and another on vacation. But usually these various 'sub-personalities' are governed by a generalized 'Federal jurisdiction', even as the States of Montana and Idaho must submit to control from the United States government. We sense a continuity of selfness at all times. It is generally unrecognized that each of us is not a unity, but more like a confederation of component segments. Sometimes these parts cooperate and smooth the way of adaptation to the world. At other times they exhibit relative autonomy from each other and, through internal conflict, give us our anxieties, depressions, headaches, phobias, and other painful symptoms.

(Watkins and Johnson 1982: 129-30)

This links in very easily with some of the other material we have already been noticing. It is interesting that these people, working from quite different premises, come to the same conclusion about the undesirability of merging all the characters into one central self or ego: 'Fusion, or the merging of two or more personalities into a 'oneness', is generally neither essential nor desirable except in special circumstances' (Watkins and Johnson 1982). They also come to the same conclusion about the function of the therapist, who is there to see fair play and make sure that all the voices in the dialogue are properly heard. 'The therapist should act like an internal diplomat, working out compromises and resolutions between the various personalities' (Watkins and Johnson 1982). But they certainly make some new points of their own, as for example when they discuss the difficulties which some clients offer when they threaten to take some extreme action:

> Underlying personalities and ego states, being 'part-persons', do not have the ability to generalize and engage in abstract thinking. They frequently think concretely and illogically like a child. It is common for an underlying personality to plot the destruction or death of the person while believing that it, itself, will survive. Suicide is thought as applying only to one of the other personalities, not one's self.
>
> (Watkins and Johnson 1982: 138-41)

This is certainly a useful hint for something to watch out for very carefully. And it may be that working with subpersonalities even makes it easier to become aware of this kind of possibility.

VOICE DIALOGUE

This leads us on to what is perhaps the most ambitious and well worked out approach to subpersonalities yet devised. Like Berne and Shapiro, the Voice Dialogue people like to give names and categories to the subpersonalities. They are Hal Stone and Sidra Winkelman, who come from a Jungian background, but have now broken away to found their own school. They have much more to say than any of the others as to all the ins and outs of actually working with subpersonalities, which they call 'energy patterns'. They justify this nomenclature by saying that this term more clearly points to the dramatic animating qualities of these selves, as they enliven us, causing us to think, feel and act in a variety of ways. They have identified at least the following:

The Protector/Controller	This arises early in development, and consists of that part of us which tries to fit in with the parental requirements. It notices what works and what does not work, what pleases and what does not please. It learns how to protect our vulnerability, and it erects a rigid set of answers to these questions. It is both cultural and familial. Can combine with the Critic.
The Pusher	This is the one which tells us that we have not done the chores, written the letter, done our exercises. It appears to be on our side, reminding us of our duties when we might forget. But in reality it is not helpful in its present form. 'As soon as we cross an item off the top of the list, the Pusher will add one on to the bottom.' Can combine with the Critic.
The Critic	This is the one which tells us we have got it wrong. It is extremely acute, and notices everything which could make us feel rotten about ourselves. It delights in using its power. It can combine and co-operate with other subpersonalities very well.
The Perfectionist	Insists on the highest standards. Cannot stand the second-rate, the shoddy, the messy, the incomplete, the shapeless. No mistakes must be made. Can combine with the Critic.
The Power Brokers	Have to do with Power, Ambition, Pusher, Money, Selfishness, all seen as subpersonalities. Very often cover up for more vulnerable subpersonalities.
The Pleaser	Wants to please everybody, and make them happy. Very often covers up for

	anger. Very nice, but compulsive about it, and unable to be anything other than nice.
The Inner Child	This can take various forms – the vulnerable child (often extremely sensitive), the playful child, the magical child. May be too young or hurt to use words.
The Good and Bad Mother, and the Good and Bad Father	These speak for themselves and do not require much explanation.

Stone and Winkelman use empty chairs or cushions in their work, and encourage the person to come to terms with the subpersonality in question. They encourage an Aware Ego to take responsibility for the dance of the subpersonalities.

> After the facilitator has finished working with whichever Voices have been facilitated during a session, the subject moves the chair back to the original Ego place and is asked to stand behind the chair. This is the position of the Awareness level . . .
> After this, the subject is invited to sit down and resume the position of the Aware Ego. Reactions to the work and possible differences of perception between the facilitator and the subject are then discussed. The session is reviewed briefly again and is then ended with the subject in the Aware Ego.
> (Stone and Winkelman 1985: 55)

This is quite clearly a rather formal and almost ritualistic performance, and it seems to be quite a feature of their work. It is perhaps this use of the Aware Ego that is the most limiting part of their work, because they insist on coming back to the Aware Ego all the time as a necessary central reference point. I think at times it is unwise to insist on this, as it seems to perpetrate all the errors of ego psychotherapy, which ignores the unconscious, or tries to reduce it to insignificance. My own view is that subpersonality work is there to do justice to the unconscious and to give us a respect for the way in which it works.

Stone and Winkelman seem to agree with this themselves at times, because they are quite happy to talk about things like the superego, which are largely located in the unconscious. The Protector/Controller is somewhat related to the Freudian 'superego' or the TA 'parent'. It is this Protector/Controller who makes sure that the disowned selves remain disowned' (1985: 86). This is an interesting theoretical point, which is not made by anyone else, so far as I have discovered. If it is true, it is a very valuable insight. It needs to be checked out further.

The language used by Stone and Winkelman enables them to make another interesting point, which seems to me to tie in with ideas earlier associated with the name of Wilhelm Reich:

> In many individuals today who have been involved in the consciousness process, we have a new phenomenon. In their pursuit of freedom they have disowned their Protector/Controllers. They have struggled for years to become free emotionally and sexually. They meditate, visualize and expand in all kinds of directions . . . . This rejection of the Protector/Controller energy is amazingly common in parts of the world where people have been involved in consciousness work for extended periods of time. Conversely, in those parts of the world where psychological work is relatively new, the Protector/Controllers are very strong.
>
> (Stone and Winkelman 1985: 94)

This may remind us of Reich's distinction between sexual freedom, where we have genuinely integrated our conflicts and got rid of our character armour, and sexual sophistication, where we resolve consciously to be free. The latter, he says, actually involves the inhibition of inhibition, and is even more tortuous and neurotic than the original sexual repression. To disown one's Protector/Controller seems very much to fall into the same trap.

These authors also handle in an interesting way the problem of the vulnerable child, which has come to our notice so acutely recently through the work of Alice Miller. It may be remembered that one of her most telling points is that the abuse of a young child may be actually repeated in the therapy room, the therapist taking up the role of the abusing parent. On this our authors say:

The Children of our inner world know how to 'be'. Most of
the rest of our personality knows how to 'do' and how to 'act'.
The gift to the facilitator in working with these patterns is that
he must learn how to 'be' with them; otherwise they cannot
emerge. When dealing with the Inner Child, the dictum is:
'There's nowhere to go and there's nothing to do.'
(Stone and Winkelman 1985: 145)

This seems a wise and deep thing to say, and if therapists could
take this more seriously they could perhaps avoid the pitfalls which
Alice Miller more than anyone else has pointed out.

They also seem to be on the side of the angels, so to speak, in
relation to the question of power. One of the perennial questions
which therapists get asked is this: 'If you are encouraging people
to be more powerful in their lives, and to take charge, as you put
it, of their lives, is this not going to make them more oppressive
and more arrogant?' After quoting a number of concrete cases,
our authors have an interesting answer:

We see again in these examples the basic difference between
being powerful and being empowered. Being and acting
powerful means that we are identified with the energy
patterns on the Power side. Empowerment means that we
have an Aware Ego that can honor, and to some extent
embrace, both Power and, ironically enough, Vulnerability.
Empowerment is certainly one of the inevitable outcomes of
this whole process we are describing.
(Stone and Winkelman 1985: 164)

So a combination of strength and vulnerability, to some people
exact opposites, seems to be a good way of looking at empowerment. And once we have seen it in this way, we can appreciate how
particularly relevant this concept is to women:

In a way, women are more likely to reach for empowerment
than men. They still do not have access to traditional power
and are forced to move ahead from an empowered position
(power plus vulnerability) rather than a power position (one
identified with archetypal parental energies) because in many
areas access to the power of the collective is denied them.

94

Because of this, many women do not develop the same kinds of Heavyweight sub-personalities as men.

(Stone and Winkelman 1985: 220)

This again is a question hardly touched on by other writers in this field, who often seem to assume that women are going to have just the same types of subpersonalities as men. But this is not necessarily the case at all, and it is good to be reminded of this.

There is in fact in the work of Stone and Winkelman a good appreciation of the special problems of being a woman in the patriarchal society of today. They talk a good deal about the types of subpersonality which it would be most useful for women to cultivate and make familiar. One of these is the Warrior. Not the kind of warrior which may spring to mind with a spear and shield, stamping and grimacing, but the kind of warrior we have become acquainted with through the work of Carlos Castaneda, Hyemenyosts Storm, and others:

The Warrior energy has been unavailable to women until recently. It was considered unfeminine, castrating, or worse yet, some form of devilish possession. One can see clearly, however, how necessary it is for self-protection and how powerless a woman can be if this energy is disowned . . . . The Killer Who Protects . . . Warrior energy is needed by all humans, both men and women, for self-protection. Needless to say, women are seen as life-givers and healers, and the thought that they might have any destructive energies spreads panic among the population . . . . To be denied access to the destructiveness in oneself is to be denied another major power source. Sadly enough, it also causes all of the destruction to be projected onto men . . . . It is interesting to note that this voice has been so thoroughly repressed in women that it rarely assumes the form of a female as a sub-personality. It is far more likely to be a jungle cat, a graceful feline killer.

(Stone and Winkelman 1985: 218-22)

So we have here a good awareness of the way in which we are living in a particular historical epoch, in a particular part of the world, with a particular subculture. They are telling us that we have to take into account the social context within which all therapy is done.

MAHRER

Someone who would agree with this very much is Alvin Mahrer, a very interesting academic working at the University of Ottawa. He presents a whole humanistic psychodynamics, based upon the notion of subpersonalities, which he calls potentials – operating potentials if they are consciously available, deeper potentials if they are unconscious.

> Each potential constitutes its own zone of experiencing, more or less distinct and independent of the other potentials. It is as if each potential is its own mini-world of experiencing. In this sense, we are indeed multiple selves, multiple conscious-nesses, even multiple personalities. Each potential is its own center, its own self system, its own personality.
>
> (Mahrer 1978: 29)

Human problems, he then contends, mainly arise from bad relationships between the potentials. It is these conflicts and maladjustments which cause all the bad feelings, all the compulsive behaviour, which make us appear neurotic.

> When potentials are *disintegrated*, their relationships are fractionated, abrasive, disjunctive, opposed, disorganized. Instead of accepting and loving one another, they fear and hate each other . . . the nature of the relationships among potentials is the major determinant of problems . . . our theory turns to the disintegrative relationship among potentials, not merely for 'neurosis', but for the whole spectrum of human suffering.
>
> (Mahrer 1978: 27-8)

What the therapist has to do is to get in touch with the deeper potentials of the client, deeper potentials which the client may not know how to meet or to face. The therapist tunes in to the client, bodily and emotionally, so deeply that he or she can speak on behalf of the client's deeper potentials. 'The radical proposition is that the therapist is thereby able to be the voice of the patient's deeper potential, to take on its identity' (Mahrer 1983: 57).

At the point where the patient is now able to take on this revealed identity of his or her own deeper potential, which may have been defended against for years, a breakthrough comes and the deeper potential reveals its positive form. There can then be good, integrative relationships with other potentials. Energy is released, and the patient is able to be himself or herself more completely. This is the actualization of the potentials.

This is clearly a radical way of handling the question, but it gets more radical yet. The theory of development is also important here. Mahrer's theory of development is that the person starts before conception, in the primitive personality field set up by the prospective parents. The foetus grows within this primitive personality field, and the baby is born into it. Within this primitive personality field are all the potentials of the parents, and the relations between them. In Mahrer's theory:

> basic personality processes refer to material within the period from a few years prior to conception to several years following birth. Therefore, a deep, broad, and profound experiential psychotherapy will deal with material from that primitive period. It will go beyond the infant as the experiencing nexus, and into the experiencings of significant figures during this primitive period.
>
> (Mahrer 1986: 286-7)

So in this approach the client is not talking to empty chairs, but to the inner potential represented by the therapist. The therapist is no longer there, so to speak, but is now speaking for that inner potential, that subpersonality. When I have done this kind of work, I have sometimes felt that I knew the subpersonality better than the client did.

This work seems to me radically different from all the other approaches to subpersonalities, but quite compatible with them in most respects.

HYPNOTHERAPY

When I started on this book, I knew nothing about hypnotherapy.

But the more I went into it, the more I found I had to go into hypnotherapy and find out more about it. And it turns out, as we saw earlier, that the whole of psychotherapy comes out of the tradition initiated by Mesmer, de Puységur, Liébault, Bernheim, Janet, Charcot and the rest. Let us just begin by going back to some of the details of that which have not yet been mentioned:

> The first magnetizers were immensely struck by the fact that, when they induced magnetic sleep in a person, a new life manifested itself of which the subject was unaware, and that a new and often more brilliant personality emerged with a continuous life of its own. The entire nineteenth century was preoccupied with the problem of the coexistence of these two minds and of their relationship to each other. Hence the concept of the 'double-ego', or 'dipsychism'.
> From the beginning, ideas diverged as to whether that other, or hidden, mind was to be considered 'closed' or 'open'. According to the first conception, the hidden mind is 'closed' in the sense that it contains only things, which, at one time or other, went through the conscious mind, notably forgotten memories or occasionally memories of impressions that the conscious mind had only fleetingly perceived, as well as memories of daydreams and fantasies. Some authors contended that this forgotten material could follow an autonomous development, independent of the conscious mind. The dipsychism theory was particularly developed by Dessoir, who wrote the once famous book *The Double Ego* (1890), in which he expounded the concept that the human mind normally consists of these two distinct layers, each of which has its own characteristics. Each of these two egos consist, in turn, of complex chains of associations. Dessoir called them *Oberbewusstsein* and *Unterbewusstsein,* 'upper consciousness' and 'under consciousness'; we get an inkling of the latter during dreams and clearer impressions during spontaneous somnambulism. Induced hypnosis is nothing but a calling forth of the secondary ego, which thus comes temporarily to the foreground. As for dual personality, Dessoir believed that the second personality had acquired such strength that it competed for predominance with the main personality. Everyone, he added, bears within himself

the seeds of a dual personality. Subsequent authors
supplemented that theory with rich material that included
inspiration, mysticism, and mediumistic manifestations.
(Ellenberger 1970: 145-6)

It can be seen here how much of what we are saying in this book
was anticipated years ago by the hypnotists. And they did not stop
there. They went on to get nearer still to present-day ideas, going
on from the idea of dual personality (dipsychism) to the idea of
multiplicity in the personality, or polypsychism.

This word seems to have been coined by the magnetizer
Durand (de Gros). He claimed that the human organism
consisted of anatomical segments, each of which had a
psychic ego of its own, and all of them subjected to a general
ego, the Ego-in-Chief, which was our usual consciousness. In
this legion each subego had a consciousness of its own, was
able to perceive and to keep memories and to elaborate
complex psychic operations. The sum total of these subegos
constituted our unconscious life . . . . The theory of polypsychism was taken up and given a philosophical elaboration
by Colsenet, who linked it with Leibnitz's concept of a
hierarchy of monads.
(Ellenberger 1970: 146)

Today, when these ideas need to be subjected to the most rigorous
testing, it is again the hypnotic tradition that has pursued some of
the best and most accurate research on subpersonalities – as can
be seen in the detailed work of Hilgard (1986). He mentions that
a whole issue of the *International Journal of Clinical and Experimental
Hypnosis* was devoted to evidence and issues related to the kind of
thing we are interested in here (April 1984, 32 (2)). And it also
turns out that much of the best current thinking about
subpersonalities comes from hypnotherapy. This was quite a
disturbing finding, because I had always mistrusted hypnotherapy
and thought that nothing very important could come from it.

The stunning book by Beahrs (1982), which I only discovered
late in the writing of the present work, gives a practical and also a
philosophical rationale for working with subpersonalities, and in it
the author gives a great deal of information about other people in

the hypnotic tradition who have made interesting and useful contributions in this area.

He has himself done a great deal of work with subpersonalities, and agrees with others that 'Our goal is not to be "rid" of a psychological process, but to shift it from the harmful or maladaptive ("pathological") dimension to where it is useful in its effect, so that what was once a symptom can truly become a skill' (Beahrs 1982: 82). He takes the same position as we have seen to be useful many times before, that mood changes, altered states of consciousness, subpersonalities, and multiple personality are points on a continuum of dissociation, with the boundaries becoming thicker and more marked as we go along that line. And he agrees with another of our positions:

> I consider dissociation to be essential for healthy functioning; in addition, I believe that it is a creative act. Kohut (1971) has taken the same position regarding vertical splitting, which I use almost synonymously with dissociation. Everyday examples of creative dissociating are dreams and fantasies, roles and specific skills, imaginary playmates, projection of both positive and negative aspects of the self on to others, selective amnesia for stimuli, and virtually any defence function. In each, an aspect of overall mental function is put in relief by dissociation in a way that enhances one's powers for action. [p. 85]
>
> A single, gigantic, undifferentiated oneness cannot necessarily be considered a healthier condition than a complex cooperative whole comprised of many functioning subparts, like orchestra members, their power for action enhanced by division of labour. [p. 113]
>
> (Beahrs 1982)

This is of course the emphasis we have already seen to be so important in the ideas of Hillman and Mary Watkins.

An interesting point Beahrs mentions about the use of subpersonalities in treatment is that the therapist may not actually need to deal with each subpersonality in detail. He gives the example of a patient he had who was dealt with on the basis of just one subpersonality, which was worked with very thoroughly and a good outcome resulted. Later, this patient was able to report an awareness of five distinct subpersonalities, all dating back to childhood. 'These had come together successfully without having been dealt with separately by the therapist' (p. 104).

Another point which was new to me comes from the work of Allison (Allison and Schwartz 1980), who classifies subpersonalities into three categories: persecutors, rescuers, and internal self-helpers. The first two of these are relatively familiar, but the internal self-helpers were new to me. According to Allison, they have characteristics differing from pathological subpersonalities and are a great potential resource in treatment.

> In his view, they differ in having (1) no identifiable time and reason for their formation; (2) no defensive function; and (3) far more accuracy of perception, to the point of being 'incapable of transference' and able to tell a therapist all his mistakes.
>
> (Beahrs 1982: 109)

This is fascinating if true, and certainly something worth looking out for and exploring in more detail. It reminds me of the important idea of Langs (1982) that the unconscious of the patient is often very accurate about the unconscious of the therapist.

More recently, Karle and Boys (1987) have given an interesting example of one way in which early child abuse can be handled. This is of course just the kind of trauma which fits so well with the model given in Chapter 7, and which has been found to be implicated in many cases of multiple personality. The client was a middle-aged woman who had been sexually abused by her father:

> She was asked to return in hypnosis to the time her father had molested her sexually, and simultaneously to observe the scene as her adult self. The scene was played out without the therapist intervening, up to the moment at which the child was ordered to her room. At this moment, the therapist asked the patient to enter the scene in her adult self, meet her child self on the stairs, pick her up, comfort and reassure her, and generally to act as she would to any child in such a situation. She was to continue in this fashion until the child was wholly reassured and at peace, and then to return to the present day. The patient reported successful performance of the task in

terms of the child's restored equanimity. Perhaps more important was the feeling that she could recognize in her adult self that her child self . . . was in fact innocent.

(Karle and Boys 1987: 250–1)

Whether the client needed to be hypnotized to do this work is a moot point, and I personally would not take if for granted that this would be so. But certainly it is an approach which fits very well with the hypnotic tradition.

In general, work with subpersonalities is no more common in hypnotherapy than it is in other modalities. John and Helen Watkins are two people who have taken this approach a very long way. They make many of the same points that others have also made in this field, but add some interesting ideas such as the thought that working with ego states is like a kind of family therapy. This is, I feel, a very fruitful thought, and it seems worth while to look at the way they put it: 'Ego-state therapy is the utilization of family and group treatment techniques for the resolution of conflicts between the different ego states that constitute a "family of self" within a single individual' (Watkins and Watkins 1986: 149).

They give the example of a student who could not study successfully. A strong ego state close to consciousness wanted him to study and was very upset when he could not do so. However, another ego state, identified as a four-year-old child, wanted more play and less study, and refused to let the student study unless he was treated better. The therapist made friends with the child, and persuaded him to play at night, thus permitting the student to study during the day. 'A week later Ed returned in great delight reporting that he had studied well during the past week and had gotten an A on his foreign language examination. He wondered, though, why he was having such vivid dreams and "in technicolor" every night' (Watkins and Watkins 1986: 150). It turned out that the child had kept his agreement and was playing at night. The student was not aware of this ego state until the therapist informed him about it afterwards.

So this is very interesting work, and I have acquired a new respect for at least some aspects of hypnotherapy since coming across it.

SATIR

A quite different and very original approach which comes from the field of family therapy was developed by the late Virginia Satir. She calls the subpersonalities 'parts' of the person:

> For one thing you probably have many parts that you have not yet discovered. All of these parts, whether you have owned them or not, are present in you. Becoming aware of them enables you to take charge of them rather than be enslaved by them. Each of your parts is a vital source of energy. Each has many uses, and can harmonize with many other parts in ways to add even more energy.
>
> (Satir 1978: 63)

So far this is similar to other approaches we have seen until now. But what Satir then does is to use the idea to create a 'parts party'. She suggests that the focal person (who may be a patient, a client, a student, a trainee, a family member, or someone else) uses imagination to bring up the faces (bodies, voices, movements) of famous people (fact or fiction, past, present, or future, same sex or different) that have some meaning, positive or negative, for the individual. When at least six such people have been brought up, an adjective is put after each one, to sum up the particular reason why they came up – the particular meaning each one has for the focal person creating the list.

The next step is to imagine the people interacting. Satir's favourite way of doing this is to work with a group, and get the people in the group to take the various roles at the request of the focal person. But the same thing can be done with just one person, by getting them to imagine their people circulating round and round on a merry-go-round, getting to know each one more deeply as he or she comes round again. As this happens, each one becomes less and less the person they were to start with, and more and more the quality they represent for the focal person. As this goes on, the negative personalities or qualities very often seem to be more approachable and more manageable – 'I cannot manage anything I do not own' – not so impossible as perhaps they were before. 'There was a time when I thought I had to kill all those parts of me that gave me trouble. Now I see they may be my greatest helpers if I decide to make them my friends' (Satir 1978: 99).

Satir likens the person to a mobile, which only works well when all the various parts are balanced. We need in a way to stand outside the whole mobile in order to be able to balance it properly. And we cannot balance it properly if we pretend that some of the parts of the mobile are not there. Furthermore, there is a continual rebalancing of the mobile as it moves through different situations.

Satir has a deceptively simple way of putting these things. For example, when she comes to discuss anger and how to handle it, we get this:

> The child who throws a rock at his brother must be taught
> that such behaviour is unacceptable and that he needs to
> develop different methods for coping with his anger. Instead,
> he is often taught that it is bad to have angry feelings.
> (Satir and Baldwin 1983: 232)

This is actually a profound point, but it sounds so simple and obvious that we may not recognize its profound simplicity. Similarly with the idea of the 'parts party'. It sounds at first quite banal, but in the hands of a fine therapist it can go very deep. There are actually four phases which can be considered: (1) meeting the parts (each part is personified and encountered as a person); (2) witnessing the conflicts between the parts (this can be brought out more vividly if there is a group, by asking each part to try to dominate the whole); (3) transforming the parts (through dialogue and negotiation until some stable balance is reached); and (4) integrating the parts, where the parts are again encountered, only now in their modified form, and symbolically accepted and unified. This is described in more detail in Satir and Baldwin (1983).

NEURO-LINGUISTIC PROGRAMMING

An approach about which we need to say somewhat less is that of Neuro-Linguistic Programming (NLP). NLP does not really believe in subpersonalities, but it does use all kinds of approximations to subpersonalities in its actual work. For

104

example, one of the NLP books spends two pages on giving a seven-step procedure for creating a part (their word, I assume taken from their work with Virginia Satir, for a subpersonality) and then they deny that there is any such thing as a part: 'The notion of parts is a good pace for most people's experience, but for me there is a bit too much anthropomorphism in the notion of parts' (Bandler and Grinder 1982: 72). To anthropomorphize sticks and stones may be dubious, and to anthropomorphize computers or robots may be dangerous, but to anthropomorphize people seems a perfectly proper thing to do, and maybe about the only thing to do. In any case, what we are talking about here is personification rather than anthropomorphization.

Possibly the reason for the lack of interest in subpersonalities in NLP is that they are so much influenced by the work of Milton Erickson, and he never did very much along these lines, so far as I have been able to discover.

However, some practitioners of NLP are more accommodating than Bandler and Grinder themselves. For example, Genie Laborde talks about subpersonalities, and makes rather a nice point about them, that 'inner conflicts are evidence of our potential flexibility' (Laborde 1987: 187). She also has her own version of Satir's parts party: she invites eight parts to sit round a table, and appoints a Conflict Manager to facilitate the negotiation between them. This seems to be a solitary activity in her book. However, in a later book, she goes into more detail about subpersonalities, regarding them largely as resulting from the process of introjection, which we will see in Chapter 7 is indeed one of the main sources of subpersonalities. She points out that the incongruence we so often notice in people (the tone of voice not matching what is being said, or the gestures not fitting what is being expressed verbally, and so on) can very often be traced back to conflicting subpersonalities within the person, some of them quite possibly unconscious. And she states very succinctly and well the main point of becoming aware of one's subpersonalities: 'By becoming aware of our internal conflicts, we can release the mental energy we have been using for repression, work out some internal negotiations, and use the released energy in our lives' (Laborde 1988: 113). What we then get, she says, is congruence – the co-operation of our various parts working in harmony, so that it is the whole person acting at once.

SASPORTAS

This kind of outcome is also found in another rather similar way of working, developed by Liz Greene and Howard Sasportas. They feel that the astrological chart, with its careful and specific delineation of influences upon the person and conflicts within the person, can be used to identify subpersonalities and suggest how they may be worked with. They say that the whole point of subpersonality work is not just to identify subpersonalities but also to disidentify from them and reconnect to the 'I' that has the subpersonalities, the 'I' that shifts from one to another.

> Diana Whitmore uses this analogy to explain the difference between being a subpersonality and *having* a subpersonality. She says that if you are a dog that bites, then you bite. But if you have a dog that bites, then you can choose to let it bite, or choose to put a muzzle on the dog, or teach it not to bite. If you are totally identified with a subpersonality, then you just act it out. But if you realise a subpersonality is something you have operating in you, then you can do something to change, alter or transform it.
>
> (Sasportas 1987)

Their outlook is rather Jungian, and Sasportas makes an interesting and novel suggestion that just as Jung says that each person (or persona) has a shadow (a negative or inferior subpersonality who embodies all the worst things we do not like or accept about ourselves), perhaps each of the subpersonalities has its own shadow:

> Someone with a strong love subpersonality might be harbouring resentment and anger: 'When is it my turn for someone to give to me and look after me for a change?' A strong masculine or animus subpersonality may have a fear of not being loved or appreciated hidden within it.
>
> (Sasportas 1987)

This is an interesting thought, and it does often happen that when one is working with one subpersonality, another voice will come through, and another subpersonality will advance and have to be

106

recognized. Sometimes this may be a shadow aspect of the same subpersonality, and sometimes it may be describable in some other way. But certainly the idea of a shadow for each subpersonality is a thought worth playing with.

Another idea which Sasportas puts forward that he says he acquired from the British psychosynthesis teacher Diana Whitmore, is that it is helpful to ask these three questions of each subpersonality:

What do you want?
What do you need?
What do you have to offer me?

Sasportas gives the example of a subpersonality who was a racing driver. He asked it, 'What do you want?', and it replied, 'A flashy car'. He comments about this that is is very gross, very specific, and very exact. He then went on to ask, 'What do you need?' The answer this time was 'I need recognition'.

The need for recognition, he says, is more subtle than the gross want of a flashy car. It could be satisfied in a number of other ways, not just through having a car, and this may suggest other means of getting the same thing which are less expensive or more satisfying. The third question – 'What do you have to offer me?' – brought the reply: 'I have energy, drive, and will-power to offer you.' There is within the person a source of those qualities, and as long as it is defined as bad, and as just wanting flashy cars, those qualities will remain denied and untapped.

Sasportas also has a discussion of the question of whether there are any standard subpersonalities, so to speak, which come up in all people at all times. He has found some of these, and considers the main ones to be the critic (judge), the saboteur (victim, martyr), and the inner child. These, he says, come up so often that they may be universal. But for the most part he does not like this solution, but would, rather, like to speak of certain conflicts which may appear quite regularly. The first of these is the conflict between subpersonalities which have love at their core, and other subpersonalities which have will at their core. Other typical conflicts he deals with are change versus maintenance, work versus play, the mystic/pragmatist split, the freedom/closeness dilemma, and the disagreements between head, heart, and belly.

107

COGNITIVE-BEHAVIOURAL THERAPY

A complete contrast to this is the way in which the idea of subpersonalities is beginning to creep in to cognitive-behavioural therapy. This has come about because a good deal of research in cognitive psychology has now established the notion of self-schemas as being empirically testable and valid. Much of Chapter 9 is devoted to this research and its ramifications into the ideas of prototypes and schemas, subselves and imagoes, and so on.

One of the most important and most recent papers mentioned in that chapter is from Hazel Markus and Paula Nurius, cognitive researchers at the University of Michigan. They talk in terms of selves and subselves, and introduce the very important notion of possible selves – projections of various aspects of ourselves into the future, an idea which turns out to have a great deal to say about the whole question of long-term motivation. They say this about therapy:

> Such thinking is, in fact, quite central to some recently
> developed therapeutic cognitive restructuring paradigms. The
> goal of such programmes is to introduce alternative self-views
> into the individual's self-system and then attempt to modify
> the social environment so that these alternative self-views can
> be more frequently activated to enhance their strength (e.g.
> Beck *et al.* 1979, McCullin and Giles 1985).
>
> (Markus and Nurius 1987: 164)

This view of therapy is very close to the general approach of what is now called cognitive-behavioural therapy, which is now well developed and advancing on all fronts.

For example, Donald Meichenbaum (one of the most eminent of those espousing the cognitive-behavioural position in psychotherapy) has made use of the idea of an internal dialogue. This is of course very appropriate for the general emphasis which he and this whole school places on self-statements – instructions to oneself, or self-putdowns, excuses, and so forth. He says that internal dialogues are generated by cognitive structures which are 'a system of concepts and judgements' (Meichenbaum 1977: 21). It is precisely this sort of cognitive structure which constitutes a subpersonality, though obviously our concept of a subpersonality is richer and contains more than just what is cognitive.

Again in personal construct psychology, which Robert Neimeyer argues is part of the cognitive-behavioural approach, there is a concept of different levels of construction, such that whole subsystems can come into existence and be differentiated. The person can then slip from one to the other construct system, depending upon the situation. Neimeyer gives the example of a woman who was extremely efficient at work, and extremely inefficient at home.

> As a consequence, therapy turned toward integrating these disparate subsystems, by importing into her personal life some of the organizational skills she used so effectively in business, and into her work some of the sharing of responsibility she accepted in other areas.
>
> (Neimeyer 1986: 238)

This sounds very similar to the kind of work which we have noticed elsewhere as appropriate to subpersonalities. The basic distinction which is so important is between detailed constructs on one level, and construct subsystems on the other.

Aaron Beck, who some would say invented cognitive therapy, has made a similar distinction between automatic thoughts and images on one level, and schemas on the other. He says that it is schemas derived from previous experience which are 'used to classify, interpret, evaluate and assign meaning to that event' (Weishaar and Beck 1986: 64) The notion of a mental schema (a whole subsystem within the personality), which is explained fully in Chapter 9, is congenial to the cognitive camp, and well founded within it.

In the same book, Richard Wessler, who has been particularly associated with the approach known as rational-emotive therapy, argues that:

> Specific thoughts and statements may be seen as generated from schemata [plural of schema, JR] about oneself, the world and other people, and should be distinguished in therapy from specific cognitions. The relationship is not unlike that between surface structure and deeper underlying meaning. In a sense, every specific cognition may reflect underlying assumptions, which may be

nonphenomenological. One important task of therapy, then, is to make clients more aware of their underlying nonphenomenological schemata. In other words (certain to be unacceptable to radical behaviourists), the task is to make the nonconscious conscious.

(Wessler 1986: 22)

This is obviously even closer to what we have been talking about elsewhere in this chapter.

Similarly, Goldfried (1982) has argued that schemas come at the level of therapeutic strategies, and that it is at this level that therapists of diverse orientations can speak a common language. (This is a point to which we will return later in this chapter.) So the language of schemas and subpersonalities may well be the language of the integration of psychotherapy.

HILLMAN'S CRITIQUE

One of the most interesting questions to arise out of this account of how the idea of subpersonalities is used by various people is raised by James Hillman. We saw earlier that he is one of the main proponents of the idea that it is not only all right but very important to personify the mental entities which we have called subpersonalities. But then he seems to take away with one hand what he has offered with the other. He warns that 'to take the archetype literally as personal is a personalistic fallacy'. He warns against literalism and externality:

We fall into externality all the time, even when internalizing in active imagination, taking the figures at face value, listening to their counsel literally, or simply by having to do active imagination at all in order to find depth, interiority, fantasy, and anima.

(Hillman 1985: 123)

And so he sees as a kind of religious neurosis the practice of talking with one's inner figures. He pours scorn on the idea of resolving the enigmas of life by means of internal dialogues with, for example, 'my anima'.

But this is very odd, in view of the commitment of Jung himself

110

and many other Jungians to precisely the sort of practice which Hillman condemns. In the very same book, for example, from which the above extract is quoted, Hillman quotes Jung as saying:

> start some dialogue with your anima . . . put a question or two to her: why she appears as Beatrice? why is she so big? why you are so small? why she nurses your wife and not yourself? . . . Treat her as a person, if you like as a patient or a goddess, but above all treat her as something that does exist.
>
> (Jung, 7 May 1947, letter to Mr O)

> [The patient] . . . is quite right to treat the anima as an autonomous personality and to address personal questions to her. I mean this as an actual technique . . . The art of it consists only in allowing our invisible partner to make herself heard. [O]ne should cultivate the art of conversing with oneself in the setting provided by an affect.
>
> (Jung, *Collected Works*, vol. 7, paras. 322-3)

Hillman's thought seems to be that to treat anima in this way is to devalue her by reducing her to just one personality, whereas she is much greater than that. But on his own showing, anima is characterized by multiplicity, and we cannot relate to multiplicity other than by taking the many entities one at a time. For example, if the Great Goddess is Maid, Mother, and Crone, it does no harm to relate to her as Crone only for a while. Perhaps later one will relate to her in one of her other aspects, and there is nothing about relating to the Crone which prevents one doing this. If I relate to my anima in the way in which she appears to me at the moment, that seems to me quite appropriate. At another time, she may appear quite otherwise.

This is clear in the work of Johnson (1986), and if we simply follow his hints we are unlikely to make the mistakes which Hillman seems to think so likely.

INTEGRATION OF PSYCHOTHERAPIES

What we have seen in these three chapters is that a number of different theoretical systems are saying very similar and quite compatible things about subpersonalities. Could it not be true, therefore, that the concept of a subpersonality could help in the integration of the psychotherapies?

All evolution is a process of differentiation and integration, and we have seen in the past thirty years an enormous differentiation and proliferation of psychotherapies. The fat book edited by Herink (1980) contains details of more than 250 different therapies: of these approximately 34 per cent come from the 1970s, 36 per cent from the 1960s, 17 per cent from the 1950s, 6 per cent from the 1940s, 5 per cent from the 1930s, and 2 per cent from before 1930. This shows the remarkable increase over the twenty years from 1960 to 1980. If a similar book were produced today, my belief is that the growth would have slowed down considerably. Today we are in a period, I believe, of integration rather than differentiation. And in this difficult period of integration, so much less glamorous and exciting than the hurly-burly of creation and innovation, we need concepts which can carry across disciplines and enable them to make sense to one another.

If we can say to the Jungians, 'Cast off the shackles, and explore the world of the complexes with greater vigour and freedom'; if we can say to the Gestaltists, 'Take seriously the archetypes, and don't reduce everything to polarities'; if we can say to the Voice Dialogue people, 'Take your own ideas more seriously and admit that that this can be a really deep and coherent form of therapy, stop being so nervous about always bringing everything back to the Aware Ego'; if we can say to the Neuro-Linguistic Programmers, 'Stop being so relentlessly trivial and adolescent and take the unconscious a lot more seriously as a realm with laws of its own which need to be respected'; if we can say to the hypnotherapists, 'Give up your insistence on speed and technique, and admit that therapy can take a long time, stop avoiding a real relationship with your clients'; if we can say to Mahrer, 'Drop your passion for polemic, and admit that you have a lot more in common with your colleagues than you usually make out'; if we can say to the cognitive-behavioural people, 'Give up this absurd notion that the cognitive can be isolated from everything else'; then we shall be beginning to create a climate in which dialogue can take place.

The odd people out, as always, are the Freudians. Guardians of the treasure as they are, they are the least free of the therapeutic groups we have considered. They are trapped in the dogma of the transference and cannot seem to get out. Yet it would be so easy and so productive to allow their clients at least to have dialogues

112

with their superegos. Actually, I am sure that some analysts have done so, and perhaps someone will write to me to tell me that this is all written up somewhere – maybe Ferenczi did it all in 1925 or something.

Psychoanalysts spend so much time enabling their clients to get in touch with their childhood selves, and it would be so easy and natural and productive to allow them to have dialogues with these internal children. The transference is just one way of making the absent present, and it is this which is the secret of psychotherapy. There are other ways, quite compatible with the ethos and theory of psychoanalysis. One could write a whole paper, perhaps, on the subpersonality as a transitional object.

I think it is the training analysis which is responsible for the rigidity of psychoanalysts. This is another dogmatic and idiotic practice which has become totally ossified, apparently, so far as I can find out. The idea that it is a good thing to stay with one person indefinitely, and to work out all one's internal problems and conflicts by projecting them on to this one person, is ridiculous as soon as stated. The result of this attempt can only be: (1) to give the trainee the illusion that all or most of his or her neurotic material has been dealt with; (2) to give the trainee an unrealistic and exaggerated attachment to everything the training analyst said or did; (3) to repeat the most neurotic of the misunderstandings which occurred in that relationship with the trainee's own clients. This sort of thing, which seems so obvious to the outsider and which has been stated so many times by various critics, leaves the psychoanalysts cold, apparently. They have the grail, the ark of the covenant, and these outsiders are simply envious, trying to pull psychoanalysis down so that they can climb up.

Yet surely, even to the most sincere and convinced psychoanalyst, there is something grotesque about a book like *Psychotherapy: a Basic Text* by the highly respected psychoanalyst and teacher Robert Langs (1982), where he says that the following things are part of the essential framework for psychoanalytic psychotherapy, and that ignoring them will have a very negative effect on the whole course of the therapy itself:

The therapist's chair should be quite different from the patient's chair (p. 364).
There should be a table between the therapist's chair and the

patient's chair (p. 364).

There should be a table between the therapist's chair and the couch (p. 364).

There should be a desk present to provide a sense of professionalism, but there should be nothing on the desk which is in any way self-revealing (p. 364).

The therapist should not respond directly to requests to change the times of sessions, and should either remain silent, or suggest that the patient continues to say whatever comes to mind (p. 421).

The therapist's fee should be maintained. If it is suggested that it be reduced, sufficient exploration will usually point to the need to keep the fee as stated (p. 421).

Any reduction in fees, or the proposal of a fee well below the therapist's usual range, is highly seductive and infantilizing (p. 435).

The patient should pay the fee by cheque, which should be endorsed by the therapist so that it is clear that the money has gone into the therapist's professional bank account (p. 439).

If an error is made with a cheque, it should be put out on the desk or on a table, so the patient can see it upon entering the next session (p. 439).

The filling in of a form for the therapy to be paid for by an insurance company precludes the patient's experience of separation anxieties in his relationship with the therapist, while reinforcing his own perverted tendencies. It is a disturbance in the therapist's therapeutic commitment to the patient and a means of driving him away (p. 486).

There will be no physical contact between therapist and patient other than the handshake with which the patient is greeted at the time of the initial consultation, and perhaps a handshake at the time of an extended vacation or at termination (p. 429).

If the patient becomes bored and wary of the therapeutic relationship because of the therapist's passivity, the therapist has no choice but to continue it (p. 431).

The therapist has three options: silence, interpretations, and the management of the ground rules; anything else is ruled out (p. 466).

If the patient finds out directly that the therapist is in

supervision, the therapist must give up supervision, even if this means that the therapy has to come to an end, because total confidentiality has been violated (p. 478).
The prerogative of cancelling hours and taking vacations belongs to the therapist, and is one of the necessary inequities (hurtful aspects) inherent to an optimal framework (p. 438).
The therapist should be careful to end the session within 30 to 60 seconds of the appointed time (p. 449).
If the therapist cannot make a particular hour, there should be no charge for the session, but there should be no offer to make the session up (p. 451).

Rules as rigid as these must be mad. There must be something wrong with a discipline which produces this sort of craziness. And if a psychoanalyst should read this, and say that he or she does not stick to these rigid rules, I ask the question, Are you not just as rigid about the rules which you got from your training analyst, and which you repeat without ever questioning them or trying anything different?

It seems clear from all the other therapies which exist that transference is not the only way in to the unconscious, not the only way to uncover the Oedipus complex, not the only way to uncover the Kleinian internal objects, not the only way to uncover the Kohutian self-objects, not the only way to be thorough.

And in experimenting within the bounds of the theoretical framework, subpersonalities seem one extremely useful way to go. If we want to get the benefit of all the discoveries of the past thirty years, we have to take some risks. We have to try new things, and just because the idea of subpersonalities does not come from any one school, it perhaps does not bear on it the mark of Cain. I have come across no less then twenty-five different names for subpersonalities in the literature I have been examining, and this means that if there is safety in numbers, then the idea of subpersonalities is a safe one.

Perhaps it can at the very least act as a kind of Rosetta Stone, enabling translations to be made between one discipline and another. This seems even more worth while now that we know so much about its development and its structure, as we shall see in the next chapter.

Part Three

THE EXPLANATIONS

Chapter Seven

DEVELOPMENT OF SUBPERSONALITIES

How do we come to need and have and use subpersonalities? In this chapter we shall look at the origin of subpersonalities in the personal unconscious, as a result of internal conflicts. As we saw in the first chapter, there are other origins too, but this is certainly one of the most important. In discussing this question, it seems useful to look at it developmentally. There is a theory of child development which has been put together by those working with very early experience, which seems to make sense of a number of puzzling phenomena.

EIGHT DEVELOPMENTAL DIAGRAMS

In putting forward this theory, I find it helps to use a set of diagrams. The conventions in these diagrams are as follows:

1 The outer circle represents the person's boundary of interaction with the world.
2 Dotted lines mean that energy can pass in or out freely.
3 Dashed lines mean that energy can pass in or out, but in a filtered, controlled or impeded way.
4 Solid lines mean that energy can pass neither in nor out. However, a blocked-off subsystem can 'take over' the whole person at times, when certain buttons are pressed. When this happens, it is felt by the person to be inexplicable and scary. Blocks tend to erode over time, and energy has to be spent keeping them in position, and in repair.
5 Subpersonalities specially marked are P for the patripsych (unconscious identification with the patriarchal system of

119

social relations), and S for the shadow (destructive, violent, frightening, or otherwise inferior).

Some people may not like such diagrams, and of course no two-dimensional picture can do justice to the dynamics of personal development. It is all right to take these diagrams with a pinch of salt, or even to disregard them completely.

Also I would not wish to pretend that this is the only way of looking at the matter. In some ways the theory of Alvin Mahrer (1978) covers the same ground in a quite different and equally plausible way. But he ends up with a very similar attitude to subpersonalities, so this will not seriously hold us up. We shall come back to him at the end of the chapter.

We shall have to run through this very quickly, without giving chapter and verse for every statement made, in order to get the wide sweep of the material clear. In other chapters, many of the points made here will be taken up again in more detail.

Let us start, then, at the beginning.

THE ORIGIN

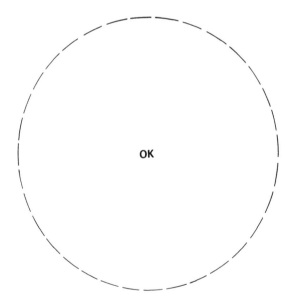

Diagram 1 The Origin

At this stage (see Diagram 1) the person is, and feels, OK. It seems quite possible to regard this stage as a myth, in the sense of an unverifiable story which somehow makes sense of things. In other words, some people may have an actual state like this which they can get back to in their experience of this life, but others may not; they may have to go back further, into previous lives (Netherton and Schiffrin 1979) or into the great archetypes of the human race (Jung 1968), before they can find anything as positive as this. This is essentially a state before trauma. Somehow we all seem to have memories of such a state, and the sense of it has regularly been projected in the form of myths of a Golden Age, the Garden of Eden, the Primordial Paradise, and so on (Neumann 1973). I postulate it only because none of the rest seems to make sense unless we do start here.

At this stage there is nothing wrong. Whatever is needed is given, without the need to ask. The self is OK, and the world is OK, and there is no need to differentiate between the two. The world understands me in a very intimate way, so that I do not need to be able to communicate my needs. It is peaceful and quiet (whoever heard of a noisy Utopia?) and when I do become aware of lights or sounds, they are filtered and muffled before they get to me. There is one sound which may become symbolic of this whole state of being – my mother's heartbeat (Verny 1982). My body is relaxed, and energy can easily flow in and flow out again. The dashed circle indicates that the energy is not trapped – I am open to the world (Boadella 1987). But it also indicates that I have no protection against harsh events which may occur. I assume that I am free, and even perhaps omnipotent (Fenichel 1945). I am totally identified with myself. I am whole. This stage may be very far back, because the foetus is a very active creature. And for some people, apparently, their first trauma was implantation (Laing 1976, 1982) or even conception (Peerbolte 1975).

It is important to see even this very early form of being as *rational*. Development is not just a question of energy flow; it is also a question of levels of rationality. At this level, rationality is trapped in a kind of naive subjectivity which is all-pervasive and very open to the subjectivity of others (Hegel 1971). I am totally in touch with my own body and my own feelings.

Ken Wilber (1980) calls this the Pleroma stage, and points out how important it is not to confuse it with the later, more spiritual, stages. Many people have done this, including Freud, Rank (1929) and others. Such lack of distinction he calls the Pre/Trans Fallacy, because it confuses what is pre-personal with what is transpersonal. We shall return to this point again later.

THE PRIMAL SPLIT

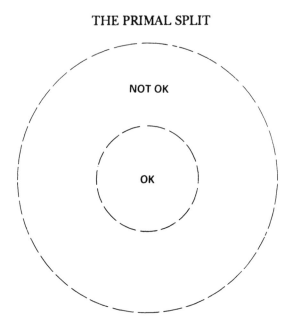

Diagram 2 The Primal Split

At some point – maybe pre-birth, maybe during birth, maybe some while after birth – an event happens which indicates that I am not in control of my world. My assumption of freedom, and perhaps of omnipotence, is contradicted, and my total identification with myself is split (Freud 1938, Klein 1948, Winnicott 1965, Balint 1968, Janov 1970, Grof 1975, Lake 1980, Rowan 1988) (see Diagram 2).

The event which happens must be one which produces panic. I seem to be invaded by some aggressive force. It could objectively be said that I am being abused. But the way I take it, whether as foetus, neonate, infant, or child, usually seems to be that I am wrong, and am being punished. How could I be hurt if I were perfect? But I am being hurt, therefore I am not perfect. In a state

122

of panic, I resort to some kind of defensive tactic. At this stage I have no resources for dealing with trauma. I cannot cobble together any complicated defence. It seems as if I am faced with extinction, annihilation. In desperation, I split into two. I turn against my original OK self, and put in its place a self which has lost the notion of being perfect and whole. So now there is an OK-me (distanced and disowned) and a not-OK-me (fostered and put forward as the answer to the insult). This is the basic split, and of course splitting is a much more drastic defence than repression (Guntrip 1961, 1971, Grotstein 1981).

> The fundamental schizoid phenomenon is the presence of splits in the ego; and it would take a bold man to claim that his ego was so perfectly integrated as to be incapable of revealing any evidence of splitting at the deepest levels, or that such evidence of splitting of the ego would in no circumstances declare itself at more superficial levels, even under conditions of extreme suffering or hardship or deprivation.
>
> (Fairbairn 1952: 8)

The non-OK-me, in order to repair itself and feel better about itself, may instantly adopt something salient from the invading and punishing entity, and incorporate it. After all, that is where the power is, and power is what it needs or lacks.

It is sometimes objected, in relation to this account, that something as early as the birth trauma cannot possibly be remembered, never mind events even earlier still. The answer to this was discovered a long time ago, and stated quite clearly by Fodor (1949), who says:

> [When the patient relives the shock of birth, he] invariably apologises and assures the analyst that he was not making up a story. This is the very reaction we should expect. At his birth emotions have never been verbalised, in putting them into words the patient is making up a story. It is a true story, in spite of the fact that it is not based on memories registered by consciousness but rests on organismic impressions. The imprints of the latter may be just as real and vivid as the rings in a cross-section of a tree showing its physical growth.

In more recent years, of course, this has been verified many times, and Janov (1977) has published photographs showing how bruises made in pre-verbal experiences may actually come to the surface as visible marks during psychotherapy. I have seen a video made with a heat camera by a Gestalt therapist which shows very clearly the marks of early trauma becoming visible as the client relives the experience. It seems clear from all the evidence that we have to accept the possibility of muscular memory and cellular memory as well as the more common kinds of memory using the cerebral cortex (Ridgway 1987). This is very important to keep in mind when we are discussing the philosophical thought experiments of Chapter 10.

Now this experience of trauma and splitting is a particularly powerful one, because it is only in this experience that I first become conscious that there is a 'me' at all, as distinguished from the world. My very first experience of being me is tied in with the first experience of being not-OK. We do not fully understand yet how this can happen with the foetus or with very young babies – it becomes more obvious about the three-year-old stage (Duval and Wicklund 1972) – but somehow it does seem to occur. There may be a whole chain of such events, one of which may be more dramatic than the rest, and may come to symbolize the rest: Grof (1975) has been clearer about this than most, and so has Janov (1977), who says:

In the maturation of the brain each new trauma is represented and then rerepresented holographically on higher and higher levels of the brain neuraxis. In this way a Primal chain is developed, with later traumas reactivating related first-line Pains. What this means is that at each stage of brain development an imprint of the trauma occurs, and as the brain develops each imprint joins other related imprints of traumas, the early imprints becoming connected to the later ones. This fusion and representation continues to occur and becomes more elaborate and complex as maturation goes on.

I want to make it clear that some birth processes are quite all right, and may well induce a feeling of triumph as having made it into the world through all obstacles (Grof 1975, Janov 1983). It is not at all suggested that birth is always a trauma, but rather that there is always some kind of a trauma which starts this process going. Balint (1968) is also very clear about this:

> One possible theoretical explanation of these differences uses the idea of trauma. According to it the individual has developed more or less normally up to the point where he was struck by a trauma. From that point on his further development has been fundamentally influenced by the method he developed at the time for coping with the effects of that particular trauma – his basic fault.

Frank Lake (1980) has been very specific about different levels of trauma and exactly how that makes a difference to how the trauma is taken and experienced. Partly it is a matter of how the mother and the other close and important figures react to various situations – the very young infant seems to be able to pick up emotional reactions very quickly.

Few of the writers in this area do real justice to the dialectical nature of the process: the non-OK self is the *negation* of the OK-self. It sees itself as the answer to the problem of the OK-self; and it devalues the real self. This is the first and most dramatic instance of something which will happen again and again throughout life: the move into objectivity and away from subjectivity. The non-OK self is, or wants to be, objective, right, or on the side of those who are right. The OK self feels itself to be defined as wrong – subjectivity is wrong – it is wrong to see things my way.

Once this split has been established, it has effects which continue long afterwards. As the psychoanalyst Rangell (1973) has well put it:

> Reflecting on the subject of psychic trauma, I suggest that the trauma an analyst is pitted against is often no longer the trauma of childhood but the cumulative traumata of a lifetime of psychic repetition of the original in an attempt to master it .... If the trauma is repeated indefinitely and mastery fails to evolve, it is like a series of reinoculations which come to exceed the original dose and restore the original disease in chronic and even more virulent forms.

And this links with the work of Alice Miller (1987), who has underlined the importance of early trauma and the way in which many analysts in the past have downplayed it and failed to do it justice. But if it is important, it must continue to be important, because the way of dealing with this first split will set the pattern for the way in which the person deals with the next trauma, and the next, and the next.

SPLITTING AND INTROJECTION

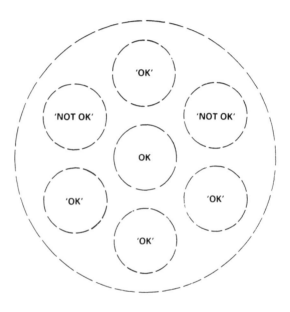

Diagram 3 Splitting and Introjection

Once the non-OK region has been established, it starts to become populated by somewhat separated subregions (Lewin 1936) (see Diagram 3). This happens by the same process as the original split – in a situation of panic some defence is thrown up, and this defence is then used in other, similar situations.

It is important to recognize that the events we are talking about here may be very unimportant to the adults, and very important to the baby. Winnicott (1971) is precise about how this can happen:

The feeling of the mother's existence lasts x minutes. If the mother is away more than x minutes, then the imago fades, and along with this the baby's capacity to use the symbol of the union ceases. The baby is distressed, but this distress is soon mended, because the mother returns in x + y minutes. In x + y minutes the baby has not become altered. But in x + y + z minutes the baby has become traumatized. In x + y + z minutes the mother's return does not mend the baby's altered state. Trauma implies that the baby has experienced a break in life's continuity, so that primitive defences now become organized to defend against a repetition of 'unthinkable anxiety' or a return of the acute confusional state that belongs to disintegration of nascent ego structure.

So if we are right that the primitive defence which Winnicott is talking about may very often be splitting, we can see how not only in the very first experience of trauma, but also in the later experiences of trauma, this defence can result in the setting up of more and more subregions within the person.

Each of these subregions is contained within the not-OK region, so that even those which seem to function well are only 'OK' in inverted commas: they are easily shaken and easily questioned. This leads to the phenomenon, often seen in group therapy, which I have called the Samurai-and-Slob pattern: the person comes forward with great confidence and confronts another person, but if this other person fights back in any way, the first person collapses.

This how the internal objects mentioned by the object relations school get set up:

The figures with whom we have relationships in our phantasies are called appropriately, by Melanie Klein, 'internal objects' because we behave with respect to them, emotionally and impulsively, in the same ways as we do towards externally real persons, though in more violent degrees of intensity than would be socially permissible. The formation of this inner world of internal objects and situations proceeds from the very beginnings of life.

(Guntrip 1961: 226)

Each subregion that is set up represents a decision – 'this is the way to lead my life' – often made in a hurry and on inadequate evidence. Some of them are complete introjects – soneone else's way of being is swallowed whole.

Stanislav Grof casts a flood of light on this whole area by his notion of the COEX system (system of condensed experience). He shows how the trauma can be represented again and again in the life of the person by successive experiences in which the original feelings are reinvoked:

> A COEX system can be defined as a specific constellation of memories consisting of condensed experiences (and related fantasies) from different life periods of the individual. The memories belonging to a particular COEX system have a similar basic theme or contain similar elements and are associated with a strong emotional charge of the same quality. The deepest layers of this system are represented by vivid and colourful memories of experiences from infancy and early childhood. More superficial layers of such a system involve memories of similar experiences from later periods, up to the present life situation. Each COEX system has a basic theme that permeates all its layers and represents their common denominator.
>
> (Grof 1979: 46-7)

If we personify a COEX system, it comes to life as a subpersonality. It may also remind us of Goffman's (1974) idea of a frame – except that this is an internal frame which we carry round inside us. It may remind us, too, of Hegel's abstract systems, inadequate because one-sided. And it may also remind us of Freud's idea of a core problem.

The central OK self is often called the 'real self', and it tries to come out from time to time, giving and receiving love, but is often countered again, and goes back inside a barrier which is further strengthened. So all the way through childhood the OK-me is retreating further and further. Reality is given away to the outside world, so that all the power seems to be out there, and none (or very little) of it seems to be in here. And when I do try to use my personal power, I may get put down or punished for it, so that it, too, gets defined as not-OK. This may happen in very ambiguous, 'double-bind' kinds of ways.

128

One of the earliest subregions to become well-defined is the sex-role one – 'I am a boy or girl' – which later becomes the ego and the patripsych (Southgate and Randall 1978).

The dashes round the non-OK-selves indicate that attempts are made to control the manifestations of these aspects of the personality. This is emphasized by the dashes on the outer circle, which indicate that energy is not as readily released into the environment from these regions.

The introjects start off by 'riding herd' on one of the subregions, telling it what to and what not to do. Then they move inside the subregion and become a part of it. This can then lead to a topdog/underdog split inside the subregion affected. We have already seen in Chapter 4 how Freud's superego is formed in just this way.

The negating and devaluing of the subjective level is going on apace here. Each success in 'getting by' leads to an inflation of one or more of the subpersonalities which are incipient. This leads to the 'puffing up' and 'selfishness' which children often display at this time. 'Being good' means denying the subjective level. All the things we accept are called 'objective' or 'true', and all the things we reject are called 'subjective' or 'false'. This is a continuous social process which goes on for years. At this stage the body is very important, and things are seen very much in terms of the body, as Wilber (1980) emphasizes.

PUTTING AWAY CHILDISH THINGS

At the next stage, shown in Diagram 4, the subregions associated most closely with childhood get blocked off and put away. They are forgotten, and barriers are erected round them to make sure that they stay forgotten. The knowledge that there is a panicky self who throws up defences is forgotten too. There is an attempt to find the 'real me' – who I am, now that I am no longer a child defined by family membership. There is much introspection, and openness to the world is cut down somewhat. But the introspection takes place only within the outer layer. And because the process is still going on, of panicky self erecting defences and setting up new subregions, the adolescent now feels more and more phony. This is very uncomfortable, so the phoniness is projected, and the world is often seen as phony. This particularly applies to those figures who were most looked up to in childhood. The attempt is then

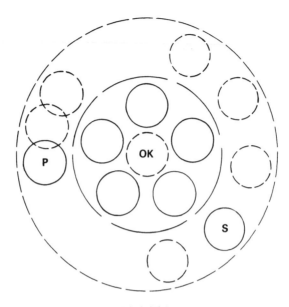

Diagram 4 Putting Away Childish Things

made to make each of the subregions into a fully-fledged subpersonality, capable of holding its own in a phony world. 'My personality' then becomes an important issue, and one of the subpersonalities is usually picked on to be the dominant one, or ego. This is usually the one most closely associated with stereotyped sex roles. Some acceptable form of personal power may be discovered at this stage: money, knowledge, beauty, goodness, overt aggression, or subtle manipulation. This then gets integrated with the dominant subpersonality or ego. The person learns to achieve an identity by identifying with one of the subpersonalities. At the same time the shadow and the patripsych take definite form, at an unconscious level. The real self feels particularly vulnerable, and retreats further.

The description here is a psychological one, but a more sociological approach would emphasize the importance of reference groups here, in giving content to the subpersonalities. Heroes and heroines may be introjected whole at this stage. There is, of course, much experiment with different subpersonalities before one is picked out to be the main one.

It is important to realize that this is a dialectical process. Just as the not-OK self negates the OK-self, so the personal identity (public-relations personality) negates the whole childhood self. But this is a false negation, because it is based on a further denial of the true self. So instead of finding the original self on a higher level, the original self is still further lost.

This is simply the same process we saw in Diagram 2, only now on a larger scale, and with far more rationalization. This is precisely why the conflicts of adolescence tend to be so dramatic and so hard to handle. They recapitulate the COEX (Grof) of the original split.

This is Wilber's transition from membership self to mental ego.

THE HOLLOW PERSON

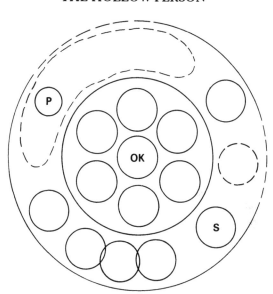

Diagram 5 The Hollow Person

At this stage (see Diagram 5), the subjective level is totally closed to view, including the childhood subpersonalities. Most of the other subpersonalities built up during adolescence are also blocked off, so that their energy is not available to the person. Energy is only allowed to flow through the main executive subpersonality, often called the ego or persona and generally

131

associated with the sex role, and maybe one or two subsidiary ones – some kind of exception which makes the person feel more individual. In effect, the person at this stage is completely hollow. There 'is no centre', and so the person is forced to concentrate on the self-image contained in the outer layers. Identity is precarious.

For this reason there is much emphasis here on there being just a single self or ego. Self-consistency is felt to be extremely important. It is a wish rather than a reality, because the person is really no more self-consistent than anyone at the previous level or the next one, but it is an anxious and driven wish, revealing itself in a positive insistence on the importance of there being just one ego. Many people, including many psychologists, are stuck at this stage.

Because so much energy is locked up, the person's body at this stage tends to be very rigid and bound up in certain ways – exactly which ways will depend on the decisions taken earlier. Very little of the person's original energies are available at this point. The person is easily manipulated because of depending unsurely on rather narrow roles – but of course for that reason is extremely wary of manipulation.

This is the stage of 'normal alienation', where the person is not even conscious of being alienated. This tends to produce a compulsive conformity which can easily tip over into schizo-phrenia – the 'nervous breakdown'. At this stage any problems are seen as out there in the world somewhere, and preferably far out there. Any problems which are quite clearly internal are projected into the outside world. The person does not want to look inside at all. If the person adopts an unusual or unconventional identity, the patripsych migrates and takes up residence inside it.

There is a precise description of this stage in Denzin (1987), who calls it 'the emotionally divided self '. He emphasizes that the extreme nature of the split means that there is a relation of hatred between the outer and the inner parts of the person. This is a self-hater. And because of this, the world of emotion and the world of fantasy are indistinguishable; both can be dismissed intellectually, but when they take over, they take over in force.

It is important to see that whenever a subsystem is blocked off it is never completely lost; in fact, quite a lot of energy has to be used to keep it blocked. It comes back in dreams and fantasies, and may in fact come back and 'take over' the whole personality at times, which can be a very frightening event for a person like this. These non-cognitive bodily experiences are usually ignored or misinterpreted by the person who is at this stage. A person like this will depend very heavily upon the opinion of others, external authorities who will set the limits and provide structures of meaning.

This is the height of objectivity, in its one-sided majesty. Our society continually encourages us to be like this – lost in roles and depending upon the esteem of others.

This is the middle, 'normal' mental-ego stage described by Wilber (1980). A strong sense that boundaries are very important goes with this stage, as does an idolization of language.

UNHAPPY CONSCIOUSNESS

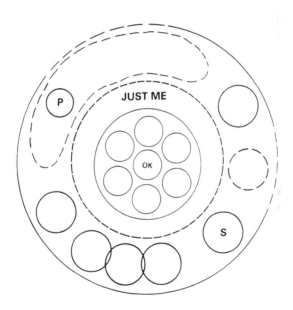

Diagram 6   Unhappy Consciousness

In Diagram 6 we are dealing with a necessary sequence, because this can only happen after what we have called stage 5. Its distinguishing feature is that the realized level emerges at first in a disguised form, as a unique role or subpersonality, and is called by some such title as 'just me' or 'only me', or 'me when I am on my own'. It is normally seen as more authentic, in some way, than the more external roles or subpersonalities. 'When I am walking on the moors, enjoying nature, than I am me without any pretences.' The person at this stage is just beginning to develop this quasi-centre, or private self. But because this construction is still seen as part of the non-OK-me region, it is still rather easily shaken and subjected to disconfirmation. Still, there is a sort of uneasy awareness that there could be a private self behind all the roles. And this may lead to a beginning awareness of alienation. There is not the same identification with roles, and this may lead to some sense of role distance – deliberately setting oneself off from one's role – 'I want you to know that I am not just a street cleaner/housewife/surgeon/model'. And this may lead to a feeling of unhappiness about role-playing: 'I am tired of playing games'. This is particularly likely to happen if the person moves from getting esteem from others to a kind of self-esteem. There may be many versions of this stage, some more stable than others.

The slight opening in the OK barrier and the childhood barrier indicates that subjectivity, always seeking to be involved with ego-consciousness, does succeed sometimes in getting through in a direct way; and also the childhood subpersonalities sometimes succeed in getting through directly. At this stage these irruptions are not so disturbing as they were at the previous stage, partly because they are not so violent and sudden, because the suppression is not so firm and continuous. Subjectivity and the childhood subpersonalities may be most likely to get through to the 'just me' role, but they may also get through to the persona. When this happens, there is a feeling of unreality about the normal role relations, which may be expressed in some such phrase as 'I am doing this, but it isn't really me.' This is the stage where people are most likely to come into therapy.

The realized level contradicts the objective level, just as the objective level contradicted the subjective level. This is more traumatic than the diagram indicates. It results in the assertion of a new, higher-level subjectivity which has been through the objective level. It may be called an objective subjectivity. This is the beginning of the process which Wilber (1980) calls passing through the biosocial bands.

OPENING

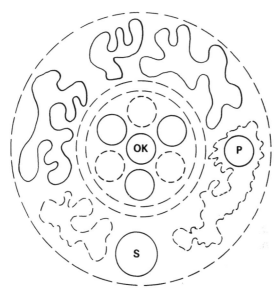

Diagram 7 Opening

If the person now gets into some process of intentional self-development, through counselling, therapy, personal growth activities of one kind or another, several things start to happen (see Diagram 7). First of all, the inner self is seen as inconsistent with the subpersonalities. The outer self is now seeen as futile, unreal, absurd, and so on, and the subpersonalities are seen as distorted and ugly. At the same time some of the childhood subpersonalities may be tapped, and their energy made available. The whole childhood world is opened up and seen to be important. Its emotions are basic and very strong. The inner self is often seen as this stage as a child self – natural, unspoilt, and spontaneous. But because what is being discovered is all part of the not-OK-me, a lot of it is also ugly and painful, and pain becomes the regular diet of the therapy sessions. However, so much energy is being released that the increased sense of aliveness makes it all seem worth while. One is suppressing much less, and owning much more of one's internal world. As each new blocked-off subsystem is reached, resistance to further exploration tends to rise, and so people tend to drop out of therapy at various points where resistance is strong. They may then get left with the knowledge that a lot is still wrong, but just try to 'soldier on' and cope with it. They have 'been through' therapy and refuse to 'go back' to it. This then becomes just a more sophisticated version of stage 6.

The COEX system can be used in therapy to get at the necessary early experiences, and this often leads to some form of catharsis, as Mahrer (1986) has emphasized. Very often after a catharsis has been experienced, the real self will take over briefly, and the person will have a glimpse of the next stage. But it will retreat again, particularly if the external environment is alienating, as it normally is under patriarchy.

The difficulty with Diagram 7 is illustrating a state of flux combined with resistance to awareness. This seems about the nearest I can get to it.

What cannot be shown is the peculiar connection between the realized level and the subjective level. Material is taken out of the subjective level and incorporated (now fully owned and highly valued, but possibly transformed) into the realized level. This is right in the middle of the process of passing through the biosocial bands – a very confusing time.

BREAKTHROUGH

As therapy progresses, at some point the person gets in touch with their own fuller rationality and truth (see Diagram 8). It becomes obvious that I create my own world. This can be an ecstatic experience, though it comes at the end of a painful search, and it makes the process of breaking down subpersonalities much easier. There is now nothing that is so marvellous or essential about the subpersonalities that one needs to hang on to. One can give up the ideal aim of being perfect, of being interesting, of being lovable, and so on – all these conscious aims start to look equally meaningless and illusory. Now one can have them without trying, and see for the first time what they really mean. One experiences what real spontaneity is like, and it is a real turn-on. The energy available is now much greater again, and it is possible to be strong and vulnerable at the same time – vulnerable because one now lets the world in, instead of keeping it out; strong because all the energy that is necessary is available for dealing with the world. The

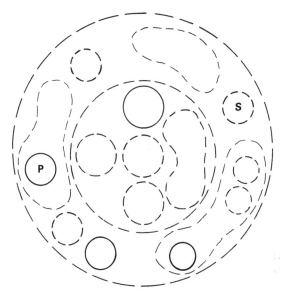

Diagram 8 Breakthrough

body changes and becomes more flexible; the face becomes more relaxed and less conventional. The person is more approachable and gives off good vibrations. There may be all kinds of difficulties to be handled about relationships at this stage, because the other people involved will often try to hang on to the existing patterns, and may succeed unless support can be obtained. Diagram 8 looks static, but all the subsystems are more fluid now, and the picture is really changing faster than at any previous time. This is not an easy stage to cope with. The COEX systems become much more easily available to consciousness. The patripsych or 'inner pig' may give particular problems at this stage, because we live in a patriarchal society. The shadow now becomes opened up and starts to change. The inner self is experienced as universal as well as particular. But unless the environment is supportive, the person may slip back to stage 7 or even stage 6.

It is important to emphasize that this may be a transient stage, certainly at first. It cannot be hung on to at will. There may be all sorts of returns to earlier stages, and this is quite normal and quite possibly inevitable. Two things, in fact, need to be said: first, that it is hard to learn how to stay at this stage; and second, that one may deliberately turn one's back on this stage and return in a voluntary way to an earlier stage. One starts here to run into the paradox of the real self: if you try to use it, it turns into just another false self, or subpersonality. Some people can cope with this paradox, and some cannot, it seems.

It is not actually a 'real self' at all: it is a realized level of consciousness, more aware and fully in touch with the subjective world. Once one realizes how rational it is, it becomes easier to maintain. Much better description of this is available now; it is precisely equivalent to Wilber's (1980) Centaur stage.

Summing up this whole developmental process (which of course continues beyond the scope of this book) we can say that the patterns discerned here are extremely important for personality theory. It accounts for both peripheral and central aspects of the personality, and shows how they are related to one another.

MAHRER

It is important to say that the theory of Alvin Mahrer (1978) is compatible with this story, even though expressed in different language. His view is at the whole set of both parental subpersonalities (which he calls 'potentials') form the psychological field within which the foetus develops. When birth takes place, these patterns remain within the infant and determine his or her consciousness in various ways. As long as the parents maintain that psychological field – and they have many ways of doing so – the infant cannot escape, even when language comes and the infant becomes a child.

So the origins of his subpersonalities are different from those given above, but the patterns which they take up, and the methods used to release them are very similar. It is rather like the way in which Freud says of the superego that it is not formed out of the infant's experience of the parents, but is taken over direct from the parents' superegos. So the origins in this way are different, but the final effect seems to be the same.

Chapter Eight

OTHER ORIGINS OF SUBPERSONALITIES

It would be wrong to jump to the conclusion that the data of the previous chapter were sufficient to account for all the phenomena associated with subpersonalities. Those facts deal entirely with the personal unconscious, which of course is extremely important: but we must also consider the cultural unconscious and the collective unconscious.

THE CULTURAL UNCONSCIOUS

By the cultural unconscious is meant that part of our unconscious minds which comes from conflicts endemic in the culture into which we were born. I first came across this possibility in the work of John Southgate and Rosemary Randall, where they discuss the problem of the patripsych:

> The patripsych is a shorthand term for what we have called the internal constellation of patriarchal patterns. By this we mean all the attitudes, ideas and feelings, usually compulsive and unconscious, that develop in relation to authority and control. This development is closely related to learning about sex roles – learning about whether you are a little boy or a little girl.
>
> (Southgate and Randall 1978)

It is the patripsych we have to contend with when we are touching on compulsive feelings of dependence on authority figures, so that I assume they know best. I want to get near them. I want to be like them, and so forth. It is also the patripsych I have to contend with when I have a compulsive need to fight authority figures, opposing them regardless of what they do, dedicating my life to their destruction and seeing them as symbols of evil. And it is the patripsych I have to contend with when I am withdrawing into myself, refusing to compete, being uncommunicative, not engaging in any way and in this way avoiding all the issues of control.

> It is important to remember that we not only develop
> compulsive ways of relating to people who are in authority
> over us but also develop compulsive ways of relating when we
> are in positions of authority ourselves. The general point
> about this is that it is very difficult for anyone to relate to
> authority (theirs or others') in a fully creative way. There is
> frequently little choice in our actions (although we may think
> there is) and power relations are mystified and confused.
>
> (Southgate and Randall 1978)

And they make the point that the patriarchal family continues to exist still, even though the outward appearance of many families may be relaxed and equal. This usually becomes more apparent when children come along, and the 'crisis of parenthood' (Neugarten 1968) pushes men and women into more one-sided roles.

This kind of insight is of course very similar to what Mitchell (1975) has said about the extraordinary way in which patriarchy has entered into our language and our thinking at deep unconscious levels. It seems closely parallel to the kind of thing which Wyckoff (1975) has been saying about the Pig Parent:

> In women's groups, women can become familiar with what
> insidiously keeps them down – not only the obvious, overt,
> male supremacy of which many of us are already aware and
> struggling against, but also oppression which has been
> internalized, which turns women against themselves, causing
> them to be their own worst enemies rather than their own
> loving best friend. This internalized oppression I have called
> the Pig Parent. It is the expression of all the values which
> keep women subordinate.

The idea of the Pig Parent is again an internal pattern of responses: the voice within us which tells us that we are no good, that we need good pure strong figures to lean on and depend on and admire, that we can never make it on our own, that it is wrong to aim at equality. Another version of this has been described as the *self-hater* by Starhawk (1982), who actually got it from Doris Lessing (1970) and her character Martha Quest. But Starhawk has taken it further.

> The self-hater is the inner representation of power-over. We have internalized it, not just from our parents, but from every institution in society with which we have contact. It is the structure in the psyche that perpetuates domination. It reminds us of our helplessness, our powerlessness. It blames the victim; it tells us we are bad when bad things happen to us, that we do not have the right to be, to feel, to do what we do. It is the inner gun that keeps us in an inner prison.
>
> (Starhawk 1982)

And this applies to men just as much as to women. Both men and women have internalized the oppression of a patriarchal society, and both have this internal voice. It is just that society tells men that they have to be leaders, and so they lead, but still with the voice telling them that they are no good, that they are unworthy, that they have no right to be equal or to be loved for themselves. And so they perpetuate the structures which will make it all seem impersonal and objective, and nothing to do with them personally.

A dream will illustrate the way in which we can recognize the patripsych when it comes up in therapy. A middle-aged man dreamed that he was in his old school – an ancient school, with wood panelling and big separate desks with heavy hinged lids, and a raised dais for the master. Somehow he found himself being the walls of the room, and saying to the boys in the class,

> I am here to make you feel small. I am here to put you down. I am here to make you feel so weak and inadequate that you will latch on the words of the master as being your only hope. I am here to reduce you to obedience to the master. I am here to make sure that you understand the conditions under which you can progress – my conditions. And if you rebel, I

141

am here to make sure that your rebellion is futile and pointless.

There is a mocking, masculine tone to this speech which usually appears in the words of the patripsych. This is the authentic voice of oppression, which in our time means patriarchy, as I have shown in more detail elsewhere (Rowan 1987). It is patriarchy which produces all the typical forms of oppression which we meet with today: racism, classism, adultism, sexism. And it produces a certain way of thinking:

> Masculine bias, thus, appears in our behaviour whenever we act out the following categories, regardless of which element in each pair we are most drawn to at any given moment: subject/object; dominant/submissive; master/slave; butch/femme. All of these false dichotomies are inherently sexist, since they express the desire to be masculine or to possess the masculine in someone else.
>
> (Dansky *et al.*: 1977)

Under patriarchy, it is the stereotyped masculine qualities which get all the acclaim and all the interest, and this is true both for men and for women.

This is all very reminiscent of the discussion about penis envy, except that, as Firestone (1972) puts it, we should talk rather about power envy. And except that we now see it as applying to men as well as women, and as being much more complex – not only wanting to be close to penis-power, but also wanting to oppose it or withdraw from it, and all these in a compulsive way, driven by unconscious demands.

It is extraordinarily difficult to deal with the patripsych in therapy; all the most successful attempts seem to have been in groups, rather than in one-to-one work. This is simply because as fast as we break down the patterns in our therapy sessions, society tries very hard to put them back again. If we really want to deal with the patripsych, it seems that we have to set up some kind of living community which will have different values; but then it seems that we lose all power to change the broader society.

Ultimately, then, we are faced with the answer that, in order to deal with this aspect of therapy thoroughly, we have to change the whole society. I have dealt with this problem elsewhere (Rowan 1978) and this is not the place to go into it fully. Enough to say that the patripsych is one of the most important subpersonalities, and that it is therefore imperative to sort out one's own personal attitude to it.

ARCHETYPES

Another origin of subpersonalities is the archetype. This is an inborn pattern of a rather general description, which takes on a more specific form depending upon personal experiences of the person involved.

It is necessary to point out once more that archetypes are not determined as regards their content, but only as regards their form and then only to a very limited degree. A primordial image is determined as to its content only when it has become conscious and is therefore filled out with the material of conscious experience. Its form, however, as I have explained elsewhere, might perhaps be compared to the axial system of a crystal, which, as it were, preforms the crystalline structure in the mother liquid, although it has no material existence of its own . . . . The axial system determines only the stereometric structure but not the concrete form of the individual crystal. This may be either large or small, and it may vary endlessly by reason of the different size of its planes or by the growing together of two crystals. The only thing that remains constant is the axial system, or rather, the invariable geometric proportions underlying it. The same is true of the archetype.

(Jung 1968)

For example, one of the most common archetypes which comes up in psychotherapy is the shadow. The shadow is that part of ourselves which we like least. In other terms, it is the negative self-image. It is what we are afraid we are like, underneath the covers and the pretences. For some people it is nasty: 'If they knew how full of hate I was, how evil are my wishes, how vicious I really am, they would all reject me.' For some people it is weak: 'If they knew how inept I am, how incapable, how lacking in all positive qualities, they would all reject me.' For others again it is more complex: 'If they knew how I put on a friendly face to allure people, and then when they are hooked I turn on them and destroy them, they would all reject me.' So the shadow is that part of us we would least like to meet.

Another archetype is the persona. The persona is that part of us we would most like other people to meet. It is the public-relations self, the mask we put on to greet the world. It has been said that in Jungian therapy there is often a movement from dealing with the persona at the start of the therapy, to the ego as the second stage, to the shadow as the third stage, to the anima or animus, to the self as the final stage. Some would interpose the Wise Old Man and the Wise Old Woman as spiritual archetypes coming before the final step of the self.

However, we are here not trying to be pure Jungians, but to see how the archetype can be a separate and distinct origin of subpersonalities. It makes sense to me that some of the things we come up with in working with people seem to be very generally applicable. In other words, they are common to more than one person. Some of these, in turn, seem to be common to more than one culture. And it is these universal subpersonalities which I think it makes sense to think of as archetypes.

In this sense Berne's parent, adult, and child ego states can be perfectly well understood as archetypes. Even in cultures where fatherhood was denied or not understood, a child would still have parents. Similarly, it would make sense to say that Hal Stone's protector/controller was an archetype, since all cultures have some such notion. This makes it obvious that archetypes are in fact very common, though as Jung says, when they come up, they come up with power and fascination.

The collective unconscious is a controversial concept, but I think if we accept the notion of an archetype, than we have to accept the notion of the collective unconscious. I would disagree, however, with the view of Sasportas (1987) that 'every sub-personality has an archetype at its core'. As he states it, this is a very useful idea, because it enables him to say that a subpersonality can be more or less adequate as it gets closer to or deviates away from its central core. He says:

An archetype is like an elevator in a department store. The same elevator can let you off on the first floor at women's

shoes, on the second floor for men's clothes, or you can go
straight to the restaurant at the top. Similarly, any archetype
can express on many different levels.

This is a tempting thought, but it seems to me that because of the
many origins of subpersonalities, it would be a mistake to attribute
them all to archetypes. It seems to me that this diminishes the very
real differences between archetypes, which are deep and
fascinating, from much more prosaic and everyday subpersonalities, which may be far from archetypal. It would be using
the word 'archetype' in an almost insulting way just to tack on to
any subpersonality which came along, and I think this would be to
rob the word of all real meaning and contrast.

THE MULTIPLE UNCONSCIOUS

This is a good point to look at the whole question of the unconscious. It has long been noted that the word can be used in more
than one way. Miller (1942), for example, shows how there at least
these sixteen definitions, all of which have been used at one time
or another by someone or other

Inanimate	Unresponsive to stimulation
Not mental	Undiscriminating
Conditioned	Unsensing
Unnoticing or unattending	Insightless
Unremembering	Instinctive or unlearned
Unrecognizing	Acting involuntarily
Unable to communicate	Ignoring
System Ucs	Unavailable to awareness

Miller makes the point that it is all too possible for a writer to slide
or slip across from one of these concepts to another without
realizing that this is what is happening. This has made for much of
confusion in talking about the unconscious.

More recently, Wilber (1980) has put forward the idea that
when talking about what goes on in therapy and personal growth
we need to keep separate five different types of unconscious mind.

Ground unconscious

The foetus has a ground unconscious. 'In essence, it is all the deep structures existing as potentials ready to emerge, via remembrance, at some future point.' All of these structures are unconscious, but they are not repressed: rather, they have not yet entered consciousness. Development or personal growth consists of a series of 'hierarchical transformations or *unfoldings* of the deep structures . . : starting with the lowest . . . and ending with the highest.' This is similar to Jung's notion of an archetype. Perhaps also we may think of this as another way of seeing the psychological field spoken of by Mahrer.

Archaic unconscious

This is 'simply the most primitive and least developed structures of the ground unconscious'. We can never get these structures into conscious awareness, so they always stay unconscious. 'They are preverbal, and most are subhuman.' They are not personal, but enter consciousness through the impersonal archaic or phylogenetic heritage. They are best treated mythologically rather than analytically.

Submergent unconscious

This consists of 'that which was once conscious, in the lifetime of the individual, but is now screened out of awareness'. It contains all those psychic contents which are incompatible with the conscious attitude, together with those which have been forgotten, and subliminal impressions too weak to reach conscious awareness.

Embedded unconscious

This is the part of the unconscious which does the repressing, which pushes stuff down into the submergent unconscious. Freud called it the superego. It is 'an unrepressed but repressing structure'. It comprises those aspects of the ego level with which the self is unconsciously identified, so much so that they cannot be objectively perceived. Wilber says that 'the superego is simply one instance of what we call the embedded unconscious: because it is embedded as the self, the self cannot totally or accurately see it'.

Emergent unconscious

The transpersonal realms are not yet repressed – they have simply not yet had the opportunity to emerge. 'At any point on the developmental cycle, those deep structures which have not yet emerged from the ground unconscious are referred to as the emergent unconscious.' The archaic unconscious is low and primitive and the emergent unconscious is high and transcendent: the former is humanity's past, the latter humanity's future. 'The ego is strong enough to repress not only the lower realms but also the higher realms – it can seal off the superconscious as well as the subconscious.'

This suggestion of Wilber's is, I think, well worth considering, because anything which helps to make useful distinctions in this very confused area must be a positive move. To say that the most common archetypes come from the ground unconscious is very helpful, because it helps us to see that some of the Jungians are confusing this with material which comes from the emergent unconscious, which can of course also be archetypal.

When we work with subpersonalities, it is usually very easy to see the difference between an archetype coming from the ground unconscious and one which comes from the emergent unconscious. The one certainly has power, but it is power of a very down-to-earth and often very limited kind, narrow and two-dimensional. The other has a mind-opening quality which leads to much deeper or higher insights, often of a spiritual character. Here, for example, is an extract from a therapy session which shows the emergence of one of the higher archetypes.

This is a dream (Perls 1976) being worked on in a Gestalt therapy group, a dream in which the woman client had seen a statue in the middle of a lake. The statue has a vase which continually poured out water. The client has just played the part of the statue.

FRITZ: Okay, play the water. Tell us. You're now the water.
MADELINE: In the vessel?
FRITZ: Yes, the water in the vessel. What's your script? What's

your story, Water?
MADELINE: (*Pause*) I don't know much about myself.
FRITZ: And again.
MADELINE: I don't know much about myself. (*Pause, begins to cry*) I come. I don't know how I come but I know I'm good, that's all I know. I would like you to drink me because I know I'm good. I don't know where I come from . . . I'm in that big vase. It's a black vase.
FRITZ: Now, get up. Say this to each one of us. Stand up. Go to each one of us and tell us this. You're the water.
MADELINE: (*Crying and sniffing*) I'm water in a vase and I don't know where I come from. But I know I'm good to drink. I'm water in a vase.
FRITZ: Use your own words now.
MADELINE: I look like water and they call me water and I'm just there in the vase. And there's no hole in the vase. I don't know where, nobody, I'm just there all the time, I'm just pouring out, and I'd like you to drink me.
FRITZ: Go on to the next.
MADELINE: I'm there and I'm white and pure, and if you ask me where I come from I can't tell you. But it's a miracle, I always come out, just for you to drink me. You have to get out of the other water and come. (*Goes to the next person, crying*) I'm in a vase, and I don't know where I come from but I'm coming out all the time, and you have to drink me, every little bit of it.

This was a very moving scene, and the beauty of Madeline's face when she was saying these things was wondrous to behold. Everyone in the group was deeply affected. Something archetypal had come from the emergent unconscious through the symbol or image of water. And it was by personifying the water that the archetype could emerge most effectively.

It is this move, of personification, that we are urging over and over again in this book.

FANTASY IMAGES

This brings us on to the question of fantasy images. We all know very well what is meant by this. Mary Watkins reminds us that

148

children engage in imaginal dialogues where they play the roles of parents (good or bad), children (good or bad), princesses, and other characters, using dolls, toys, animals, or other children as helpers, or doing without them. 'Through introjection and identification the child shares in the strengths and qualities of the other, thereby redressing the inordinate lack of equality in most child-adult relations' (Watkins 1986: 24). Not only through imaginary companions and transitional objects (certainly through these too), but also through the whole process of play that most children engage in, fantasy images come up. Winnicott (1971) tells of a woman he saw who described how in her childhood she had an imaginary white horse which was very real to her. She 'would ride it everywhere and hitch it to a tree and all that sort of thing'. (p. 27). And Watkins explains that we do not leave behind this ability or this practice:

> We should recall that it is not only children who invite
> imaginal others to the dinner table. Machiavelli had
> imaginary dinner conversations with historical personages.
> Petrarch wrote letters to the eminences of classical antiquity.
> Landor wrote volumes of imaginal dialogues between sages
> and stars of different centuries. Pablo Casals told his listeners,
> 'Bach is my best friend'. Indeed, art, drama, poetry, music, as
> well as the spontaneous appearence of personifications, keep
> us in conversation with imaginal others. From this point of
> view, these imaginal others affect our interactions with
> 'actual' others just as surely as the other way around.
>
> (Watkins 1986: 69)

For this reason Mary Watkins argues throughout that, although such identities, derived from imagination, may be based on child's play and imaginary companions and teenage crushes, they are actually very healthy and may show a mature appreciation of our own inner complexity: 'We would not judge a play or novel with one character as necessarily better or worse than another with several characters. So why should we impose this kind of ideal on the richness of our own thought?' (Watkins 1986: 106). We have just mentioned the idea of a teenage crush. Here is an example of how this works, just in case we have forgotten how powerful this sort of thing can be:

The first hero I ever fastened on for any length of time was
Greta Garbo. She was glamorous, beautiful, sophisticated – all
the things that I wanted to be at that time. I wanted to be like
her very much. I thought she was wonderful. I was hungry for
any scrap of information I could get, any movie magazine
which told what she was like, how she dressed. I wanted to
familiarize myself as completely as possible with her life. I
found out that she was a sad person, and I affected a sad
attitude although I was by nature an exuberant person. I let
the corners of my mouth turn down and my hair hang
straight. I thought she was lonely and sad, and I felt lonely
and sad.

(Woman, 50, recalling teenage heroine, in Klapp 1969: 216)

She had taken on a Greta Garbo subpersonality, and reacted to the
world in terms of this subpersonality much of the time, until she
did not need it any more.

But there are more serious ways in which this may be done.
Stanislavsky, in his famous work *An Actor Prepares*, is really quite
often giving instructions as to how to set up an inner
subpersonality corresponding to the character in the play. One of
the definitions of Method acting might be, that form of acting
which depends upon subpersonalities for its success. A good
example of how it works came up in a recent magazine report,
relating how Bob Hoskins, an experienced actor, prepared for a
role in which he had to have long scenes with an imaginary
cartoon rabbit, who would not be present on the set, but would be
painted in later: 'I had to build a relationship with thin air – to
actually hallucinate that Roger was there,' says the actor, who
prepared for his role by watching his toddler daughter, Rose, play
with an invisible friend' (*Newsweek*, 4 July 1988). This is actually also
similar to the way in which animators in cartoon films have to get
inside their characters in order to put in those tiny touches which
bring the character to life. In a programme shown on TV, a Disney
animator told of how when he had to portray Pinocchio being
embarrassed and ashamed, he acted out the scene in front of a
mirror in order to get the body language right. In other words, he
was deliberately and consciously setting up in himself a
subpersonality corresponding to the cartoon character. These
examples may remind us of how Mary Watkins speaks of the

150

developmental way in which we learn as children to converse with imaginary characters, some of which may be inner characters of our own.

John Watkins (1978) speaks of the technique he calls 'resonance' in psychotherapy. The therapist sets up an ego-state (subpersonality) corresponding to the client, and invests energy (cathexis) in that. In that way the therapist can be with the client from the inside, and share the client's subjectivity. He defines resonance as that inner experience within the therapist during which he co-feels (co-enjoys, co-suffers) and co-understands with his patient, though in mini-form. Watkins explains it using the analogy of two pianos which are put side by side; if you then hit the 'A' on one piano, the 'A' string on the other piano resonates in sympathy. He argues that this is different from empathy:

> Rogers says that empathy means the *understanding* of the feelings of another. He holds that the therapist does not necessarily himself experience the feelings. If he did, according to Rogers, that would be identification, and this is not the same as empathy. Resonance is a type of identification which is temporary.
>
> (Watkins 1978)

And similarly he argues that resonance is not the same as the psychoanalytic notion of countertransference.

In much the same way, Mahrer (1983) speaks of what he calls 'experiential listening', in which the therapist sits beside the client, and sets up in his or her own body the very same sensations which the client owns up to having. This again leads to a kind of identification which is temporary:

> There is another way. It is derived from the existential idea that one person (the therapist) is capable of merging into the identity of another (the patient), literally aligning with or sharing or 'being' the deeper personality process of another .... The radical proposition is that the therapist is thereby able to be the voice of the patient's deeper potential, to take on its identity.
>
> (Mahrer 1983: 57)

This is to say that the therapist can set up internally the self-same subpersonality that the client is experiencing at the time, and speak on its behalf if necessary. Mahrer has many examples of how this is done.

Mary Watkins is careful to point out that this is not the same as encouraging hallucinations. She says very clearly that the whole trouble with hallucinations is that there is no real dialogue with the voices which are heard or the entities which are seen, and therefore there is no real benefit to be obtained from them. What we are talking about here is a healthy process, not a pathological one.

We can even use this approach to get at parts of ourselves which are more than just healthy. The type of guided fantasy which has become so popular now can lead us in the direction of extra powers and unknown talents which may be there for the taking. For example, Brown (1970) shows how we can get in touch with a creative subpersonality within us, which can be very helpful in enabling us to be more creative. I have used this technique on many occasions, and can testify to the fact that it works very well in the majority of cases.

So fantasy images are not just something to which we make use of as teenagers and leave behind for ever, but something which we have access and which can be used all through life.

ARCHETYPE OR FANTASY?

This brings us on to one of the most difficult areas within the study of subpersonalities. We saw in Chapter 1 that two of the origins of subpersonalities were, on the one hand, the collective un- conscious, and, on the other, fantasy images. Those from the collective unconscious were archetypes, and those from our own fantasy could be anything we chose. How do we tell the difference?

In practice this becomes extremely important in psychotherapy when there is a possibility that the client is psychotic. Just the same feeling of being in touch with something marvellous and meaningful may on the one hand be a very positive archetypal experience which, with careful handling (avoiding the dangers of inflation) may be extremely important for the person involved, or may, on the other hand, represent the beginning of a bout of craziness.

152

Someone who has tried with some success to sort this out is David Lukoff. In a very convincing paper, he argues that there are two things which can very easily be confused with one another – mystical experiences and psychotic episodes. But in between the two there can be a mixture, which may be described either as mystical experiences with psychotic features, or as psychotic disorders with mystical features. The difference will be in the prognosis. If a positive outcome seems likely, given all the facts, then we have to ask the further question, is there a high risk of some kind involved, or is this a low risk case? If the latter, then Lukoff (1985) suggests that a formal diagnosis of Mystical Experiences with Psychotic Features be assigned, a new psychiatric category which at present is not featured in the standard lists. If a high risk seems to be involved (such as suicide or homicide), then the person needs to be 'put on hold', so to speak, until the risk has passed, and then looked at again.

I think we can adopt this general approach to the whole question of archetypes versus fantasy. If something arising in a person's experience is an archetype, it may be hard to handle, but it will be essentially positive and will probably help the person along the path, so to speak. If it is fantasy, it may either be something conscious, in which case it will share in the general neurotic picture presented by the client in question, or it may be something psychotic, in which case the Lukoff considerations will apply.

There may be some exceptions to this. Hannah (1981) gives the example of a patient in Jungian analysis who, on the night before a crucial examination, had a great vision in which a Holy Voice spoke to her and told her that it was not her vocation to become a famous person herself, but to become the mother of a man of genius. She totally accepted this apparently archetypal message in ecstasy and humility, and the next day passed the examination brilliantly, and was very happy for a while. However, by the time she came into analysis this experience had passed away, and she had been through a very unsatisfactory Freudian analysis as well. Her new analyst said that this supposedly Holy Voice was actually the voice of her animus, and the statement made was just a staggering animus opinion. The analyst then advised her to get in touch with another archetype, such as the Great Mother, which she duly did, with very good results. This is mentioned to illustrate the fact that just because something is a genuine archetype, this does not necessarily mean that it has to be taken at face value in every respect. It still has to be treated with discernment. We shall return to this question in Chapter 12.

Chapter Nine

ACADEMIC RESEARCH AND SUBPERSONALITIES

One of the most exciting developments of recent years in relation to subpersonalities is the way in which they have been adopted into academic psychology. This is still only a tiny movement, hardly visible unless you look closely, but it seems to be growing fast.

MARTINDALE

The first I heard of it was in 1980, when I came across the fascinating paper by Colin Martindale, slipped into a general compendium of papers in and around the subjects of personality and social psychology. Martindale's paper is very well based and sophisticated, giving much of the history of the idea of subunits within the personality in brief form, and pointing out that there have for many years been three basic views about the personality. One says that there is just one self or ego: this was popular at the beginning of the nineteenth century, and is again popular today. The second says that there are multiple selves coming on and off the scene; this was popular at and around the turn of the twentieth century. And the third says that there are multiple subselves, but that these are or can be connected to or integrated with a deeper-level unitary self; this view, he says, goes back at least to Myers (1961, originally published 1903), and is explicitly espoused by Jung (1956), Assagioli (1975), and Vargiu (1974). As to his own view:

> The basic argument of the cognitive theory to be proposed is that personality is best conceived of as being ultimately composed of a set of subselves. A subself is defined as a

155

cognitive unit that receives input from a number of sources (e.g., information concerning the situation one is in, one's self-concept, and one's emotional state) and sends output to a number of cognitive units coding dispositions for action.

(Martindale 1980: 194)

After showing that there is ample theoretical justification in cognitive theory for the existence of subselves, Martindale asks what is the structure of subselves within the personality. One obvious line of enquiry is simply to ask people about their subselves. This is certainly possible, and people generally give positive answers to this kind of question, so that the structure can be built up quite readily.

Another line of enquiry is to use hypnosis. Hilgard (1986) has, as we have already noted, reported the existence of 'hidden observers' during a hypnotic session, and has investigated these empirically, and Watkins and Watkins (1979) have found that subjects often have more than one hidden observer, and have given evidence to show that these are in fact enduring sub-personalities rather than transient states.

Other lines of enquiry include multiple personality, dissociative states, conversion reactions, creativity of certain kinds, sudden conversion experiences and so forth, and Martindale goes into some detail about these.

A number of very interesting implications of this model are drawn out, showing that cognitive theory can be much enriched by such a way of seeing the world. There is in this paper, however, no empirical test of the model being proposed. Hence it is promising and titillating rather than fully satisfying.

ROGERS

The following year another pioneering paper appeared, this time from T. B. Rogers. He used the concept of a prototype, a kind of schema of the self which is available to consciousness.

Our starting point here is to postulate that the self is a prototype that contains a collection of features the person sees as describing him or her. Its organization is probably not unlike those considered to underlie semantic memory. Cantor

156

and Mischel (1979) offer a detailed description of such a structure as it relates to categories of people. In our case the elements of the prototype are self-descriptive terms such as traits, values, and possibly even memories of specific behaviors and events. These terms are organized hierarchically, becoming more concrete, distinctive, specific, and less inclusive, with increasing depth into the hierarchy. Making a self-referent decision involves comparing the stimulus item with the prototype to determine if it 'fits' into the structure. Presumably the self-prototype is a fuzzy set in that no feature is necessary or sufficient for category membership. Moreover, the self-referent decision is probabilistic in nature, in that positive and negative decisions will not always correspond perfectly with the presence or absence of the category in the self-prototype.

(Rogers 1981: 196)

Rogers is aware that these ideas are not new, and goes back to William James as an early exemplar of the kind of thinking he is engaged with here. We saw earlier that James was one of the earliest people to bring the concept of subpersonalities into psychology proper, rather than leaving it hanging around the medical fringes.

A review of the classic self theories shows that affect has been accorded a key role in almost all cases. James (1890) argued that the spiritual self (this is similar to our prototype) is 'the most felt and at the same time the most objectively obscure' . . . . Our model of the self – defining it as a cognitive prototype – is, at present, clearly deficient in its handling of affective phenomena.

(Rogers 1981: 206)

So he goes on to examine the affective side of the matter, having to do with emotions and feelings. If all we can talk about is the intellect, clearly this is not going to be enough to describe a human being (though it may be fine for describing a computer). To deal with human beings, we must bring in the question of emotion, the whole affective side. And this Rogers goes on to do quite effectively:

The person can be thought of as 'maintaining a watching brief' for indicators of self-relevant events. When such an indicator is encountered, the person's attention is directed toward it. In this way the self becomes involved in encoding personal information by directing attention to certain aspects of the current environment. This attention direction is toward information that is personally relevant and also toward information that the person is already an 'expert' at analyzing. Affect, then, is thought to direct the person's attention toward a specific environmental occurrence. An event indicative of kindness may not be signaled for a person whose self-concept is centered on independence, but for a person with kindness in his self-prototype, it would evoke an affective response, thereby drawing the person's attention to it . . . . This model suggests that the encoding of a unit of personal information will be a combination of the actual cognition plus an affective signal or tag . . . . Possibly a strong, but negative, affective response moderates the cognitive processing by diverting attention elsewhere or overloading the system.

(Rogers 1981: 208-209)

This is of course right in line with the enormous body of research generated by Osgood and others over the years (see, for example, Ajzen (1988) for an up-to-date summary), showing that the evaluative dimension is the first and largest factor by far in our appraisal of things and people. In other words, our first question on meeting any new thing or person is, 'Will it do me good, or will it do me harm?' Or to put it round the other way, 'Do I like it or do I dislike it?' This is to say that all our perception is whole person perception in which the self is deeply involved at every point. And Rogers goes all the way to saying that we must, we have to, take into account the whole mind of the person. He says quite boldly:

Ours is a commitment to a *neomentalistic* approach to the self, as outlined by Paivio (1975). This emergent approach embraces:

mental phenomena as its subject matter and behavioural approaches as the method of study. It aims to understand both the form and function of ideas, images, meanings, and anything else that can be conceptualized as cognitive information by studying their behavioural manifestations and relating these to a theory of mind [p. 264].

The major characteristic of a neomentalistic approach to self is its commitment to thoroughgoing empirical analysis of any theoretical propositions that are advanced.

(Rogers 1981: 210)

Such a firm theoretical commitment is rare in psychology these days, and it is good to see someone sticking his neck out and making a statement like this. Of course our definition of 'empirical' must now include new paradigm research (for example, Reason 1988) rather than the old paradigm which has been shown to be so unsuitable for human beings.

MARKUS AND SENTIS

The next paper I discovered took quite a different tack. It also came from the broad area of cognitive psychology, but did not refer to Martindale or any of his references – rather strange in one way, but quite impressive in another, as demonstrating that such a concept has to be invented or discovered simply because of the nature of the problems within cognitive psychology itself, and not because of the spread of any fashion or fad from one campus to another. This was from a very interesting researcher, Hazel Markus, together with her colleague Keith Sentis. She developed the notion of self-schemata, which we have already come across in Chapter 6, as her version of subpersonalities. What is a schema, exactly? She says:

Schemata are the central cognitive units in the human information-processing system (Neisser 1976, Rumelhart and Norman 1978). We view schemata as memory structures of conceptually related elements that guide the processing of information. They are conceptual frameworks for representing relationships among stimuli that are built up on the basis of experience with reality. They are active in the categorization, interpretation and comprehension of social events and behaviour . . . . An important characteristic of schemata is their dual nature: A schema is at once a *structure* and a *process*.

(Markus and Sentis 1982: 43-4)

Having established the notion of a schema, which of course goes back to Bartlett, and is a very well-established theoretical entity, Markus and her colleague go on to say that some of these schemata have to do with the self. In other words, they have to do with the system as a whole:

> From our perspective, the self can be conceptualized as a system of *self-schemata* . . . . A schema integrates all the information known about the self in a given behavioural domain into a systematic framework used during processing (Neisser 1976, Palmer 1977). A schema is a conceptually advantageous analogue for the self because it can potentially represent what James (1890) called the two distinct aspects of the self – 'the self as the knower and the self as that which is *known*' . . . . More specifically, self-schemata are generalizations about the self derived from the repeated categorizations and evaluations of behaviour by oneself and by others. The result is a well-differentiated idea of the kind of person one is with respect to a variety of domains of behaviour . . . . Self-schemata search for information that is congruent with them and direct behaviour so that it is commensurate and consistent with them.
>
> (Markus and Sentis 1982: 45)

As with Martindale, they see this as a hierarchically organized model such that a kind of bureaucracy operates, keeping the whole under control even though there is a relative degree of autonomy amongst the subunits. This is spelt out very thoroughly in the chapter:

> The self-structure can be seen as a system of substructures, as a hierarchy of universal, particularistic and idiosyncratic knowledge structures about the self that are embedded within each other. These structures will be activated as processing units depending on the nature or goal of the processing act or task and the nature of the external stimuli. The repeated

160

activation of some self-structures causes them to become strong and well-articulated. They structure new inputs according to their constraints and thus influence the course of information processing.

(Markus and Sentis 1982: 66)

So here again we have cognitive psychology coming up with a very plausible model for how subpersonalities might be organized within the whole personality of a given person. Whether the structure should best be regarded as hierarchical is another question, and one to which we shall return later.

ROSENBERG

However, it took another three years for the next ground-breaking paper to come along, this time from a different source again. Seymour Rosenberg and Michael Gara brought out a paper – again in a book containing rather a mixed bag of different essays with quite different topics – which contained some empirical research on the subject.

People are asked to describe, in their own terms, each of from 20 to 50 personal identities, one at a time, and to list as exhaustively as possible the characteristics and feelings (features) associated with each of these.

(Rosenberg and Gara 1985: 97)

This is done in quite a complex way, and the interviews take several hours to complete, spread over several sittings. They cover negative as well as positive identities. They are open-ended rather than giving predetermined responses to choose from. Analysis is carried out using hierarchical algorithms which are supposed to yield an objective structure of the personality.

The authors point to the difficulties involved in doing this work, particularly in the tricky area of negative identities, to deal with which requires a sense of trust between the researcher and the subject. This whole question of the relationship between the researcher and the subject has of course been much under scrutiny in recent years, and I have made some contribution to that discussion myself (Reason and Rowan 1981).

161

In one investigation the subjects were asked of each identity, 'If you were to wake up one morning and find that this identity had been taken away or lost its significance, to what extent would your life be affected?' The researchers were then able to test whether this subjective importance rating tied in with the more objective prominence in the identity hierarchy obtained through the factor analysis. In most cases it did. In those cases where it did not, the person was in fact going through some sort of crisis of identity.

The authors of this paper also show how the same approach can be adopted in relation to existing sources of information such as diaries, ordinary conversation, letters, and literary material. They perform a detailed analysis of Thomas Wolfe's novel *Look Homeward, Angel* to show how this may be achieved. This analysis is then compared with a psycho-biography of Thomas Wolfe, and it is shown that there is in fact a very convincing correspondence.

So here we have a well-wrought piece of work, which explores the notion of subpersonalities (identities) in an objective and replicable way. The question of hierarchy arises again, and is settled here by using a computer program which works hierarchically. This is, of course, to assume hierarchy rather than to test for it.

McADAMS

In the same volume, there is another chapter which approaches the same topic from quite a different angle. This is by Dan McAdams, who starts off by examining the development of ego identity in the life of George Bernard Shaw. He says there are three central protagonists in Shaw's life story – the Snob, the Noisemaker, and the Diabolical One.

> Each of these internalized identity structures is associated with characteristic roles, recurrent behavioural scripts, consistent attitudes, hopes, fears and goals. Each, moreover, appears to be 'born' in a specific biographical episode in Shaw's life, generally an episode from childhood. More encompassing than the mere 'roles' that Shaw plays in daily living, these images of self cut across a host of identity domains while integrating essential information about the self to be found in

Shaw's past, his present situation, and his expectations for the future.

(McAdams 1985: 116)

These identities, these subpersonalities, McAdams calls imagoes. 'An imago is an idealized and personified image of self that functions as a main character in an adult's life story.'

McAdams calls on Jung (1943) and Sullivan (1953) to show that others have used much the same idea in much the same way, Jung saying that the imago may be derived from an archetype, and Sullivan saying that personified images of self are organized within the child's self-system. He then goes on to show that Freud and the object relations school also postulated the emergence of internalized images of loved and hated objects in the person's world. He follows this with a discussion of the way in which Transactional Analysis postulates the emergence of ego states and scripts: the personified scripts described by Steiner (1974) include (for men) Big Daddy, Playboy and Jock (athlete), and (for women) Mother Hubbard, Poor Little Me and Queen Bee.

The author goes on to suggest that imagoes are often arranged in the self as dialectical opposites. This was the general view of Jung, who also agrees with McAdams that the synthesis of opposing imagoes is a hallmark of the mature self.

At this point McAdams makes the leap over into cognitive psychology, quoting the work of Markus and Sentis (1982) which we have just looked at above, and also other work on schemata. He quotes Cantor and Mischel (1979) and Rogers (1981) as saying that a particularly well-formed self-schema constitutes a prototype, and concludes that an imago is a kind of prototype in this sense.

Imagoes, therefore, may function as superordinate schemata that are structured like prototypes and that are utilized by the person to organize and evaluate self-relevant information. As such, imagoes reduce the multitude of motley information about the self to manageable personified categories and fill in the gaps when self information is occasionally missing or deficient.

(McAdams 1985: 124)

And he quotes Martindale (1980) as supporting this view, as we have again seen above. He also quotes Markus on the concept of possible selves, which we shall be meeting later in this chapter.

However, his main emphasis is on imagoes as main characters in our personal myth – the story we tell to ourselves and others about the meaning of our lives.

> Beginning in late adolescence, each of us constructs a self-defining narrative – a life story – that promises to consolidate the synchronic and diachronic dimensions of identity in order to answer the twin identity questions [Who am I? How do I fit in to the adult world?] and to provide our lives with a sense of inner sameness and continuity. This is precisely what the formation of identity means. A process akin to this has been described by a number of other psychologists in terms of a 'mythological rearranging' of one's life attempted in young adulthood (Hankiss 1981), the creation of a 'personal fable' in adolescence (Elkind 1981), the construction of a personal 'myth' that draws upon a 'library of scripts' offered by one's embedding society (Bruner 1960), the coalescence of 'nuclear scenes' within life 'scripts' (Carlson 1981, Tomkins 1978), and the creation of a 'fictional finalism' that orients one's reconstruction of the past and one's present situation to an envisioned future (Adler 1927).
>
> (McAdams 1985: 127-8)

The author's own version of this life-story model of identity holds that life stories are made up of at least four identifiable components: an ideological setting, nuclear episodes, a generativity script (extending the narrative into the future), and imagoes. These latter, he says, are semi-autonomous guises of the self whose exploits and conflicts provide some of the most illuminating identity material in the life story.

Again, McAdams and his colleagues actually carried out some research to explore these ideas. Fifty subjects took part in two sessions each. In the first session they filled in personality tests and questionnaires; in the second, they were asked to tell their life stories.

> The subjects were asked to think about their lives as books, dividing them into chapters and describing the content of each chapter. Other questions in the interview concerned

significant life experiences and turning points, one's plans for the future, heroes and role models, philosophy of life, and the underlying theme of the person's life story. The life-story interviews lasted between one and two hours.

(McAdams 1985: 189)

From this the researchers derived a set of criteria for the presence of a given imago in a life-story interview. In a number of cases, two imagoes appeared to be in conflict with each other.

From this point on the research went, in my opinion, sadly astray, with McAdams with enormous *hubris* constructing a taxonomy of imagoes based on the Greek gods and goddesses. I feel he gets this wrong at all sorts of points, and exhibits a great ignorance of what these gods and goddesses traditionally stand for. He also tries to bring in the two dimensions used by Bakan (1966) of Agency and Communion. The whole thing becomes a mish-mash which I for one cannot take seriously. This is a great pity, because up to that point McAdams was making a good deal of sense and exhibiting a very encouraging sense of connections and meaningful networks. In any case, his work is clearly of importance both conceptually and in the area of research methodology.

GAZZANIGA

The next piece of work which we need to examine comes from quite a different context – the field of brain research. Michael Gazzaniga is a well-known researcher, particularly in the area of the split brain – the brain where the *corpus callosum* (the bridge between the two sides of the brain) is cut for some surgical reason. He spells out in detail, with a wealth of actual experiment, that more and more evidence accumulates to suggest that the brain is organized into modules, rather than acting as a whole.

I think this notion of linear, unified conscious experience is dead wrong. In contrast, I argue that the human brain has a modular-type organization. By modularity I mean that the brain is organized into relatively independent functioning units that work in parallel. The mind is not an indivisible whole, operating in a single way to solve all problems. Rather, there are many specific and identifiably different units of the

165

mind dealing with all the information they are exposed to. The vast and rich information impinging on our brains is broken up into parts, and many systems start at once to work on it. These modular activities frequently operate apart from our conscious verbal selves.

(Gazzaniga 1985: 4)

He raises some very interesting questions, such as why cognitive dissonance theory should operate at all. You may remember that cognitive dissonance says that if we have beliefs about what we do which are contradicted by what we actually seem to be doing, we feel very uncomfortable and have to do something to release the tension thus set up. So we engage in all sorts of self-justification, which can take numerous forms.

What has never been clear in dissonance theory, however, is why the organism engages in the behaviour that is at odds with a belief in the first place. Why do all the conflicts develop? Enter the answer from our review of brain research. I suggest it is because our brains are organized in terms of independent modules, each capable of action, of carrying out activities that test and retest the beliefs that are being maintained by our dominant left brain's language and cognitive systems. The conflict is produced by a mental module eliciting a behaviour, a module that can function independently from the dominant, language-based system of the left half-brain.

(Gazzaniga 1985: 139)

In other words, a subpersonality is involved here. The conflict is between two subpersonalities, and that is why it is so lively and personal. It may be worthwhile to underline the fact that no hierarchical structure is being assumed here, and to realize that no hierarchical structure is necessary. Gazzaniga's contribution is to show that subpersonalities are not just a psychological concept, but have an objective anatomical basis. So how is it that we feel like a single person all the time? He has an answer to that, too:

According to my model, the brain is constructed in a modular fashion in which particular modules would be free to respond to the literalness of environmental contingencies. Yet a brain system built in a modular way would also need a single interpreter to explain the various behaviours emitted over time by the modules, enabling a human to construct a unified theory of self, an activity most of us have carried out. It turns out the brain is organized in precisely such a fashion.

(Gazzaniga 1985: 195)

So here we have a fascinating confirmation, from a different angle again, of the basic idea of subpersonalities and how they work within the individual.

ORNSTEIN

In the following year came another independent sally into the field, this time from Robert Ornstein, who has also written a great deal about the brain and consciousness. In this new book he outlines a theory which combines extremely well with what we have found so far. His synonym for subpersonalities is small minds:

Instead of a single, intellectual entity that can judge many different kinds of events equally, the mind is diverse and complex. It contains a changeable conglomeration of different kinds of 'small minds' – fixed reactions, talents, flexible thinking – and these different entities are temporarily employed – 'wheeled into consciousness' – and then usually discarded, returned to their place, after use.

(Ornstein 1986: 25)

Like some of the others we have seen, he goes for a hierarchical model of how all this operates. He has rather a full chart showing how the various levels within the personality might relate to one another. Again, as with some of the earlier papers, this is based mostly on other people's research, and he has done little of his own to check out the model. But it looks plausible enough (see Table on p. 168).

The policies are not really part of the chart: they underlie everything, and are very general; but, mainly talking about the small minds, Ornstein is able to tackle some interesting puzzles. For example, we have all met the case of the person who behaves

> consciousness
> 'small minds'
> the talents and smaller single abilities
> the domain-specific data-processing modules
> reflexes, set reactions
> the basic neural transformations
>
> ---
>
> The policies: sensitivity to recent information;
> emphasis on vivid information; simplifying by
> comparison; focus on meaning – all influence
> activities at all levels.

in ways which are very uncharacteristic, and which may actually go against espoused rules or principles.

> What might have been considered hypocritical behaviour or examples of repression might well now be seen as a normal mental mechanism: the small mind operating at any time may not have the appropriate memory in store or the behaviour in its repertoire. We may well be able to decide how to behave in a situation when we are calm and can see many ways of acting, but that does not mean that it can be done. The small minds that we think we may choose from may be unavailable to consciousness when we need them.
>
> (Ornstein 1986: 143-4)

But Ornstein urges that this is not inevitable. Through the process of coming to self-awareness (perhaps through counselling or psychotherapy) it may be possible to acquire more self-control in the good sense:

> It is a question of who is running the show. In most people, at most times, the automatic system of the MOS [Mental Operating System] organizes which small mind gets wheeled in, most likely on that automatic basis of blind habit. But there is a point when a person can become conscious of the multiminds and begin to run them rather than hopelessly watch anger wheel in once again.
>
> (Ornstein 1986: 185)

Nor is this the only question which this approach can tackle. Ornstein comes to the issue of how we relate to other people once we have the notion of small minds clearly in view. It makes it easier to see how we could relate better to people who seem difficult or frustrating to us:

> You may not like some parts, perhaps entire 'subperson-alities', of someone, but there is a problem: people come in large and inconsistent packages, like other groups, teams, companies, and the like. These people may swing in different small minds at times, some of which you may find objectionable . . . . Considering others in the same way we consider groups or crowds, like our company, favourite team, or restaurant, might be the shift in understanding we need to make. 'I like the food, but not the decor,' neatly separates different functions, and we can decide whether to go to the restaurant again. The same approach could be used in marriage and in other close relationships.
>
> (Ornstein 1986: 189-90)

That is perhaps a little optimistic, but at least it shows how we can free up our approaches to other people, much as we saw in the work of O'Connor in an earlier chapter.

CANTOR AND KIHLSTROM

Much more technical is the next piece of work to come our way, this time from Nancy Cantor and John Kihlstrom. They take the whole idea one step further by postulating the existence of different levels within the subpersonalities, which they call selves. They find that the self-concept, usually spoken of as something unitary, depends in fact upon this system of selves:

> Sarbin (1952) . . . spoke of each individual having a variety of 'empirical selves' corresponding to different social roles, as well as a unitary 'pure ego' representing the cross-section of all of these empirical selves. Perhaps another answer resides in viewing the self as a family of selves: a fuzzy set . . . . The unity of self comes from the many overlapping resemblances among the different selves . . . (Wittgenstein 1953) . . . . Of

169

course, just as with any fuzzy concept, some of these selves are more central, more important to 'who you are' than are others (Markus 1977). These central selves are more representative of one's self than are the peripheral selves because they exhibit many features shared by other selves in the family of selves – they are closer, then, to the meaning of who you are (Rosenberg and Gara 1985, Gara 1986). Additionally, these central selves are representative because they more clearly differentiate self from others (Kihlstrom and Cantor 1984). The self-concept, therefore, must represent both the variety and the unity within each person's family of selves. In that respect, recent theorists have likened the self-concept to an implicit theory (Epstein 1973) or a network of linked concepts of self (Kuiper and Derry 1981, Markus and Smith 1981, T. B. Rogers 1981).
(Cantor and Kihlstrom 1987: 124)

How does this relate to the idea of a schema, which we came across before? In a very interesting way: these authors say that it is the more central selves which are closer to the idea of a schema. In fact, by concentrating attention on these central selves, they become schematic and acquire a richness and a solidity which may be extremely important in the person's life.

One of the structural features of the family of self-concepts that greatly eases the process of accessing self-knowledge is the organization of selves according to degree of centrality (or importance) in the current self-definition . . . . For example, Jack is 'schematic' (Markus 1977) in the professional domain, and the self-concepts that relate to this important identity will be far more elaborated, well-organized, and readily accessible for him than will be less central self-concepts (e.g. 'self as neighbour'). A person's particular domains of self-expertise are quite likely to have many possibilities for self and to figure heavily in the person's action plans (Markus 1983).
(Cantor and Kihlstrom 1987: 134)

This now links with the idea of a narrative and a life story, along the lines suggested by McAdams, though these authors do not in fact mention his work. It is the personal myth represented by the life story which links together the different selves and makes sense of the relationships between them:

> Together, the concepts of self and the autobiographical record provide a very complex, multifaceted subjective self-definition, but one for which there is a core gist (provided by the continuity of the narrative and the overlapping resemblances between the different selves). Additionally, this self-definition is a dynamic one, incorporating new visions of self and revising old ones to fit the present definition.
>
> (Cantor and Kihlstrom 1987: 125)

Thus their idea of selves is much more dynamic than some of those we have come across so far, and they broach much more fully the subject of the future projection of the subselves. In other words, we are now allowed to become interested in the possible selves which may appear in the future, and look at the question of how they might affect present-day actions:

> For example, in a questionnaire study with over two hundred undergraduates, Markus and Nurius (1986) observed a great deal of attention being accorded to past and future selves. Fully one-third of the sample reported 'thinking about past selves a great deal' and sixty-five percent of the students reported 'thinking about future possible selves a great deal'. These students clearly believed in the potential for the development of new self-concepts: sixty percent of them believed that 'the majority of their self-concept was still to be developed'. Ninety-five percent of these students had very definite ideas about the domains in which they would be likely to acquire new 'possible selves'.
>
> (Cantor and Kihlstrom 1987: 128-9)

MARKUS AND NURIUS

This leads very naturally on to the next contribution, which appeared in book form, the chapter by Hazel Markus and Paula Nurius in a very interesting British compilation of papers on self and identity. In it they go into this whole question of possible selves, and we are clearly in a much more sophisticated realm of discourse by this time. They say:

> Possible selves are conceptions of the self in future states. The possible selves that are hoped for might include the powerful or leader self, the elegant and glamorous self, the revered and esteemed self, the rich and famous self, or the trim, toned, in-shape self. The dreaded possible selves may comprise an equally vivid and compelling set. One's fears and anxieties can be concretely manifest in visions of the alone and unwanted self, the addicted or dependent self, the violent or aggressive self, or the undervalued and unrecognized self.
>
> (Markus and Nurius 1987: 158)

These possible selves, say the authors, have a great deal to do with motivation. They are, in fact, the concrete manifestation of enduring goals, aspirations, and motives, and provide an essential link between the self-concept and motivation. But now, of course, the self-concept is not seen as unitary, but rather as a system of salient identities or self-schemas that lend structure and meaning to one's self-relevant experiences. 'Self-schemas are our unique and fundamental self-defining elements.' They have been shown, in all the work we have quoted up to date, to have a systematic and pervasive influence on how information about the self is processed. So the possible selves which we are now considering actually move the person into action and outline the likely courses of that action. In sociological terms, say the authors, possible selves are the link between salient identities and role performance. They are the cognitive bridges between the present and the future.

> This universe of self-conceptions includes the good selves, the bad selves, the hoped for selves, the feared selves, the ideal selves, the ought selves. Some of these self-conceptions qualify as self-schemas. That is, they define areas of expertise about the self, areas where one has a great deal of knowledge and involvement. These are the self-defining elements, the domains of investment and commitment.
>
> (Markus and Nurius 1987: 163)

In other words, they are the subpersonalities. Coming on now to their own research, the authors make an important structural distinction between schematics (people with self-schemata in a particular area, who therefore pay a lot of attention to that particular area) and aschematics (who do not have self-schemata in the area under consideration).

> To explore this idea we (Wurf and Markus 1985) selected individuals who had self-schemas for independence, outgoingness and shyness (these were individuals who rated themselves extremely on these attributes and also thought these attributes were important for their overall self-evaluation). We compared these schematics with individuals who did not have schemas in these domains (aschematics). The schematics had many more selves, both positive and negative in the domain of these self-schemas than did the aschematics. The schematics could also supply a great deal of detail about the nature of their possible selves in the domain of these schemas that aschematics could not. The schematics and the aschematics did not differ in number or elaboration of possible selves in domains for which neither group had a schema.
>
> (Markus and Nurius 1987: 166)

These authors conducted a number of other studies, all of which circled around the idea of possible selves and how they influenced social action. They come to the conclusion that motivation can only be fully and adequately understood by reference to the notion of the self-concept and the elements of self-knowledge which come from an awareness of the self-schemata or subpersonalities.

In the same volume there is an interesting but quite different paper by Norman Denzin, which is well worth a look, but which will not be noticed in detail here because it is not so central to our concerns.

MINSKY

The last book which has come to my notice is from a quite different origin from any of those we have mentioned so far, and therefore constitutes a further independent corroboration of the importance of the idea of subpersonalities in understanding how the human mind actually works. This is from Marvin Minsky, who is an expert in the field of artificial intelligence, the study of how computers can by analogy throw light on how the mind might be organized. He talks about agents within the mind – agents which may have more or less responsibility, more or less specifically assigned, and who may group together into broader agencies. After a long but very readable discussion, he comes to the conclusion that

> All this suggests that it can make sense to think there exists, inside your brain, a society of different minds. Like members of a family, the different minds can work together to help each other, each still having its own mental experiences that the others never know about. Several such agencies could have many agents in common, yet still have no more sense of each other's interior activities than do people whose apartments share oppposite sides of the same walls. Like tenants in a rooming house, the processes that share your brain need not share one another's mental lives.
>
> (Minsky 1988: 290)

So here again we have the same message, this time built up step by step from a logical consideration of what must be involved to make human action possible.

This has been a fascinating journey, moving through this world of experiment and observation, questionnaire and survey, putting together much research from many different sources. We can see that our concept of subpersonalities is indeed well supported empirically in psychotherapy, and checks out in terms of structure from several different lines of enquiry. We shall come back to the question of hierarchy in the next chapter.

174

Chapter Ten

OBJECTIONS TO SUBPERSONALITIES AND SOME REPLIES

If, as we have seen all through this book so far, the idea of subpersonalities makes so much sense and is so useful, why is it not found in the textbooks on personality theory or in the chapters on the self?

THE SOUL AND THE MIND

The explanation seems to be something like this. All through the years up until recent times, there was a view, in the western world at least, that each person had a soul. And since the soul came from God and was basically like God – made in His image – and since there was only one God, there had to be a singleness, a unity about the soul.

In more recent times the idea of the mind came in instead of the soul. In order to make the mind respectable and acceptable, much of the thinking about the soul was simply transferred wholesale into the thinking about the mind, and again the mind was supposed to be single and united.

This is not really worth going into in detail. Spearman (1937) long ago produced a book dealing with this. He quotes or mentions Xenophanes, Parmenides, Plato, Aristotle, Plotinus, Augustine, Busse, Stout, Drobisch, Wolff, Fries, Kant, Baldwin, T H Green, Hartmann, Clifford, Schuppe, Ardigo, Ward, Ebbinghaus, Sully, Lotze, Höffding, Spencer, and Locke – all to say that unity is very important or essential. With such a show of support, it seemed that that was really all there was to say about the matter.

Of all these, by far the most influential down to this day was Kant (1933), who talked about 'the original synthetic unity of apperception'. His point was very simple: it must be possible for the 'I think' to accompany everything which I represent to myself or others. He also called it 'the transcendental unity of self-consciousness', to emphasize that new knowledge could emerge from it. But all that this says is that I must have the sense of 'I' in everything I do. We have already seen how this works in the case of subpersonalities: the sense of 'I' just automatically migrates to and goes with that specific subpersonality which happens to be in charge at a given moment. We always feel that sense of 'I', however bizarre our experience may be.

When the idea of the unconscious came in, it made a stir for a while, as we saw in Chapter 1, and as we saw in Chapter 2 it had a big influence on literature and the media generally. But the moment it looked like being influential, the basic materialism of scientific (some would say scientistic) psychology took over and made for unity in quite a different way.

MATERIALISM

From a materialist point of view – and this is still dominant at the moment, though there are hopeful signs of change – there can only be one personality because there is only one body, only one brain. Since everything mental is biologically based (and therefore reducible to physiology, neurology, immunology, and so forth), nothing mental can escape from the limitations of the body or brain. Some say that the mind actually is the brain; others, more sophisticated, say that mental phenomena are mediated by the brain. But either way, a person could on this reasoning only have subpersonalities if he or she had more than one body, more than one brain.

So how did the fact of multiple personality and all the rest of the phenomena discovered by the magnetizers, the mesmerists, and the hypnotists, which seemed to speak for a basically multiple identity, which might perhaps be forged into a single identity, get explained away? According to Ellenberger, it was through doubt being cast on its genuineness:

> After 1910, there was a wave of reaction against the concept of multiple personality. It was alleged that the investigators, from Despine to Prince, had been duped by mythomaniac patients

and that they had involuntarily shaped the manifestations
they were observing.

(Ellenberger 1970: 141)

The idea seemed to be that, with the advent of Freudian analysis,
it was much clearer how strong was the power of transference,
particularly where the patient was a young woman and the
therapist was an older man – and this was the most common
pattern, then as now. If the therapist had the idea that there was
such a thing as multiple personality, the patient gladly took up the
hint and duly produced multiple personalities. (Today such a view
seems absurdly insufficient, of course, in the light of the manifold
different sources of evidence offered in earlier chapters of this
book.)

So whether the psychologist was an old-fashioned religionist, or
a modern idealist, or an up-to-date materialist, the message was
still the same – think of the person as a unity. Any departure from
such a unity must be abnormal, temporary, and illusory. It was
probably due to repression, splitting, or some other mechanism of
defence, and should be dealt with as such, not as any kind of
secondary personality.

THE TOTALITARIAN EGO

This process of historical movement towards unity has resulted
today in psychology committing itself to what Greenwald (1980)
calls the 'totalitarian ego', characterized by egocentricity,
beneffectance (the tendency for self to be perceived as effective in
achieving desirable ends while avoiding undesirable ones), and
cognitive conservatism. These biases resemble the information
control apparatus of a totalitarian dictatorship, says Greenwald.

THE PERSON

In case it may be thought that some oversimplification is involved
here, let us look in more detail at some of the philosophy which is
relevant to the question of unity. We shall start with Strawson,
because in some ways he is a philosopher who is highly regarded
in this area. Strawson in his book on individuals looks at the notion
of a person, and after some argument, comes to the conclusion

that in order for us to be able to talk about a person, there must be a body, and there must be a mind, and they must work together:

> What we have to acknowledge, in order to begin to free ourselves from these difficulties, is the primitiveness of the concept of a person. What I mean by the concept of a person is the concept of a type of entity such that both predicates ascribing states of consciousness and predicates ascribing corporeal characteristics, a physical situation etc. are equally applicable to a single individual of that single type. . . . A necessary condition of states of consciousness being ascribed at all is that they should be ascribed to the *very same things* as certain corporeal characteristics, a certain physical situation etc. That is to say, states of consciousness could not be ascribed at all, unless they were ascribed to persons, in the sense I have claimed for this word.
>
> (Strawson 1959: 101-2)

This seems to take us back to unity again. But all that he is really saying is that the person *starts* from a position of unity. Once this primitive proposition is admitted, we can start to make concessions from that solid foundation. He goes on to say this:

> The concept of a person is logically prior to that of an individual consciousness. The concept of a person is not to be analysed as that of an animated body or of an embodied anima. This is not to say that the concept of a pure individual consciousness might not have a logically secondary existence, if one thinks, or finds, it desirable. We speak of a dead person – a body – and in the same secondary way we might at least think of a disembodied person. A person is not an embodied ego, but an ego might be a disembodied person, retaining the logical benefit of individuality from having been a person.
>
> (ibid. 103)

This now seems to admit the possibility of subpersonalities. For the concept of a subpersonality is clearly derived from the notion of a personality, which is a perfectly proper derivation from the idea of a person.

There is a very good discussion of these matters in the work of the sociologist Erving Goffman. He says:

When an individual utters the statement, 'I feel I have to tell you I was upset that night and told Mary everything,' three standard entities are implied. There is the animator (a fully situated transmitting machine); there is the 'addressing self', the one the speaker refers to as currently responsible and accessible to the listener, the self that the speaker has come to be up to and as of this moment, the self, incidentally, that is to be taken as closely geared to its possessor's capacity as animator; and there is the self-as-protagonist, the principal of the embedded, reported action, this latter person being someone the speaker may feel is no longer like the he in whose name he is now speaking. Nor need the speaker work through these standard entities. Take this bit of melodrama: 'There is no excuse. You are right to hate me. I am coming to do so myself.' Warmly animated, this utterance is something of a paradox. After all, anyone who identifies himself with the standards against which the culprit is being judged (and is found wanting) can't himself be all bad – and isn't, and in the very degree that he himself feelingly believes he is. A self-deprecator is, in a measure, just that, and in just that measure is not the self that is deprecated. He secretes a new self in the process of attesting to the appraisal he is coming to have of himself.

(Goffman 1974: 520-1)

It is hard to deny such an argument as this, which comes out of a different tradition again.

But the commonsense difficulty remains: if there is only one body, how can it house several subpersonalities? Would not each of them have to have its own body?

BODY AND BRAIN

In order to help with this, a story told to me by a very good group leader may be in order. In his work, he carries round with him a number of toys – small things which can be easily transported from group to group. One of these is a metal gorilla. The exercise he generally does is to invite participants to pick out one of the toys and identify with it, to say 'This is me' and talk about what it feels like to be this particular toy. In one group a man chose the gorilla

179

and spoke through it as a strong, powerful creature who was physically able to get what it wanted and dominate the environment; it enabled him to get in touch with his wild man, his hairy and primitive masculinity. In another group a woman chose the gorilla, which had quite a bad scratch on it, as a representation of her wounded part, the part which felt very hurt and vulnerable and attacked by the outside world. The gorilla, being a blank and innocent toy, could take both of these projections with equanimity. But one day these two individuals found themselves in the same group, and both wanted the gorilla. She couldn't see why he would want this wounded creature; he couldn't see why she would want this arrogant male. They were both upset by the other's interpretation, which seemed to both of them to spoil their identification with the gorilla. But the group leader encouraged them to work out these feelings in the group, and the whole group was very moved by the depth of understanding which then emerged between them, as they each saw how the other could be right, too. Ever after that, all those who had been involved in that group, faced with an apparent difference of opinion, could often get to a better place about the argument by saying, 'That's *your* gorilla!'

In the same sort of way, I may have the same body in different situations, but it may be seen very differently by the people involved. One person may be impressed by how tall I am; another may be disgusted by how fat I am; one may be excited by the spate of my eager speech; another may be upset by the words I use; one may be pleased that I have all my own teeth; another may be put off by my glasses and hearing aid. It may be true that I have the same body in all these contexts; but it may still be seen differently by others. And for them it will be a different body each time. Even for me, my body is at one time a vibrant instrument, and at another time an aching burden. And so on. So I think this problem about the body simply evaporates.

Now when we come to the argument about the brain, it becomes even more interesting. If we said that because there is only one brain, there can be only one mind, this now seems a complete non-starter as an argument. After the work of MacLean (and his division of the brain, well described in Hampden-Turner (1986), into three differently functioning parts), after the work of Ornstein (and his idea of multiminds), perhaps most of all after

180

the work of Gazzaniga (which we looked at in an earlier chapter), this argument cannot hold up even for a moment. The whole point of all this work is that there is more than one region within the brain, more than one module of the brain. And these modules are capable of acting independently. It must be possible, therefore, for there to be subpersonalities acting independently.

This argument has in recent years exercised several philosophers, who have discussed the difficulties involved in, for example, the hemisphere research. After reviewing a great deal of this recent philosophical argument, Jonathan Glover says:

> It seems that, when the left hemisphere has been removed, the right hemisphere can be associated with consciousness. It is hardly likely that the presence in the same skull of a disconnected left hemisphere changes this. And so it is reasonable to see the disconnected right hemisphere of the split brain patient as a centre of consciousness. If this is right, the experiments do demonstrate divided consciousness.
>
> (Glover 1988: 40)

Similarly, after discussing a thought experiment where he had the power to separate the two halves of his brain at will, Derek Parfit concludes:

> It might be objected that my description ignores 'the necessary unity of consciousness'. But I have not ignored this alleged necessity. I have denied it. What is a fact must be possible. And it is a fact that people with disconnected hemispheres have two separate streams of consciousness – two series of thoughts and experiences, in having each of which they are unaware of having the other. Each of these two streams separately displays unity of consciousness. This may be a surprising fact. But we can understand it. We can come to believe that a person's mental history need not be like a canal, with only one channel, but could be like a river, occasionally having separate streams. I suggest that we can also imagine what it would be like to divide and reunite our minds.
>
> (Parfit 1984: 247)

It is perhaps only because so much of this work is so recent that it has still not made much impact on the world of academic psychology.

Another recent development in philosophy is the recognition that there is such a thing as 'folk psychology' as distinct from 'scientific psychology'. I don't much care for this terminology myself, as the distinction seems to me much more between realist psychology and anti-realist psychology. But be that as it may, the conclusion has been that any attempt to construct a psychology free from commonsense notions like subpersonalities is doomed to failure.

> We have excellent reason to believe that the concept of action, as opposed to mere bodily motion, is a thoroughly folk psychological concept. For, in the extensive philosophical literature on action theory, there is overwhelming agreement that whatever else an action is, it is a piece of behaviour that is explainable by certain folk psychological states of the agent which rationalise it under some description (e.g. Davidson 1963; Goldman 1970; Brand 1984). But if the concept of action is folk psychological in this way, then the anti-realist position entails that we never do anything – persons never act. And if we never do anything, then anti-realists cannot assert anti-realism, for asserting is a form of acting. Indeed, for a vocal noise to count as a speech act requires an especially rich set of intentions, beliefs, desires, etc., as causes of the noise – as Grice (1957,1969), Bennett (1976) and other philosophers have argued. Therefore, if nobody ever has propositional attitudes, as anti-realists assert, then nobody ever speaks either. In particular, nobody else asserts anything, because asserting is a form of speaking. So, there is a virulent pragmatic contradiction inherent in anti-realism: When someone asserts this view, the very content of his assertion entails that he is not actually asserting anything, and indeed is not even speaking.
>
> (Graham and Horgan 1988: 72)

This seems to me a good knock-down argument, and I cannot see any way round it. But coming back specifically to subpersonalities, it is interesting to see how those psychologists who in effect deny the idea actually carry out their work. It is not, repeat not, the case that psychology argues against the idea of subpersonalities, or tries to prove that the idea is in error. It simply organizes things so that it is quite impossible for such a concept to emerge.

AVOIDING THE ISSUE

Take for example a recent book edited by Terry Honess and Krysia Yardley (1987), excellent researchers and editors, capable of selecting and publishing papers sympathetic to the notion of subpersonalities, and editing a book here which is right on the topic of self and identity. The first chapter simply takes for granted that there is just one self. So does the second chapter. The third chapter teases us by apparently suggesting that there could be false self structures, but takes away with the one hand what has been given by the other. The fourth chapter tantalizes us by mentioning false selves, but says of them that they 'are selves that mostly feel empty, lack their own ambitions and are enfeebled'. It is only the true, cohesive self that is any good, says this chapter. The fifth chapter speaks of a piece of research in which there was no opportunity given for subpersonalities to appear. The sixth chapter is about identity constancy, which is simply assumed and taken for granted. The seventh chapter is on the conservation of selfhood, but again it is simply assumed that this is necessary. The eighth chapter is on the meaning and development of identity. The research asked questions like 'If you change from year to year, how do you know you are always you?', and 'What makes you different from everyone else in the world?', and 'What kind of person are you?', and 'How would you describe yourself?'. These questions simply do not allow any notion of subpersonalities to appear or be counted. The ninth chapter congratulates itself on 'the use of a demanding and unusual approach' but still takes totally for granted that 'the subjective experience of self ' (the title of the article!) is the subjective experience of just one self – whereas we know that it is not. The tenth chapter arouses our hopes by its title, 'The self as observer of the self ' – but no, all that happens is that we investigate the subjective self along four lines: individuals' conceptions of (1) continuity of the self, (2) distinctiveness of the self, (3) the self as agent (volition), and (4) self-reflection. It is 'the self ', 'the self ', all the way along the line.

The eleventh chapter takes unity for granted. The twelfth chapter is on self-esteem, a term which takes unity for granted. The thirteenth chapter is on depersonalization, not relevant in any case. The fourteenth chapter reports research on the definition of self among young women which was so worded that no concept of subpersonalities could emerge, though it would have been highly relevant. The fifteenth chapter looked promising, as it was about personal projects of adolescents, but again unity was taken for granted. The sixteenth chapter again looked promising, as it offered a case history approach, but again the opportunity was missed due to a too directive questioning procedure. The seventeenth chapter takes unity for granted. The eighteenth chapter appears to veer close to acknowledging subpersonalities at one point, but quickly veers away from it again. The nineteenth chapter excited some expectations at first, because it has a diagram very close to those in Chapter 7 of this book, and it does actually use the word 'subidentities' at one or two points. But the concept is not pursued or worked with in any way. The twentieth chapter used a research design which does not permit the emergence of subpersonalities. The twenty-first chapter does actually raise the question of unity versus multiplicity of selves. But the research reported does not make it possible for anything about the multiplicity to emerge; the research questions were all about 'the self' and about 'others'. The twenty-second chapter is about adoption, and again takes unity for granted.

After this rather tedious examination, it becomes obvious that these people are not considering the possibility of subpersonalities to any great extent. Even when they sail close to it, they sail away again just as fast as the wind will take them. It is as if there were a consensus, arrived at in some mysterious way, to ignore the possibility of multiple selves, and therefore to organize all the research in such a way that they cannot emerge, even in principle.

THE ONE AND THE MANY

At one time I was quite occupied with the question of how it could be true that a person could be one and many at the same time. For this seems to be the real question. I see it as a quite false question to say, 'Is the person one or many?' We do not have to make this choice. Rather, the question is, 'How can the person be one and many at one and the same time?' The best account I came across in philosophy was from Harold Joachim, who was a British Hegelian and wrote a good deal about the human mind. He starts off by saying: 'The unity of a mind throughout its experiences is the unity of a "self-consciousness", what one may call, in order to have a distinctive name, a spiritual unity; and the experiences, being the many of what is thus one, are a spiritual plurality' (Joachim 1948: 86). What we are emphasizing now is that this plurality does not only consists of experiences, but also of potentially distinct subunits, each of which itself behaves like a mind. We can then understand better what he goes on to say:

> The mind is one throughout its many experiences: but its
> unitary being – its individual character – depends upon, is
> made and moulded by, the special variety it experiences. The
> 'many' in this case contribute to determine the character of
> their 'one'. And at the same time, what each experience is
> depends essentially upon the individual character of the mind
> which is experiencing. The 'one', in this case, contributes to
> determine the character of every item of its 'many' –
> contributes to make and mould each single experience.
>
> (Joachim 1948: 86-7)

In other words, each subpersonality is *my* subpersonality. Ultimately I have to take responsibility for it and own up to it. If we say with Stone and Winkelman that vast numbers of people have a protector/controller subpersonality, my own version of that is still my own, my very own protector/controller, and it has to be reckoned as something which in a very real sense *is me*. As Joachim continues:

> To be 'a mind' is to be a self-conscious subject of experiences;
> and the unity of the subject in its many experiences conforms
> (more or less, at different levels and in different degrees) to a
> certain type of union-of-a-manifold. Wherever, whenever, in
> so far as, there actually are 'experiences', or there actually is
> 'a mind', there, then and so far, the only way to conceive the
> facts without distortion is to think of them in terms neither of
> a mathematical sum, nor of a mechanical system, nor of an
> organic whole, but of a 'spiritual' union of a 'spiritual' variety.

185

> If anything is 'one subject acquiring and owning many
> experiences' it must be (and be conceived as) immanent in
> them and modified by them – in some sense, therefore, it
> must make and mould, and be made and moulded by, its
> many. And if any plurality is (and is to be conceived as) a
> many, of which the items are experiences, they must
> 'interpenetrate one another' (in Bergson's picturesque
> phrase); they must be, and be conceived as, modes and phases
> of a single immanent subject. In some sense, therefore, they –
> these modifications of its 'substance', these varied expressions
> of its unitary being – must go to make it what it is; must go to
> mould and individualize their 'one', to constitute it '*this*
> subject of *these* experiences'.
>
> (Joachim 1948: 87)

Now Joachim admits that this is an ideal – a philosophical account
of what must be the case if we are to understand what a mind is and
how it works. But do our real minds in the real world actually
measure up to this ideal? Is there, in fact, any point in saying all
this, if very few people can have this total sense of being one and
many at one and the same time? Joachim has something to say
about this, too:

> it may be objected that the type of unity demanded by our
> general principle for a mind-in-its-experiences is a mere ideal,
> unrealized and unrealizable in fact. No actual person – not
> even the most perfect and fortunate specimen of humanity –
> is, or even approximates to being, throughout his life, a
> 'spiritual union of a spiritual plurality'. The self-consciousness
> of any actual person is broken and fitful, interspaced by
> regular and occasional interruptions (by sleep, reverie, and
> inattention – to say nothing of swoon, delirium, or of the
> breaches that may be caused by, for example, anaesthetics). If
> to be a mind is to be a single self-conscious unity, pervading,
> constituting, and moulding – and yet also constituted, varied,
> and moulded by – many mutually interpenetrating
> experiences; – where are we to find examples of mind in the
> actual world? The utmost that could be said of any actual
> person, of any actual self-conscious subject, is, not that in
> some degree, or at some level he is, or has, a mind, but that

he is, or has, a series of imperfect and fragmentary minds –
that, from time to time in his historical life, there occur
evanescent unions of a manifold which approximate *longo
intervallo* to the ideal 'spiritual union of a spiritual plurality' of
which we have spoken.

(Joachim 1948: 88)

This, then, shows how subpersonalities can actually be allowed in
in terms of the philosophical account itself. They are expressions
of the fact that we are not whole, not unified. They are expressions
of the fact that we have not yet achieved integration or actualization of what it is to be a fully functioning human being. And
Joachim accepts that:

The actual persons (as they are called) are, in fact,
precisely that which they appear themselves to be
when measured by the general principle. Each of them
is, at most, a series of evanescent and fragmentary
'minds'; modes of a 'mind': imperfect and transitory
individuations of the human spirit. If we are to look for
actual examples of that 'spiritual union of a spiritual
plurality' which is distinctive of a 'mind-in-its-experiences',
we must now turn to the 'spiritual realities' to which
reference was made in a former context. We must
consider the so-called actual persons – the so-called finite
intelligences and wills – in respect solely to the 'infinite'
self-conscious subject, the 'universal' mind, *potentia infinita
cogitandi,* which fulfils itself (in part, at least) in and through
them; which, in their fragmentary knowings and willings,
creates, develops, and sustains the realm in which it knows
itself (the realm of knowledge-or-truth); the realm in which it
wills and enacts itself (the realm which is man's ordered life
of freedom and right).

(Joachim 1948: 89)

What he is now finally saying is that we are part of a greater whole,
and that the truth is this whole. Our own individual minds are best
regarded finally as just a part of a greater mind, which lives and
breathes through us just as we live and breathe through our
subpersonalities.

187

PLURALISM AND HETERARCHY

Of course, he uses rather formal and philosophical language, which is not easy for us as denizens of a rather unphilosophical decade. Another way of putting the matter would be to say something like this:

> Just as a free society requires a plurality of Somes, themselves each containing enough persons to support each individual in his resistance against the socializing Other, so each individual contains a plurality of selves who must in turn manifest yet another dimension of pluralization. Just as each statusphere is a Some in a social context, so each intrapersonal self must be a Some in the personal context . . . .
>
> Third realm rationality eschews the search for some basic level to which others may be reduced. Relieved of the quest for a lowest or highest level, relational thought can pursue the sense in which each dimension can alternate with other dimensions, in playing the role of pluralized content or determining context . . . . In short, a hierarchy is like an unambiguous pecking order. A heterarchy on the other hand has a structure like the game of paper, rock and scissors: paper covers rock, rock crushes scissors, but scissors cut paper. Scissors do not always lose. Instead they play a role analogous to what McCulloch (1945) calls a 'diallel'; that is, a synaptic link that cuts across a hierarchical neural net (or 'drome') to produce a heterarchical pattern of preference.
>
> (Ogilvy 1977: 113)

With this understanding, we can now see that a person can be integrated without falling into the error of the 'monarchy' or 'monotheism' which our authorities have warned us against. This is a most important point: to be integrated is not to lose or to play down or to be superior to the subpersonalities. To be integrated is to be more in touch with more of one's subpersonalities, particularly the ones which have been feared, hated, and denied. And this enlarges the realm of our consciousness.

> With the dilation of the domain of the operating potentials [subpersonalities now made conscious, JR], I now am free to

be anywhere in this expanded domain. This new freedom significantly expands the array of behaviors which can flow forth from me. I literally can be this potential or that other potential, and I can accomplish this switch with ease. In effect I am free to be each of these potential selves, and in each there is a distinctive set of behaviors. As a result, the total repertoire of behaviors which can flow forth from me is considerably increased.

(Mahrer 1978: 504)

What we are talking about here is freedom, and the absence of compulsive fear. Instead of finding ourselves pushed around by our own processes, we are free to choose among them.

Becoming more integrated means that the center of the self is freer to move easily from one operating potential to another along channels of integrated relationships. Integrating persons enjoy their potentials far more than the rest of us.

(Mahrer 1978: 505)

And this means that new possibilities are opened up. Things which before may have seemed quite out of the question now seem within our reach, and within our world.

What is even bolder and more audacious, the integrating person is willing to relate to deeper potentials [which] are not yet a part of the operating domain, not yet integrated into his sense of self . . . . The weakness and uncertainty which are the deeper potentials can speak to him, can relate to him – and he listens. He is able to engage in a relationship with his deeper potentials, a relationship which enables him to engage in a more or less integrated fashion with potentials which are not yet fully integrated.

(Mahrer 1978: 506)

This in turn means that we can trust ourselves much more, and over a much wider range of decisions and possibilities. By doing justice to the one and the many, and being fully in the one and the many at one and the same time, we arrive at a new way of being: 'In the major decisions of one's life, the integrating person turns in complete trust to those deeper potentials which have something to say' (p.510). All this may sound very complex and hard to grasp firmly, but it seems to be accurate enough, and if we want a much simpler version of the same points we can find them very succinctly stated in a little-known but first-rate book by Beahrs, where he says:

> * When is it useful or not useful to look upon an individual as a single unit, a 'Cohesive Self'?
> * When is it useful or not useful to look upon any one as being constituted of many parts, each with an identity of its own?
> * When is it more useful to see ourselves as part of a greater whole?
> I use the term 'useful' rather than 'true' since all are true – simultaneously and at all times.
>
> (Beahrs 1982: 4-5)

What a succinct statement this is! As we saw earlier, the third point on this list, though less commonly stated than the other two, is equally important from a philosophical point of view. Not only Joachim, but also many other philosophers have argued the case for this, from Hegel onwards. The British philosopher of the nineteenth century, Bosanquet, says this:

> The true life is that of the whole, of which thought in the finite mind is a partial and incomplete revelation. The contrast of 'pensiero pensante' and 'pensiero pensate' precisely inverts the true relation. What really thinks is something more than any thinking act of ours.
>
> (Quoted in Joachim 1948: 101)

This may go further than we are willing to travel at the moment, and it is not essential to the idea of subpersonalities to agree with it, but it would be unfair to hold back on this. In the hands of Beahrs, such a view seems quite a sober statement of the obvious.

And it certainly agrees with the views of Stone and Winkelman, who, as we have seen, have done so much to illuminate all these questions by their painstaking practical work in the field:

> From our perspective, all energy is part of the Universal Energy Source that may be referred to as God. When the

voice in Siri's vision speaks to her, it is expressing the reality that belongs to any disowned energy pattern. Each kind of energy wishes to be claimed by us if it has been disowned. Each pattern returns to us in our dreams, in the personal reactions of our friends, in our meditations – each one of them is turning to us and saying – 'Be still and know that I am God. Claim me, for I am that part of the Universal Energy Source that has been left unclaimed.'

(Stone and Winkelman 1985: 278)

We do not have to believe it in these terms, because the idea of subpersonalities makes a lot of sense even if we never push to the limit in this way, but it is good to have the whole picture in front of us even if we ultimately decide to ignore part of it for the sake of utility.

To sum up, therefore, it is not so much that there is any real conceptual objection to the idea of subpersonalities, nor is it the case that researchers are prejudiced against the notion (we have seen that Yardley and Honess, for example, could edit one book which did admit the concept, and another which did not), but rather that history has pushed people in the direction of ignoring or downplaying any such schema, and that for many years philosophy appeared not to give it house room.

This is something which has now been put right, and it is a case of waiting for the new thinking to work its way through the system.

Part Four

THE POTENTIAL

Chapter Eleven

WHITHER SUBPERSONALITIES?

It is now time to ask the question, 'If all this is true, where do we go from here?' There seem to be at least seven directions in which further research could go.

MORE DATA ON MORE PEOPLE

The first thing we can do is to get data on more people. Whether we are talking about my own research, where the people involved in the project were very favourably inclined to the basic idea being put forward, or whether we are talking about more old-paradigm types of research, we just need to know much more about the conditions under which it is meaningful and proper to introduce the notion of subpersonalities. What happens if we try to use this approach in less well-motivated settings? Are we talking about something which has a 10 per cent chance or a 90 per cent chance? Well, now, from the further research which has been done in a number of areas, it seems that the basic groundwork is there, in computer science, in psychology, and in neurophysiology. Considered as an approach to the study of personality and motivation, it is now a long way forward. Considered as an approach to psychotherapy, it also seems to have many ramifications and to be applicable in a variety of ways. It may be that, like most forms of therapy, it works when carried out by someone who believes in it. But this is of course both a strength and a weakness. It is a strength because the research motivation and impetus can be very powerful; it is a weakness because of all the dangers of subjectivity and special pleading which are inherent in such an approach.

It seems to me now that the more we can move towards a new paradigm approach (Reason and Rowan 1981) in research, the more we can discover of the scope and limits of the notion of subpersonalities. On the other hand, what still gets the plaudits and the funds in academic circles is old paradigm research. I have no answer to this.

REGULARITIES

The second thing we can do is to discover regularities. It would perhaps be possible to see how many subpersonalities seem to be common to large numbers of people. It seems already that many people have at least one very unpleasant subpersonality, which frightens them very much. But there is usually at least one other subpersonality who is not at all scared of this one, and can help in dealing with it. It seems that also there may be a very small scared person in quite a lot of us, who is easily disconcerted and appears very weak; this particular subpersonality often turns out to be surprisingly strong, once some of the self-deception and self-definitions are removed. It seems unlikely that anything as regular as the superego or the id will be found, but we have now left the age when everyone had to have the same subpersonalities completely. The people who seem to have gone furthest with this particular question have been Stone and Winkelman (1985), but Berne's idea of the internal parent, adult, and child is now very well known and well accepted (as we have seen, Shapiro finds much profit in it), and must obviously have a big part to play in any final synthesis that might be attempted, and Perls's topdog and underdog, as we have seen, have made important contributions too. It is fascinating, however, to see how certain subpersonalities, very important in one system, do not come up at all in another. For example, the shadow, so important in the Jungian approaches, hardly appears at all in the Stone and Winkelman approach. Conversely, the protector/controller, so important in the latter approach, hardly appears at all in the Jungian approach. You will look in vain in the Berne framework for the anima, or in Jung for the topdog and underdog. It seems now that there is a good argument for trying to clarify this whole area both conceptually and practically. We do not have to be limited any more by the predilections of the founders.

ELICITATION

The third thing we can do is to find optimum elicitation procedures. It seems likely that there are better and worse ways of asking people about their subpersonalities, and of unearthing hidden subpersonalities, which may not be immediately conscious. Ways which have been tried include straight elicitation, Gestalt fantasy, Gestalt therapy, co-counselling, dream analysis, association tests, active imagination, psychosynthesis exercises, and the Voice Dialogue techniques. This ties in with the question of the origin of subpersonalities. As we saw in Chapter 1, there seem to be at least six sources of subpersonalities which cannot be reduced to one another: (1) the collective unconscious – if Jung is right, this is where the archetypes come from; (2) the cultural unconscious – the patripsych and all that material; (3) the personal unconscious – the complexes and internal objects described by Jung, Klein, and others; (4) conflicts or problems – sometimes the two or more sides of an internal conflict or problem situation may become vivid enough and frequent enough to seem to require an identity each, as is frequently found in Gestalt therapy and the Voice Dialogue technique; (5) roles – the way we appear to one group may be quite different from the ways we appear to another, and each role may bring out a different subpersonality. This may also apply to social frames, as described in Goffman's work. And (6) is fantasy images – we may identify with a hero or heroine, or with an admired group, and take on some of their characteristics; perhaps sometimes two or more heroes or heroines may merge. Amd these fantasy images may come from the past or future, as well as from the present. They may even be constructed to order, as Stanislavsky or Watkins (1978) have suggested.

Now, each of these six sources may ideally require quite different elicitation procedures to do them full justice: this remains to be seen. Most of the research, it seems, has restricted itself to (5) – the question of roles, though the very interesting work of Hazel Markus on possible selves is clearly about (6). The work which has been done on this suggests that virtually any form of psychotherapy brings out whatever is necessary as a normal part of its process, and that it is only when research is being carried out that we need specific elicitation procedures.

WORKING WITH SUBPERSONALITIES

The fourth thing we can do is to find ways of working with the subpersonalities and compare them. It may be quite painful and personal at times to bring out subpersonalities, and any researcher in this area would have to have some skills in counselling or psychotherapy in order to be able to help the person to work through any hurtful experiences. It is probably impossible to work in this area without having been into some form of therapy oneself. In any case, different therapeutic approaches need to be tried and properly evaluated.

The questions which seem to have been of most value in making subpersonalities concrete and explicit are the following:

What do you look like?
How old are you?
What situations bring you out?
What is your approach to the world?
What is your basic motive for being there?
What do you want?
What do you need?
What have you got to offer?
What are your blocks to full functioning?
Where did you come from?
When did you first meet (name of person)? What was going on?
What would happen if you took over permanently?
What helps you to grow?
How do you relate to women/men/children?

There are many others which can be used, but these seem the most effective ones we have discovered so far for making concrete each subpersonality as it appears and making it more solid. Another valuable move which can be very important is giving the subpersonality a name. This helps very much if we want to go back to it later, and it also makes it seem more human and more approachable. Such names can be very variable. For example, one person had these subpersonalities: Galaxy; Mighty Dam; Train; Rocket; Watch; and Bomb. Another had these: Adventurer One; Adventurer Two; Honourable Felicity Flippant-Gregarious; Calm

Enjoyer One; Calm Enjoyer Two; and Miss Crumble. One person had just these two: Controller; and Disapprover of Control.

On the other hand, some people cannot work with names. One person in our 1974 group thought his personality was as complex as anyone else's, but was all in one piece. He could find no conflicts, no fighting between parts, nothing separate within. And in quite a different way, another person could not work with names because he had too many subpersonalities to cope with: he then developed a field system, with three main nodes: a competent node, including physical, emotional, intellectual, and spiritual aspects; a sado-masochistic node; and a baby node. Each of these nodes could be represented in an authentic or in an inauthentic way, and the inauthenticity could be inner-compensatory or outer-manipulative. Each of these could have a positive or negative representation, and could be active or passive. This is not really a suitable case for treatment by subpersonalities, and so it is clear that this way of working is not for everyone, though the evidence seems to be that it is for the majority.

I have developed a very interesting way of doing primal work with subpersonalities. On discovering what Grof calls a COEX, I encourage the client to personify the COEX, and talk to it, and talk back as it. In this way we can deepen the COEX very easily, and carry experiencing forward into the deeper areas where the most fruitful work can be done.

Sometimes in recent work we find subpersonalities arising spontaneously, in such a way that we have no choice but to work with them. This is particularly the case because of the current emphasis on the importance of abuse, both physical and sexual, which is particularly likely to bring on the kind of traumatic splitting we referred to in Chapter 7. When sexual abuse occurs, it is as if there is a sane but helpless child who is witnessing the whole scene. This witness is fascinated by the scene, and cannot look away even though he or she does not want to see what is happening. And so may develop a child who is overtly split into two or more co-conscious subpersonalities. For example, Sinason (1988) worked with an eleven-year-old girl:

> She spoke in three distinct voices: a harsh mocking voice, a
> prissy voice which was an exact imitation of her housemother,
> and a shy childish voice. In the classroom and playground she

usually kept to one voice, but whenever anyone distressed her all these voices would alternate, becoming an ongoing dialogue between her fragmented selves.

(Sinason 1988: 351)

The therapy mainly consisted in giving her dolls which could stand in for the voices, and simply letting her talk out the dialogue in the presence of the therapist. Very quickly the abusive situation was acted out and clarified, with the therapist facilitating and witnessing what was enacted.

SUBPERSONALITIES AND CHANGE

The fifth thing we can do is to work at changing the subpersonalities. The first step is always, of course, simply to get to know the subpersonality, by getting it to talk and interact, firstly, perhaps, with the therapist, asking the questions we have outlined above, and then with the client and often one or more of the other subpersonalities. Once this has been done, there seem to be three main possibilities for approaching the question of change.

One is to challenge the structure or content of a subpersonalitiy directly, by confronting it in some way. This might be from outside (the therapist or group leader or one of the group members) or from the central self speaking as an integrated whole, or from one or more of the other subpersonalities. In the latter case a form of internal psychodrama might emerge. This is the so-called left-hand path, which works through conflicts and brings about a synthesis in this way. An example is to be found in a chapter (Rowan 1987a) where I describe dealing with a 'tyrannical superego' along these lines.

Another possibility is to concentrate on developing the real self, which is not identical with any one of the subpersonalities, which are now seen as all false, so that they sink back into being harmless aspects of a greater reality. This is the method of meditation and of psychosynthesis, and also of the disciplines of T'ai Chi and Aikido. It represents the so-called right-hand path, which works through the vision of a higher unity, seen as a pre-existing higher self, in the light of which the conflicts drop away and are seen as no more than aspects in correlation. This approach does not appear to have been written up very much anywhere, though it is referred to by Stone and Winkelman (1985).

There is also a third possibility, which is to strengthen one or more of the other subpersonalities, so that they can take over the functions of a subpersonality which has got too big and over-important, and which can then sink into the background and become less important. This approach seems more like behaviour therapy or NLP, and I would regard it as perhaps only a stop-gap or temporary measure, to bring about the relief of immediate symptoms and make the main job easier. There is another angle on this which has become important in recent years, however, and this is the question of befriending the hurt child within, and helping it to find its own inner strength. This is of course Alice Miller (1987) territory, and extremely important for any therapist to understand, because of the possibilities of recreating the original abuse all over again in the therapy situation itself.

It seems to me that all three of these approaches are worth trying in a systematic way, to see what different effects come about, both in the short and long term.

THE INTERNAL GROUP

The sixth thing we can do is to explore the possibility of reasoning from one's own internal group to the society outside, and vice versa. If one's first reaction to a subpersonality judged to be bad is to to say, 'Cut it out, destroy it', then this will perhaps be one's attitude to social, financial, or political enemies. If one's attitude to one's business or academic rivals is to manipulate them without their awareness, then this may also be one's attitude to those subpersonalities which seem to be a threat. Research could show whether the inner and the outer correspond in this way, or whether different rules apply in each of the two worlds. Let us look at this in a little more detail, and see some of the possibilities here, in the form of the following research hypotheses which might be put forward:

Better decisions are made by bringing out the counter-arguments and integrating them, than by allowing one side to dominate, or making some kind of mean compromise. This would fit with the work of Janis and Mann (1977) on decision making, and the more philosophical work of Follett (1941), the research of

Eiseman (1977) and with the work on psychotherapy of Rogers (1961) and Perls (1969), as well as with the clinical work on subpersonalities already mentioned. The implications of this would be that one should deliberately look for countervailing viewpoints whenever one decision seems particularly attractive or particularly unpleasant. This seems a very important hypothesis in the field of professional disillusionment, as Edelwich (1980) has suggested.

It is good to have a trained process observer at each meeting to give feedback on how each person was acting and relating to others, as opposed to what they are saying in terms of content. In this way dysfunctional relations and actions can be raised to awareness and thereby changed. This is fairly well established as a management technique (Schein 1969), and as a form of self-awareness it has been suggested by people like Shapiro (1976), Beahrs (1982), and Stone and Winkelman (1985), as we have seen above.

Cohn (1971) suggested that the rule that 'disturbances take precedence' should be applied in good working groups; the same seems to apply to the internal group. We do better to pay attention to what is going wrong with us and do justice to it fully – feel it deeply – rather than try to override it and carry on as if it did not matter to us. This idea can be checked out both in the group and in the individual context; or as we have now learned to put it, both in the external and in the internal group.

One of the things that seems to happen with great regularity in all sorts of psychotherapy is that people are released from the domination of their 'topdog' or 'superego' or 'critical parent' or 'bad breast' or 'bad womb', and so on. They do not need an internal autocrat any more. This seems to parallel some of the things which happen in groups, particularly in T-groups – for some very interesting thoughts in this area, see Mann (1975). But what happens instead? What we need are some really good studies of how leadership changes within the internal group; I do not know of any at the moment, but someone like Markus or Kihlstrom might well be capable of working on such a project. *My hypothesis would be that different leaders would be able to come forward at different times, in quite a healthy way – the person would be able to use the subpersonalities, rather than being used by them.* Or it might be that the subpersonalities become much less separate and distinct, and the personality much more unified, along the lines of Jung's concept of individuation. I am slightly sceptical about the likelihood of the latter, because of the very strong social pressures within our very complex culture, which make it hard indeed to avoid some kind of role playing. And also, as Mary Watkins has argued, it may not even be desirable to have such an aim.

People in the group change and develop the more they are open to one another and trust one another, as Golembiewski and McConkie (1975) have described. But also in therapy this quality of mutual trust tends to grow between the subpersonalities – certainly this is the outcome of my own research into this area, and I think Vargiu, Shapiro, and others would probably concur. Rogers (1961) has for long made the point that one of the major signs that therapy is working is that the person displays more self-trust. This seems to be a theme which could be very fruitfully explored using both the external and the internal group, and going back and forth between the two.

In the social world, it is very convenient to give one person one job; this is called the division of labour. But it has been pointed out often that this narrows people (Rowan 1976) and alienates them from their work, from other people, and from themselves. It is a distortion of the human being to make him or her merely a social functionary, and the process also makes it harder for the person to change and develop. *A very striking instance of this, to which much attention has been drawn in recent years by the feminist movement, is the gender role. Jung (1959) has suggested that it is also true within the individual* – the gender role has been so exaggerated in our culture that most individuals have within them an equally exaggerated representation, at the unconscious level, of the opposite sex; this is the notion of the anima or animus. One answer to this has been the concept of androgyny, as described by Bem (1977) and in a different way, by June Singer (1977). But there are difficulties with this concept, as Miller (1976) rightly says:

> Likewise Jung's 'woman hidden inside the man' is not the same as its reverse. The idea remains a fanciful notion unless we ask seriously who really runs the world and who decides the part of each sex that is suppressed. The notions of Jung and others deny the basic inequality and asymmetry that exists; they are also ahistorical.

There are at least three things involved in this area: sexual preferences; gender roles; and sexual identity as a man or woman. In order to tease out the very difficult distinctions which need to be made if we are to put right the injustices of the past without introducing cures which are worse than the disease, it seems that the idea of going back and forth between the external group and the internal group could be of great value.

No one can represent or speak for a whole group. Even if information is gathered from all the members (which is often not done) the focal person still sees things from his or her own angle, and is *parti pris. This is a hypothesis from group work, and which seems equally valid in the person-as-group.* If I get into one of my subpersonalities, I invariably find that it is richer and more complex than I would have expected, and has things to say which I could not have predicted. Similarly when I ask group members what they really think about some matter on which they have perhaps voted, I find that the vote often misrepresents their real position, which has many reservations and qualifications, perhaps to the extent that they do not really go along with the decision in any significant sense. This again seems to me something which could well be investigated in both contexts with advantage, and results from the one reflecting back on the other.

The real structure of a group can be very different from its ostensible structure: in particular, it can be dominated by one strong character. However, if the external world changes, other characters may come to the fore: this is the understudy or standby or substitute phenomenon. It happens in genetics, with dominant and recessive genes, as well as in sociology and in psychology. It also happens in information theory, where what was background noise may become the message, and vice versa. *This phenomenon can very readily be studied using the internal group, and the conclusions then tested with greater difficulty at the external group level.* It is in this sort of investigation that the internal group is perhaps of greatest use.

One interesting possibility here is to see whether it might make sense to say that *subpersonalities are to the whole self as social classes are to the whole society.* For some purposes, it may make most sense to see the subpersonalities as just two – topdog and underdog – or the classes as just two – capitalists and workers. But for other purposes it may be better to think in terms of several subpersonalities, or several classes – as, for example, Marx in *The Class Struggles in France* names nine different classes as being important to keep separate. If we can find out how to deal with the internal society, this may help us in our understanding of the larger society we live in.

STRUCTURES

Finally, the seventh thing we can do is to explore the structural relations existing between the subpersonalities. Are they all on the same level, or are they arranged in a hierarchical manner, or are there a fixed number of different levels, or what? There are a number of hints about this in Jung, and Assagioli has formalized and simplified Jung's thoughts into his 'egg diagram'. Berne and Shapiro have outlined a version which is compatible with Freud's structural ideas. There are a number of eastern models which might be relevant, and the mandala is a very suggestive way of looking at the whole question: here, for example, is a quote from Argüelles and Argüelles (1972) on the mandala:

> The Mandala of the Transmutation of Demonic Powers requires the painful recognition and acceptance of the existence of negative or demonic forces at work within oneself. Once this difficult task is achieved, what is required is a visualisation and projection of these aspects into an ordered whole. The purpose is not to eliminate these forces – that is impossible considering the nature of energy – but as indicated in the Dance of the Five Directions, to recognise and transform them.

The only difficulty with the mandala, as with Assagioli's diagram, is that it is two-dimensional. There is nothing to say that the relationships between the subpersonalities have to be describable in two-dimensional terms. But the similarity between the writing on the mandala and the work I have been reporting here is too close to ignore.

We have seen that most of the authorities we have quoted have gone for a hierarchical model (or for a holarchy, which sounds nicer but is really similar), but that is of course suspect in a patriarchal society, which has an interest in justifying oppressive systems. There is no particular reason to suppose that a hierarchy is the only way of looking at the matter. We can adopt such positions as pluralism, of heterarchy, of anarchy (the anarchist version, not the conservative version, of course), of polytheism rather than monotheism, and so forth.

My own tentative view is that subpersonalities are for the most part rather poorly organized, as one might expect when they are in such inadequate communication with one another. As they become more connected up, through the process of self-knowledge, they seem to adopt various formations, depending on the person involved, and become more like communes (if the person is of a democratic disposition) or like committees (if the person is more hierarchically inclined). In other words, increasing knowledge gives greater choice.

At the same time, when the person gets in touch with the real self, or the greater self, the question of the subpersonalities becomes less important in any event. They move gradually from being great feudal barons to being colourful banners brought out on appropriate occasions. But this brings us on to the topic for the next chapter.

Chapter Twelve

BEYOND THE
SUBPERSONALITIES

It must have been obvious that all the way through this discussion we have been avoiding a certain area, and it is now time to give that area some due attention. What we have been avoiding is the whole question of whether there is anything beyond the subpersonalities. We have left it ambiguous as to whether there is such a thing as the Real Self, or the Higher Self (Transpersonal Self, Greater Self, Deeper Self, Inner Self, Self with a big S, and so on), or whether there is such a thing as the soul.

In a way this is not a particularly important issue. There is plenty of work to be done, as we saw in the previous chapter, regardless of how we may wish to answer this question. But at the same time it would be cowardly not to admit that there is a real question here, even though it may be difficult to answer.

The person who seems to me to have grasped this nettle most successfully is Ken Wilber, so let us first of all see if we can understand what he is saying about the matter.

PSYCHOSPIRITUAL DEVELOPMENT

What Wilber says is that there is a process of psychospiritual development which we are all going through, both as individuals and as members of a historically located culture. In a series of books he has outlined this process, and shows that we are very familiar with its early stages. The later stages are much more controversial, but follow exactly the same form.

The easiest way to describe this model seems to be by going through the diagram 9.

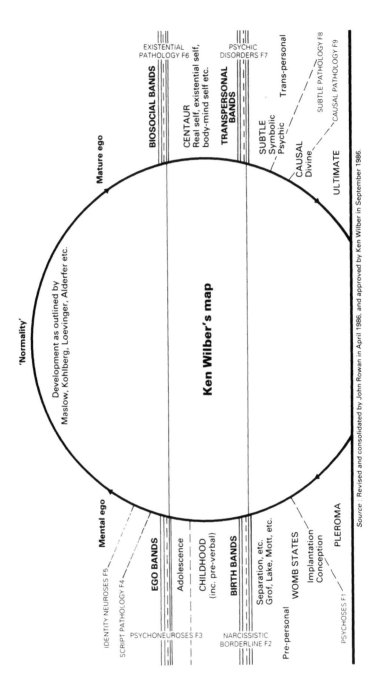

'Normality'

Development as outlined by
Maslow, Kohlberg, Loevinger, Alderfer etc.

Mature ego

BIOSOCIAL BANDS

EXISTENTIAL
PATHOLOGY F6

CENTAUR
Real self, existential self,
body-mind self etc.

TRANSPERSONAL
BANDS

PSYCHIC
DISORDERS F7

Trans-personal

SUBTLE
Symbolic
Psychic

CAUSAL
Divine

SUBTLE PATHOLOGY F8

CAUSAL PATHOLOGY F9

ULTIMATE

Ken Wilber's map

Mental ego

IDENTITY NEUROSES F5

SCRIPT PATHOLOGY F4

EGO BANDS

Adolescence

CHILDHOOD
(inc. pre-verbal)

BIRTH BANDS

Separation, etc.
Grof, Lake, Mott, etc.

Pre-personal

WOMB STATES

Implantation
Conception

PLEROMA

PSYCHOSES F1

NARCISSISTIC
BORDERLINE F2

PSYCHONEUROSES F3

Source: Revised and consolidated by John Rowan in April 1986, and approved by Ken Wilber in September 1986.

Diagram 9 Ken Wilber's map

It can be seen from this that there are three broad sections, labelled as prepersonal, personal, and transpersonal. One of Wilber's most insistent themes is that we tend to suffer from the pre/trans fallacy – that is, we confuse what is prepersonal with what is transpersonal. Some do it (like Freud) by saying that the transpersonal does not really exist – it is just a projection from the prepersonal; others do it (like Jung) by saying that the prepersonal does not really exist – anything beyond the personal must be transpersonal.

The term 'transpersonal' is still unfamiliar enough that it needs some explanation. I like Grof's (1979) succinct description, where he says it is concerned essentially with 'experiences involving an expansion or extension of consciousness beyond the usual ego boundaries and beyond the limitation of time and/or space'. Many of us have had moments at least of this kind of experience: surveys show (Hay 1983) that something like a third of the population have had peak experiences at one time or another. These are experiences where, as Maslow (1968) says, 'the whole universe is perceived as an integrated and unified whole' and where the ego boundaries seem to be stretched or removed. (Such an experience can sometimes be remembered for the rest of a person's life, and can have a profound effect on how the person lives that life.) Many people working in this field feel that the proportion is probably much higher, except that people push the experience away as too disconcerting, and do not like the idea of changes in consciousness which go so far.

Now what Wilber (1980) says is that these experiences are really intimations of a possible transition from one level of consciousness to another. What is so reassuring about Wilber is that he says this is no great leap into the deep waters of spirituality (or religion, or occultism), but a change no greater than that which we have experienced several times before, in the course of our development so far. We have already gone from symbiosis with the mother to separation, and from body-self to membership-self, and from there to the mental ego. At each of these transitions we had to revise our whole notion of who we were, and even what kind of self we were. So we know what it is like to revise our self-definition. The move from mental ego to the next stage is just another such change, and peak experiences are a very common harbinger of this particular transition.

I suppose this trip from mental ego to unified bodymind self (centaur) through the biosocial bands is one of the most interesting changes in consciousness, because it is quite close at hand for many adults. It always seems to involve a lot of pain and discomfort, because it means questioning all the roles one has been playing. Like all these transitions, it is dialectical: it involves negating the previous stage of development.

Incidentally, what Wilber means by 'bands' is a set of experiences, possibly but not necessarily traumatic, which follow one another in quick succession, rather like going on a roller-coaster, or through the white water in a set of rapids; once the process starts, it seems to take over and to be inescapable. So far we are following the basic process outlined in more detail in Chapter 7, and there is nothing too controversial about this, perhaps.

Wilber (1983: 231-9) is particularly interesting on the process of transition from one stage to another. He says that two dimensions are necessary to it: first a creative urge or impulse or drive (creative as opposed to destructive); and second, a willingness or desire to let go (as opposed to holding on). If we have the creative urge, but also a desire to hold on, many good things may happen, but they will all happen at our present level – no development will take place. If we have the destructive urge, but also a desire to hold on, many interesting things may happen, such being a good fighter for our cause, but again no development will take place. If we have the willingness to let go, but also a destructive urge, we may actually move back to an earlier level. Real development, he says, always involves incest and castration – incest because we want to hold on to the one thing we have to let go of, and castration because we fear we may have our power cut off anyway, whether we like it or not. By letting go creatively, we can overcome this and move on round the arc of development. It is this creative letting go that is essential to developmental change.

The relevance of all this to social science is that most of us stick to the central, upper part of the chart. We say, as it were, 'I am only interested in the personal.' And this is very plausible and very safe, because it is at this level that both language and mathematics reach their height, and science becomes a watchword. This is the area in which what Kuhn (1970) calls 'normal science' comes into its own. But just as in recent years research has shown (Verny 1982, Ridgway 1987) that there is far more than we thought in the early stages – the baby is far more competent than we thought, the birth process is far more meaningful than we thought, the foetus is far more competent than we thought, and so on – now we have to recognize that there is much to take account of in the later stages too. I have noticed people talking about the transpersonal and about spirituality generally in a way which was not on even five years ago. People are coming out of the closet, as it were, and admitting or affirming that they have indeed had subjective experiences which fit in with Wilber's objective analysis. Certainly, in my own case I have found Wilber to be a very good guide to my own experience, making sense of it all along the line.

THE REAL SELF

Let us then start by looking more closely at the transition from the mental ego to the centaur. The developmental task here is to move to a self which works on a basis of what Wilber calls vision-logic rather than formal logic. It entails the integration of many splits in the person, most particularly the split between mind and body. Wilber uses the image of the centaur to refer to the difference between the horse-and-rider separation of the previous stage and the unification of the present stage. At the mental ego stage we tend to think of the mind as in charge of the body; the mind has to guide and discipline the body, as a rider guides and disciplines a horse. At the centaur stage the horse and the rider become one. At this level we have the experience of authenticity; a combination of self-respect and self-enactment. At this level we get what Maslow (1987) calls 'self-actualization', what Rogers (1961) calls 'the fully functioning person', and what Perls *et al.* (1951) call 'the self' as opposed to 'the self-image'. In this book we have already touched many times upon this movement.

Now certainly the subjective experience here is an experience of unity. It seems to us as if we are for the first time one and single, and as if the subpersonalities are no more than aspects as seen from outside. It feels as if we are real, and as if there is one person taking responsibility for all that we say and do. All the stirring phrases of existential philosophy seem to have come true: 'Free and alone, without assistance and without excuse'; 'There are no limits – our own choice is everything'; 'To be that self which one truly is'; 'The encounter is here and now'; 'I create my world'. So what has happened to the subpersonalities? After a while, I believe, we find that they are still there, even though they may have been transformed in various ways. But because we are now more sure of who the 'I' is, we actually have more freedom to move around between the different 'mes' that there may be at different times and in different places, not compulsively this time, but by choice. This is a very important stage, but it has been described so many times by people in the humanistic camp (Fromm 1947, Perls *et al.* 1951, May *et al.* 1958, Bugental 1965, May 1969, Mahrer 1978) that it does not seem worth while to dwell on it here.

That is all very well, but Wilber says that it is not the end of the road. What we now come on to, if we continue with the process of development – and we now have some choice over this too – are the transpersonal bands. Here the task is to form a transpersonal self which will not flinch from entry into the spiritual field, perhaps first of all into the area of meditation, and the cultivation of intuition, healing, and psychic qualities of one kind and another. As before, we may resist the process of transformation, and this fixation might be to do with what Maslow (1987) calls 'the Jonah complex' and what Haronian (1971) calls 'repression of the sublime'. This means retreating from any involvement with the transpersonal and the psychic on the grounds that one is not worthy or not brave enough to enter upon this new territory. But if one is prepared to go through the transition here, one comes out into the next part of the diagram, the subtle stage. It is in the subtle stage that we get in touch with the higher self, just as it was in the centaur stage that we got in touch with the real self. Some of us object to the word 'higher', because it follows a phallic patriarchal model of what is good and desirable: we would rather talk about the deeper, inner or greater self, or the transpersonal self.

Voice Dialogue creates the possibility of connecting to energies on the spiritual continuum. One can ask directly to talk to the higher mind or one can lead a person into the higher mind through a meditative procedure and then shift to Voice Dialogue . . . .
   In dealing with the higher mind, we must be very careful as facilitators that we do not confuse an inner Pusher with the actual spiritual energy . . . . Jennifer's Higher Self gives her a 'view from the bridge'. It gives a perspective. It does not solve

212

problems. It does not create pressure. Amazing insight can come from such parts of ourselves. When such a voice is contacted, a strong empowerment may take place. We are helping the subject connect to inner sources of strength and wisdom.

(Stone and Winkelman 1985: 279)

We are still talking about things which we can observe in the therapy room, but this time we are giving scope to something which has gone beyond the level of the subpersonalities. We are now definitely in the realm of spirituality, of the transpersonal.

THE TRANSPERSONAL SELF AND THE SOUL

One of the errors which can strike at this point is for someone to say that what we are talking about here is the superego, or the ego-ideal. The superego, as the voice of conscience, seems to come to us sometimes from outside, or as a still small voice from inside, but just in the way we have suggested as the voice of the guru or inner teacher.

We saw just now how Stone and Winkelman caution against this error, but the person who has most clearly spelt out the error in this is Frances Vaughan, a follower of Wilber. This is what she says:

One way of becoming more aware of the transpersonal Self is to differentiate it from the super-ego. This distinction is useful in avoiding the pitfalls of confusing the two in the desire for self-transcendence. It is sometimes easy to mistake what one thinks one should do for guidance from the transpersonal Self as a source of inner wisdom. The Self can be differentiated from the super-ego as follows:

Super-Ego	Transpersonal Self
Judgmental	Compassionate
Fearful	Loving
Opinionated	Wise
Intrusive	Receptive
Dominating	Allowing
Limited	Unlimited
Rationalizing	Intuitive
Controlled	Spontaneous

213

Restrictive	Creative
Conventional	Inspired
Anxious	Peaceful
Defensive	Open
Separated	Connected

(Vaughan 1985: 42-3)

What we are saying, then, is that the transpersonal self is a further stage of development beyond the centaur, and that it has characteristics of its own which make it different both from the centaur and from the superego. One of the main differences has to do with the question of boundaries. What the ego, the superego, and the real self have in common is that they all have strict boundaries. All the humanistic writers are very clear about this: 'I am I and you are you', and so forth. But at the transpersonal stage all this changes quite radically.

At this stage the separative egoic and existential identifications dissolve. We can take down the barriers which divide us from other people, and experience our common identity. If we can imagine a hilly country which sinks into the sea, leaving the peaks above the waves, we can easily imagine how the islands so formed could become very different, with different flora and fauna and different histories of invasion or cultivation. From many important and valid points of view, they are now separate and distinct. But if we look beneath the waves, we can see that they are still part of the same mainland, still the hills they always were, rising above a common plain. In just the same way, it is true to say that we are separate individuals: it is also true to say that we are members one of another, that we are all part of something greater; and this is what we realize and experience beyond the transpersonal bands. It is very important to realize that this is not a should or an ought – it is simply our experience at this stage, which we have reached through our own changes, and not through taking on someone else's ideas.

Increased awareness of the transpersonal self can enhance the capacity for viewing reality in terms of relationships. If one willingly surrenders separateness in accepting interdependence, one may become more accepting of others as they are.

However, Vaughan also cautions us against another possible confusion here, with the idea of the soul.

214

The transpersonal Self as conscious witness of existential, mental, emotional and physical experience is not identical with the term soul. However, since the terms are sometimes used interchangeably, it seems appropriate to discuss the soul in relationship to psychotherapy in order to differentiate it from the transpersonal Self. The term soul is commonly used to designate only the simple subject of awareness of any level of consciousness. The soul, as simple subject of awareness, may be identified with any level of consciousness, whereas the transpersonal Self as witness has disidentified from contents of consciousness and transcends former identifications.

(Vaughan 1985: 45-6)

This seems to me an important and useful distinction, which is actually very helpful in sorting out our experience at this stage. In case this still does not appear quite clear, Vaughan goes on to spell this out in more detail again:

The transpersonal Self is further distinguished from the soul since its recognition implies a transcendence of egoic and existential self-concepts, the same self-concepts that are sometimes attributed to the soul as a subtle separate entity. So while the transpersonal Self includes awareness of the soul, it is not exclusively identified with it.

In contrast to the transpersonal Self, neither psyche nor soul designates a particular stage of development. The term *soul* is commonly used to refer to the subtle separate self-sense that travels the spiritual path through various realms of existence. The term *psyche* is more often used to refer to the ground of psychological self-awareness at any level on the spectrum of consciousness.

(Vaughan 1985: 47, 48-9)

Having looked at these distinctions, it is time to come back to the position which we have now reached on the diagram, which is the region of the subtle self – on the one hand higher than the egoic and the centaur (existential) self, and on the other, below the causal realm and therefore not identical with spirit.

If we succeed in all this, Wilber says we now have to go on to another transition which can be just as hard as any of the others, if not more so.

215

THE CAUSAL SELF

This transition will possibly take just as long to carry through as any of those met before. Here we have to move from the subtle realm into the causal realm. We have to differentiate between ourselves as symbolic explorers in the foothills of the transpersonal realm, and people who can do without symbols altogether.

> Spirit, which is differentiated from soul in being both the ground and the goal of the process of human evolution, is all encompassing. It is already as it has always been. The spiritual journey is therefore described as one of eternal return, not to a prior condition in time, but to the awareness of unity in reality, despite the appearance of separation.
>
> (Vaughan 1985: 49)

In the subtle realm, we are quite aware of separation even though we know how to overcome it; our acquaintance with symbols has taught us new ways of handling these things, but we are still subject to them. But at this causal stage, we have to abandon what was so painfully learned.

The main sign that we have entered into this new phase is that we do not find symbols of any use any more. This is a huge difference, because all through the subtle stage we are learning more and more and better and better to use symbols and to be with symbols. It is a vast and fascinating field, and to leave it for the bare and featureless realm of the causal seems risky. But this is always the case, at each of these transitions. To leave the familiar ego for the unknown real self seems risky. To leave the real self for the unknown transpersonal self seems risky. At each stage we are letting go creatively of the hard-won achievements of the previous stage, and it never becomes easy.

In a later book (1986), Wilber becomes much more specific about what is happening to consciousness at each stage, and how at each stage of development the process can be halted or distorted, thus producing different needs for different types of therapy. He outlines what he calls nine fulcrums – turning points or crises where things can go right or wrong and be dealt with in healthy or pathological ways.

One interesting outcome of all this is that a dream can be

interpreted at any one of the nine fulcrums, and might have important meanings at more than one of them. This opens up a large realm of further exploration, but there is no space to deal with it here.

LOOKING BACK AT SUBPERSONALITIES

Having taken a very quick ride through the Wilber levels – and really one cannot do justice to the complexity of all this material in a brief chapter – let us go back and see how this relates to our story about subpersonalities.

It seems to me that working with subpersonalities is for the most part a good method of crossing the biosocial bands and moving from the mental ego stage into the centaur stage. The reason for this is that it is a very good method of healing the splits in the personality, enabling us to work out the splits in their own terms, doing justice to what is positive about them as well as what is negative. It is a very good path to self-knowledge. When we have done all the work with our subpersonalities we really know ourselves very well, and do not need neurotic projections and other psychological defence mechanisms to carry us through. We have done our therapy, so to speak.

And it seems to me that if we do not do this, we are going to move too fast into the transpersonal (the subtle realm, as Wilber calls it), and run real risks of very bad experiences. It is well known that people who experiment with the Ouija board in order to obtain psychic communications can experience some frightening encounters with 'bad psychic characters' who, as it were, take the opportunity to play tricks and upset the applecart (Hunt 1985). These apparently discarnate entities may very often be just projections of our own nastiness, our own disowned energies which we have not yet dealt with or come to terms with.

And more generally, it is all too easy for us to go into the apparently higher realms of the transpersonal carrying all the baggage of our unworked-out subpersonalities, which then by the process of projection become voices which inspire us or actually give us books, music, art works, spiritual communications and the like. Recently Jon Klimo (1988) has investigated the whole question of channelling information from discarnate entities such as Seth, Ramtha, Lazaris, and so forth in a very full and sympathetic way, and he quotes one estimate that 85 per cent of these communications, come straight from the personal unconscious of the individual affected.

> Experienced channeling teachers, such as Canada's Joey Crinita, are the first to tell us that most of what novice channels think is channeling is rather the product of self-delusion brought on as a result of psychic immaturity. Or, through a kind of self-hypnosis, some so-called channeling is simple imagination creating its own characters.
>
> (Klimo 1988: 321)

But some of it does come from the higher (transpersonal, deeper, greater, inner) self; it is important here, as elsewhere, not to commit the pre/trans fallacy. We do not want a reductionist 'nothing but', but simply a sober realization that we are always subject to that which we have not dealt with in ourselves, on whatever plane we may be.

A good example of this came to my notice in the autobiography of a famous medium. She knew she had psychic abilities from an early age, and cultivated them, and became much in demand to demonstrate her powers. For several years she became more and more famous. And then one day, as she was coming down from the stage after a performance, she overheard two women talking, and one of them was saying that it was obvious that it had all been a cheat and a fake. This so upset her that she gave up the work, and became a nurse for five years. Now this is an example of how harmful it can be to omit doing your own therapy. If she had really worked through her own material properly, her ego would not have been so easily put down. She would have gone beyond the stage of depending upon other people's opinions in that way.

Over and over again it seems to be shown that unless we move from level to level in a sure and grounded way, we shall be subject to inflation and deflation. We have to be aware that a glimpse of the subtle level is perfectly valid – but only a glimpse. We have to accept that a glimpse of the causal level can be perfectly meaningful and important – but only a glimpse.

And some of it does come from the causal level, not just the subtle level. That, too, has to be allowed. We can develop, we can grow into these further levels, difficult and rare though it may be, and we can certainly have glimpses of levels which we have not reached yet.

This is one of the most important findings in the best book we have had yet about the whole question of spiritual development. Dick Anthony and his co-workers tell us that genuine glimpses of spiritual reality are quite common and very important when they do occur. But they can lead to spiritual inflation, a quite disastrous occurrence which makes us think we have got much further along the road than we really have.

> The term 'glimpse experience', which we are introducing
> in this volume, is intended specifically to be a counter-
> inflationary term, emphasizing that the great majority of
> mystical or transpersonal experiences are only temporary
> glimpses beyond mundane ego-consciousness and do not
> involve true transformation to a more transcendent,
> encompassing state.
>
> (Anthony *et al.* 1987: 188)

And of course particular temptation arises from the idea of channelling, because in channeling we do not say, 'I am the spiritual being'. We make the apparently much more modest statement: 'I am the humble and unworthy channel through which this spiritual being communicates.'

However, I suggest that we apply here exactly the same thinking as we saw in the case of subpersonalities generally, and take responsibility for our voices. No matter what the voice says, it is still my business what I do about it.

> Discernment is called for, whether the intuited material
> comes from one's own unconscious or from beyond oneself.
> One must look the gift horse in the mouth in each case in
> which the gift is not clearly accurate or useful, and one must
> do this regardless of source. We were told earlier by many of
> the channeled sources not to accept messages just because of
> their seeming otherworldly status. Test what we tell you
> against experience and weigh it within, they said.
>
> (Klimo 1988: 309)

So in other words, we have to take it that it is we who are doing it, in just the same way as we saw before that we could not use

219

subpersonalities as an excuse for our actions. Even if it really is the highest Deity giving us messages, that still does not excuse us from the duty of deciding what to do about it.

CONCLUSION

And so we come to the final question: in the end, are we one or many? There is a great temptation to assume that the Wilber story says that the answer must be One. The whole thrust of his approach, we perhaps assume, is to say that we have to talk ultimately about the single Atman, the single Void, the single Ground.

But when we come to look at the small print, this is not so. Wilber (1980) says that the final stage, even supposing that we reach it, and even supposing that reaching it is a meaningful phrase, is 'both One and Many, Only and All, Source and Suchness, Cause and Condition', and in his earlier book, which goes into this phase in much more detail, he says: 'Reality is actually neither one nor many, singular nor plural, transcendent nor immanent – it is a non-dual experience' (Wilber 1977: 64). He quotes from the Hua-yen school of Buddhism the view that:

> when we see through the illusion that separate things exist, we
> reach a level of experience wherein each 'thing' – because it
> is in itself unreal – contains or is penetrated by all other
> things, an experience called *hu-ju*, 'mutual interpenetration'.
> Hence the universe is likened to a net of glittering gems,
> wherein each jewel contains the reflections of all other jewels,
> and its reflection in turn exists in all the other gems: 'one in
> all, all in one', or 'unity in diversity, diversity in unity'.
> (Wilber 1977: 72)

This net is the net of Indra, which is referred to often by Joanna Macy in her lectures on the importance of networking in human affairs. And so we are back to the idea that the inner world and the outer world have the same laws and the same features and the same structures. The personal and the political are one.

If, then, the ultimate is not single in any meaningful sense, by the same token none of the stages leading to it can be just single, only single, nothing but single. They can, however, appear to be single, and be perfectly meaningful as single; but it would be better for us not to exclude the possibility of multiplicity as equally meaningful.

Going down to the causal stage, then, it makes perfect sense to say that there is One God, so long as we are prepared to say that that One God can have a multiplicity of aspects or persons. Christianity is perfectly all right on this one, with its doctrine of the Holy Trinity, and paganism is perfectly all right on it, with its doctrine of the Triune Goddess. But Islam and Judaism will have more difficulty with this view, though in both their traditions there are possibilities in this direction.

Lower down the line, at the Higher Subtle stage, it is tempting to say that there is just one Higher Self, and in the days of discovery it may well seem as if this must be the truth. But I see no reason why we should not be guided by more than one high archetype at different stages in our development, and why this should not be allowed for. In the days when we are discovering these things, of course it will seem important to believe in and hang on to the one vision, the first vision; but at a later stage this may well not seem so necessary.

Further back again, at the lower subtle stage, it is quite common to have more than one voice coming in through trance or seance or other ritual observance or spontaneous illumination. Klimo (1988) has given many examples of this.

Further back still, at the centaur stage, it seems all important to have the sense of being just one single self, and I think this must be allowed at this stage as being a very important and quite necessary illusion. Unless we genuinely have an experience of authenticity and singleness of vision, we cannot go on to any of the later stages with any authority or safety. But if we get locked in at this stage, we may deny ourselves the possibility of further development. It is a watershed or turning point, and as such its purity is essential, but it is only a watershed or turning point, not a place to stay for ever. The attempt to hang on to it brings intolerance and narrowness.

So our conclusion must be that, while at certain stages unity may be very tempting and even apparently necessary, in the end multiplicity is just as real and just as important, all the way down the line. There never comes a time when we can simply abandon our multiplicity and lie down in a perfect and final unity. We may not have subpersonalities in the sense that they fight with one another, but we shall still have many angles, many colours, many quirks. We shall still be human.

BIBLIOGRAPHY

Adler, A. (1927) *The Practice and Theory of Individual Psychology*, New York: Harcourt, Brace & World.

Ajzen, I. (1988) *Attitudes, Personality and Behaviour*, Milton Keynes: Open University Press.

Allison, R. and Schwartz, T. (1980) *Minds in Many Pieces*, New York: Rawson-Wade.

Allport, G. W. (1937) *Personality: a Psychological Interpretation*, New York: Holt.

Anthony, D., Ecker, B., and Wilber, K. (eds) (1987) *Spiritual Choices: the Problem of Recognizing Authentic Paths to Inner Transformation*, New York: Paragon House.

Argüelles, J. and Argüelles, M. (1972) *Mandala*, Boulder, Co: Shambala.

Assagioli, R. (1975) *Psychosynthesis: a Manual of Principles and Techniques*, London: Turnstone Press.

Bakan, D. (1966) *The Duality of Human Existence*, Boston: Beacon Press.

Balint, M. (1968) *The Basic Fault: Therapeutic Aspects of Regression*, London: Tavistock.

Bandler, J. and Grinder, R. (1982) *Reframing*, Moab, Utah: Real People Press.

Baumgartner, P. and Perls F. S. (1975) *Gifts from Lake Cowichan and Legacy from Fritz*, Palo Alto, CA: Science & Behaviour Books Inc.

Beahrs, J. O. (1982) *Unity and Multiplicity: Multilevel Consciousness of Self in Hypnosis, Psychiatric Disorder and Mental Health*, New York: Brunner/Mazel.

Beck, A. T., Rush, J. A., Shaw, B. F., and Emery, G. (1979) *Cognitive Therapy of Depression*, New York: Guilford Press.

Bem, S. L. (1977) 'Beyond androgyny: some presumptuous prescriptions for a liberated sexual identity', in C. G. Carney and S. L. McMahon (eds) *Exploring Contemporary Male/Female Roles: a Facilitator's Guide*, La Jolla, CA: University Associates.

Bennett, J. (1976) *Linguistic Behaviour*, Cambridge: Cambridge University Press.

Berne, E. (1961) *Transactional Analysis in Psychotherapy*, New York: Grove Press.
—— (1972) *What Do You Say After You Say Hello?*, New York: Grove Press.
Binet, A. (1892) *Les altérations de la personnalité*, Paris: Alcan.
Blatner, H. (1970) 'Psychodrama, role-playing and action methods: theory and practice', Mimeographed.
Bleuler, E. (1924) *Textbook of Psychiatry*, New York: Macmillan.
Boa, F. (1988) *The Way of the Dream: Dr Marie-Louise von Franz in conversation with Fraser Boa*, Toronto: Windrose Films.
Boadella, D. (1987) *Lifestreams: an Introduction to Biosynthesis*, London: Routledge.
Bolen, J. S. (1984) *Goddesses in Everywoman*, New York: Harper & Row.
Brand, M. (1984) *Intending and Acting: Toward a Naturalized Action Theory*, Cambridge: Bradford Books.
Brown, G. (1970) 'The creative subself', in H. Otto and J. Mann (eds) *Ways of Growth: Approaches to Expanding Awareness*, New York: Pocket Books.
Brown, M. Y. (1979) *The Art of Guiding: the Psychosynthesis Approach to Individual Counselling and Psychology*, Redlands, CA: Johnston College, University of Redlands.
Bruner, J. S. (1956) 'Freud and the image of man', *Partisan Review* 23: 343.
—— (1960) 'Myth and identity', in H. A. Murray (ed.) *Myth and Mythmaking*, New York: George Braziller.
Bugental, J. (1965) *The Search for Authenticity*, New York: Holt, Rinehart & Winston.
Cantor, N. and Kihlstrom, J. F. (1987) *Personality and Social Intelligence*, Englewood Cliffs, NJ: Prentice-Hall.
Cantor, N. and Mischel, W. (1979) 'Prototypes in person perception', in L. Berkowitz (ed.) *Advances in Experimental Social Psychology*, New York: Academic Press.
Carlson (1981) 'Studies in script theory: 1. Adult analogs of a child nuclear scene', *Journal of Personality and Social Psychology* 40: 501-10.
Carlson, E. T. (1986) 'The history of dissociation until 1880', in J. M. Quen (ed.) *Split Minds/Split Brain*, New York and London: New York University Press.
Chertok, L. and de Saussure, R. (1979) *The Therapeutic Revolution: from Mesmer to Freud*, New York: Brunner/Mazel.
Cohn, R. C. (1971) 'Living-learning encounters: the theme-centred interactional method', in L. Blank, G. B. Gottsegen, and M. G. Gottsegen (eds) *Confrontation: Encounters in Self and Interpersonal Awareness*, London: Collier-Macmillan.
Corsini, R. J. (1981) *Handbook of Innovative Psychotherapies*, New York: John Wiley.
Crabtree, A. (1988) *Multiple Man: Explorations in Possession and Multiple Personality*, London: Grafton Books.
Dansky, S., Knoebel, J., and Pitchford, K. (1977) 'The effeminist

manifesto', in Jon Snodgrass (ed.) *A Book of Readings for Men against Sexism*, New York: Times Change Press.

Davidson, D. (1963) 'Actions, reasons and causes', *Journal of Philosophy* 60: 685-700.

Decker, H. H. (1986) 'The lure of nonmaterialism in materialist Europe: investigations of dissociative phenomena 1880-1915', in J. M. Quen (ed.) *Split Minds/Split Brain*, New York and London: New York University Press.

Delay, J. (1957) *La Jeunesse d'André Gide*, Paris: Gallimard.

Denzin, N. K. (1987) 'A phenomenology of the emotionally divided self', in K. Yardley and T. Honess (eds) *Self and Identity: Psychosocial Perspectives*, Chichester: John Wiley.

Dessoir, M. (1890) *Das Doppel-Ich*, Leipzig: Günther.

Duval, S. and Wicklund, R. A. (1972) *A Theory of Objective Self-awareness*, New York: Academic Press.

Edelwich, J. with Brodsky, A. (1980) *Burn-out: Stages of Disillusionment in the Helping Professions*, New York: Human Sciences Press.

Eiseman, J. W. (1977) 'A third party consultation model for resolving recurring conflicts collaboratively', *Journal of Applied Behavioural Science* 13(3).

Elkind, D. (1981) *Children and Adolescents* (3rd edn) New York: Oxford University Press.

Ellenberger, H. (1970) *The Discovery of the Unconscious*, New York: Basic Books.

Epstein, S. (1973) 'The self-concept revisited: or, the theory of a theory', *American Psychologist* 28: 404-16.

Faber, M. D. (1977) 'Don Juan and Castaneda: the psychology of altered awareness', *The Psychoanalytic Review* 64(3): 323-79.

Fagan, J. and Shepherd, I. L. (eds) (1970) *Gestalt Therapy Now*, Palo Alto, CA: Science & Behaviour Press.

Fairbairn, W. R. D. (1952) *Psychoanalytic Studies of the Personality*, London: Tavistock.

Faraday, A. (1974) *Dream Power*, London: Pan.

Federn, P. (1952) *Ego Psychology and the Psychoses*, E. Weiss (ed.) New York: Basic Books.

Fenichel, O. (1945) *The Psychoanalytic Theory of Neurosis*, New York: W. W. Norton.

Ferenczi, S. (1909) 'Introjection and transference', in *First Contributions to Psychoanalysis*, London: Hogarth Press (1952).

Ferrucci, P. (1982) *What We May Be*, Wellingborough: Turnstone Press.

Fingarette, H. (1963) *The Self in Transformation*, New York: Harper & Row.

Firestone, S. (1972) *The Dialectic of Sex*, New York: Bantam.

Fodor, N. (1949) *The Search for the Beloved*, New York: University Books.

Follett, M. P. (1941) *Freedom and Coordination*, London: Pitman.

Franklin, M. (1981) 'Play as the creation of imaginary situations: the role of language', in S. Wapner and B. Kaplan (eds) *Toward a Holistic Developmental Psychology*, Hillsdale, NJ: Lawrence Erlbaum.

Freud, S. (1938) 'Splitting of the ego in the process of defence', *Standard edition* Vol.23, London: Hogarth Press.

Frey-Rohn, L. (1974) *From Freud to Jung: a Comparative Study of the Psychology of the Unconscious*, New York: G. P. Putnam's Sons.

Fromm, E. (1947) *Man for Himself*, New York: Farrar & Rinehart.

Gara, M. A. (1986) 'Personal prototypes and their organization in the perception of self and others', unpublished manuscript, Rutgers University Medical School.

Gazzaniga, M. (1985) *The Social Brain*, New York: Basic Books.

Gergen, K. J. (1972) 'Multiple identity: the healthy, happy human being wears many masks', *Psychology Today* 5(12): 31-5, 64-6.

Glover, J. (1988) *I: the Philosophy and Psychology of Personal Identity*, London: Allen Lane.

Goffman, E. (1959) *The Presentation of Self in Everyday Life*, New York: Anchor.

—— (1974) *Frame Analysis*, New York: Harper & Row.

Goldfried, M. R. (1982) 'On the history of therapeutic integration', *Behavior Therapy* 13: 572-93.

Goldman, A. (1970) *A Theory of Action*, Englewood Cliffs, NJ: Prentice-Hall.

Golembiewski, R. T. and McConkie, M. (1975) 'The centrality of interpersonal trust in group processes', in C. L. Cooper (ed.) *Theories of Group Processes*, Chichester: John Wiley.

Graham, G. and Horgan, T. (1988) 'How to be realistic about folk psychology', *Philosophical Psychology* 1(1): 69-81.

Greenberg, I. A. (ed.)(1974) *Psychodrama: Theory and Therapy*, London: Souvenir Press.

Greenwald, A. G. (1980) 'The totalitarian ego: fabrication and revision of personal history', *American Psychology* 35: 603-18.

Grice, H. P. (1957) 'Meaning', *Philosophical Review* 66: 377-88.

—— (1969) 'Utterer's meaning and intentions', *Philosophical Review* 78: 147-77.

Grof, S. (1975) *Realms of the Human Unconscious: Observations from LSD Research*, New York: Viking Press (British edn, London: Souvenir Press, 1979).

—— (1985) *Beyond the Brain*, New York: State University of New York Press.

Grotstein, J. S. (1981) *Splitting and Projective Identification*, New York: Jason Aronson.

Guntrip, H. (1961) *Personality Structure and Human Interaction*, London: Hogarth.

—— (1971) *Psychoanalytic Theory, Therapy and the Self*, New York: Basic Books (now Maresfield Reprints, London, 1977).

Hampden-Turner, C. (1986) *Maps of the Mind*, London: Mitchell Beazley.

Hankiss, A. (1981) 'Ontologies of the self: on the mythological rearranging of one's life history', in D. Bertaux (ed.) *Biography and Society*, Beverly Hills, CA: Sage.

Hannah, B. (1981) *Encounters with the Soul: Active Imagination as Developed by C. G. Jung*, Boston: Sigo Press.

Haronian, F. (1971) 'Repression of the sublime', in J. Fadiman (ed.) *The Proper Study of Man*, New York: Macmillan.

Hawkins, P. (1988) 'A phenomenological psychodrama workshop', in P. Reason (ed.) *Human Inquiry in Action: developments in new paradigm research*, London: Sage.

Hawthorn, J. (1983) *Multiple Personality and the Disintegration of Literary Character*, London: Edward Arnold.

Hay, D. (1983) *Exploring Inner Space*, Harmondsworth: Penguin.

Hegel, G. W. F. (1971) *Philosophy of Mind*, Oxford: Clarendon Press.

Herink, R. (1980) *The Psychotherapy Handbook*, New York: New American Library.

Hesse, H. and Bradac, J. (1975) *Treatise on the Steppenwolf*, London: Wildwood House.

Hilgard, E. R. (1986) *Divided Consciousness: Multiple Controls in Human Thought and Action*, (Expanded edn) New York: John Wiley.

Hillman, J. (1975) *Re-visioning Psychology*, New York: Harper & Row.

—— (1981) 'Psychology: monotheistic or polytheistic' (rev. version), in D. L. Miller, *The New Polytheism*, Dallas: Spring.

—— (1985) *Anima: an Anatomy of a Personified Notion*, Dallas: Spring.

Hofstadter, D. (1985) *Metamagical Themas*, New York: Basic Books.

Honess, T. and Yardley, K. (eds)(1987) *Self and Identity: Perspectives across the Lifespan*, London: Routledge.

Hunt, S. (1985) *Ouija: the Most Dangerous Game*, New York: Harper & Row.

James, W. (1890) *Principles of Psychology*, New York: Holt.

—— (1961) *The Varieties of Religious Experience*, New York: Collier.

Janis, I. L. and Mann, L. (1977) *Decision making: a Psychological Analysis of Conflict, Choice and Commitment*, New York: The Free Press.

Janov, A. (1970) *The Primal Scream*, New York: Putnam.

—— (1977) *The Feeling Child*, London: Abacus.

—— (1983) *Imprints: the Lifelong Effects of the Birth Experience*, New York: Coward-McCann.

Janov, A. and Holden, E. M. (1977) *Primal Man: the New Consciousness*, London: Abacus.

Joachim, H. H. (1948) *Logical Studies*, Oxford: Clarendon Press.

Johnson, R. A. (1986) *Inner Work: Using Dreams and Active Imagination for Personal Growth*, San Francisco: Harper & Row.

Jung, C. G. (1928) 'A psychological theory of types', in *Collected Works*, vol. 6.

—— (1936) 'Psychological factors determining human behaviour', in *Collected Works*, vol. 8.

—— (1943) 'On the psychology of the unconscious', in *Collected Works*, vol. 7.

—— (1946) *The Psychology of the Transference*, in *Collected Works*, vol. 16.

—— (1956) *Two Essays on Analytical Psychology*, Cleveland, OH: Meridian.

227

—— (1959) *Aion: Researches into the Phenomenology of the Self*, in *Collected Works*, vol. 9 (Part 2).

—— (1968) 'Archetypes of the collective unconscious', in *Collected Works*, vol. 9 (Part 1) 2nd edn.

Kant, I. (1933) *Immanuel Kant's Critique of Pure Reason*, trans. Norman Kemp Smith, London: Macmillan.

Karle, H. W. A. and Boys, J. H. (1987) *Hypnotherapy: a Practical Handbook*, London: Free Association Books.

Kihlstrom, J. F. and Cantor, N. (1984) 'Mental representations of the self', in L. Berkowitz (ed.) *Advances in Experimental Social Psychology 17*, New York: Academic Press.

Klapp, O. (1969) *Collective Search for Identity*, New York: Holt, Rinehart & Winston.

Klein, M. (1948) *Contributions to Psychoanalysis*, London: Hogarth Press.

Klimo, J. (1988) *Channeling*, Wellingborough: Aquarian Press.

Kohut, H. (1971) *The Analysis of the Self*, New York: Internatonal Universities Press.

Kuhn, T. S. (1970) *The Structure of Scientific Revolutions*, Chicago: University of Chicago Press.

Kuiper, N. A. and Derry, P. A. (1981) 'The self as cognitive prototype: an application to person perception and depression', in N. Cantor and J. F. Kihlstrom (eds) *Personality, Cognition and Social Interaction*, Hillsdale, NJ: Lawrence Erlbaum.

Laborde, G. Z. (1987) *Influencing with integrity*, Palo Alto, CA: Syntony Publishing.

—— (1988) *Fine Tune your Brain*, Palo Alto, CA: Syntony Publishing.

Laing, R. D. (1976) *The Facts of Life*, Harmondsworth: Penguin.

—— (1982) *The Voice of Experience*, Harmondsworth: Penguin.

Lake, F. (1966) *Clinical Theology*, London: Darton, Longman and Todd, London (abridged edn, 1986).

—— 1980) *Studies in Constricted Confusion*, Oxford: Clinical Theology Association.

Langs, R. (1982) *Psychotherapy: a Basic Text*, New York: Jason Aronson.

LeShan, L. (1973) *Toward a General Theory of the Paranormal: a Report of Work in Progress*, New York: Parapsychological Foundation.

Lessing, D. (1970) *The Four-Gated City*, New York: Bantam.

Lewin, K. (1936) *Topological Psychology*, New York: McGraw-Hill.

Lieberman, S. (1956) 'The effects of changes in roles on the attitudes of role occupants', *Human Relations 9*.

Loevinger, J. (1976) *Ego Development*, San Francisco: Jossey-Bass.

Lukoff, D. (1985) 'The diagnosis of mystical experiences with psychotic features', *Journal of Transpersonal Psychology* 17(2): 155-81.

McAdams, D. P. (1985) 'The "Imago": a key narrative component of identity', in P, Shaver (ed.) *Self, Situations and Social Behaviour*, Beverly Hills, CA: Sage.

McCall, G. J. and Simmons, J. L. (1966) *Identities and Interactions*, New York: Free Press.

McCullin, R. E. and Giles, T. R. (1985) *A Cognitive-Behaviour Therapy: a Restructuring Approach*, New York: Grune and Stratton.

McCulloch, W. S. (1945) 'A heterarchy of values determined by the topology of nervous nets', *Bulletin of Mathematical Biophysics.*

McKellar, P. (1979) *Mindsplit: the Psychology of Multiple Personality and the Dissociated Self*, London: J. M. Dent & Sons.

Mahrer, A. R. (1978) *Experiencing*, New York: Brunner/Mazel.

—— (1983) *Experiential Psychotherapy*, New York: Brunner/Mazel.

—— (1986) *Therapeutic Experiencing*, New York: Norton.

Mair, M. (1977) 'The community of self', in D. Bannister (ed.) *New Perspectives in Personal Construct Theory*, London: Academic Press.

Mann, R. D. (1975) 'Winners, losers and the search for equality in groups', in C. L. Cooper (ed.) *Theories of Group Processes*, Chichester: John Wiley and Sons.

Markus, H. (1977) 'Self-schemata and processing information about the self', *Journal of Personality and Social Psychology* 35(2): 63-78.

—— (1983) 'Self-knowledge: an expanded view', *Journal of Personality* 51(3): 543-65.

Markus, H. and Nurius, P. (1987) 'Possible selves: the interface between motivation and the self-concept', in K. Yardley and T. Honess (eds) *Self and Identity: Psychosocial Perspectives*, Chichester: John Wiley and Sons.

Markus, H. and Sentis, K. (1982) 'The self in social information processing', in J. Suls (ed.) *Psychological Perspectives on the Self*, vol.1, Hillsdale, NJ: Lawrence Erlbaum.

Markus, H. and Smith, J. (1981) 'The influence of self-schemata on the perception of others', in N. Cantor and J. F. Kihlstrom (eds) *Personality, Cognition and Social Interaction*, Hillsdale, NJ: Lawrence Erlbaum.

Martindale, C. (1980) 'Subselves: the internal representation of situational and personal dispositions', in L. Wheeler (ed.) *Review of Personality and Social Psychology* 1, Beverly Hills, CA: Sage.

Maslow, A. H. (1968) *Toward a Psychology of Being*, New York: Van Nostrand.

—— (1987) *Motivation and Personality* (3rd edn), New York: Harper and Row.

Mavromatis, A. (1987) *Hypnagogia*, London: Routledge.

May, R. (ed.) (1969) *Existential Psychology*, New York: Random House.

May, R., Angel, E., and Ellenberger, H. F. (eds) (1958) *Existence*, New York: Basic Books.

Meichenbaum, D. (1977) *Cognitive-Behaviour Modification: an Integrative Approach*, New York: Plenum Press.

Merton, R. K. (1957) *Social Theory and Social Structure*, New York: Free Press.

Middlebrook, P. N. (1974) *Social Psychology and Modern Life*, New York: Alfred A. Knopf.

Miller, A. (1987) *For Your Own Good: the Roots of Violence in Child-rearing*, London: Virago Press.

Miller, G. A. (1956) 'The magical number seven, plus or minus two: some limits on our capacity for processing information', *Psychological Review* 63: 81-97.

Miller, J. B. (1976) *Toward a New Psychology of Women*, Harmondsworth: Penguin.

Miller, J. G. (1942) *Unconsciousness*, London: Chapman and Hall, New York: John Wiley.

Miller, K. (1987) *Doubles: Studies in Literary History*, Oxford: Oxford University Press.

Minsky, M. (1988) *The Society of Mind*, London: Picador.

Mitchell, J. (1975) *Psychoanalysis and Feminism*, Harmondsworth: Penguin.

Mushatt, C. (1975) 'Mind-body-environment: toward understanding the impact of loss on psyche and soma', *Psychoanalytic Quarterly* 44: 93.

Myers, F. W. H. (1961) *Human Personality and Its Survival of Bodily Death*, New York: Arno (originally published 1903).

Neimeyer, R. A. (1986) 'Personal construct therapy', in W. Dryden and W. Golden (eds) *Cognitive-Behavioural Approaches to Psychotherapy*, London: Harper and Row.

Neisser, U. (1976) *Cognition and Reality*, San Francisco: W. H. Freeman.

Netherton, M. and Shiffrin, N. (1979) *Past Lives Therapy*, New York: Ace Books.

Neugarten, B. L. (ed.) (1968) *Middle Age and Ageing*, Chicago: University of Chicago Press.

Neumann, E. (1973) *The Origins and History of Consciousness*, Princeton, NJ: Princeton University Press.

O'Connor, E. (1971) *Our Many Selves: a Handbook for Self-Discovery*, New York: Harper and Row.

Oesterreich, T. K. (1974) *Possession and Exorcism*, New York: Causeway Books.

Ogilvy, J. (1977) *Many Dimensional Man*, New York: Oxford University Press.

Ornstein, R. (1986) *MultiMinds: A New Way to Look at Human Behavior*, Boston: Houghton Mifflin.

Paivio, A. (1975) 'Neomentalism', *Canadian Journal of Psychology* 29: 263-91.

Palmer, S. E. (1977) 'Hierarchical structure in perceptual representation, *Cognitive Psychology* 9: 441-74.

Parfit, D. (1984) *Reasons and Persons*, Oxford: Clarendon Press.

Peerbolte, L. (1975) *Psychic Energy in Prenatal Dynamics*, Wassenaar: Servire Press.

Perls, F. S. (1969) *Gestalt Therapy Verbatim*, Moab, Utah: Real People Press.

—— (1976) *Eyewitness to Therapy*, New York: Bantam.

Perls, F. S., Hefferline, R., and Goodman, P. (1951) *Gestalt Therapy*, New York: Dell.

Rangell, L. (1973) 'On the cacophony of human relations', *Psychoanalytic Quarterly* 42: 333-34.

Rank, O. (1929) *The Trauma of Birth*, New York: Harcourt Brace.
Reason, P. (ed.) (1988) *Human Inquiry in Action: Developments in New Paradigm Research*, London: Sage.
Reason, P. and Rowan, J. (eds) (1981) *Human Inquiry: a Sourcebook of New Paradigm Research*, Chichester: John Wiley.
Redfearn, J. W. T. (1985) *My Self, My Many Selves*, London: Academic Press.
Ridgway, R. (1987) *The Unborn Child*, Aldershot: Wildwood House.
Rogers, C. R. (1961) *On Becoming a Person*, London: Constable.
—— (1986) 'Client-centred therapy', in I. L. Kutash and A. Wolf (eds) *Psychotherapist's Casebook*, San Francisco: Jossey-Bass.
Rogers, C. R. and Stevens, B. (eds) (1967) *Person to Person: the Problem of Being Human*, Moab, Utah: Real People Press.
Rogers, T. B. (1981) 'A model of the self as an aspect of the human information processing system', in N. Cantor and J. F. Kihlstrom (eds) *Personality, Cognition and Social Interaction*, Hillsdale, NJ: Lawrence Erlbaum.
Romains, J. (1958) *Souvenirs et confidences d'un écrivain*, Paris: Fayard.
Rosenberg, S. and Gara, M. A. (1985) 'The multiplicity of personal identity', in P. Shaver (ed.) *Self, Situations and Social Behaviour: Review of Personality and Social Psychology*, vol.6, Beverly Hills, CA: Sage.
Rowan, J. (1975) 'A growth episode', *Self and Society*, 3/11: 20-7.
—— (1976) *The Power of the Group*, London: Davis-Poynter.
—— (1978) *The Structured Crowd*, London: Davis-Poynter.
—— (1983) *The Reality Game: a Guide to Humanistic Counselling and Psychotherapy*, London: RKP.
—— (1987) *The Horned God: Feminism and Men as Wounding and Healing*, London: Routledge.
—— (1987a) 'Siding with the client', in W. Dryden (ed.) *Key Cases in Psychotherapy*, London: Routledge.
—— (1988) 'Primal integration therapy', in J. Rowan and W. Dryden (eds) *Innovative Therapy in Britain*, Milton Keynes: Open University Press.
—— (in press) 'A late developer', in L. Spurling and W. Dryden (eds) *On Becoming a Psychotherapist*, London: Routledge.
Rumelhart, D. E. and Norman, D. (1978) 'Accretion, tuning and restructuring: three modes of learning' in J. Cotton and K. Klatsky (eds) *Semantic Factors in Cognition*, Hillsdale, NJ: Lawrence Erlbaum.
Sarbin, T. R. (1952) 'A preface to the psychological analysis of the self', *Psychological Review* 59: 11-21.
Sasportas, H. (1987) 'Subpersonalities and psychological conflicts', chap. in L. Greene and H. Sasportas *The Development of the Personality: Seminars in Psychological Astrology*, London: Routledge.
Satir, V. (1978) *Your Many Faces*, Berkeley, CA: Celestial Arts.
Satir, V. and Baldwin, M. (1983) *Satir Step by Step*, Palo Alto, CA: Science and Behaviour.
Schein, E. H. (1969) *Process Consultation: Its Role in Organization Development*, Reading: Addison-Wesley.

Schwartz, R. C. (1987) 'Our multiple selves: applying systems thinking to the inner family', *Networker* (March/April 25-31): 80-3.

Searles, H. F. (1986) *My Work with Borderline Patients*, Northvale, NJ: Jason Aronson.

Shapiro, S. B. (1976) *The Selves Inside You*, Berkeley, CA: Explorations Institute (see also [1962] 'A theory of ego pathology and ego therapy', *Journal of Psychology* 53).

Shorr, J. E. (1983) *Psychotherapy through Imagery*, 2nd edn, New York: Thieme-Stratton.

Sidis, B. and Goodhart, S. P. (1904) *Multiple Personality: an experimental investigation into the nature of human individuality*, Englewood Cliffs: Prentice-Hall.

Sinason, V. (1988) 'Dolls and bears: from symbolic equation to symbol: the significance of different play material for sexually abused children and others', *British Journal of Psychotherapy* 4 (4): 349-63.

Singer, J. (1977) *Androgyny*, London: Routledge.

Southgate, J. and Randall, R. (1978) *The Barefoot Psychoanalyst*, London: Association of Karen Hornsey Psychoanalytic Counsellors.

Spearman, C. (1937) *Psychology Down the Ages*, London: Macmillan.

Starhawk, (1982) *Dreaming the Dark*, Boston: Beacon.

Steiner, C. M. (1974) *Scripts People Live*, New York: Grove Press.

Steiner, C., Wyckoff, H., Goldstine, D., Lariviere, P., Schwebel, R., Marcus, J., and members of the Radical Psychiatry Centre (1975) *Readings in Radical Psychiatry*, New York: Grove Press.

Stone, H. and Winkelman, S. (1985) *Embracing our Selves*, Marina del Rey, CA: Devorss and Co.

Strawson, P. F. (1959) *Individuals: an Essay in Descriptive Metaphysics*, London: Methuen.

Sullivan, H. S. (1953) *The Interpersonal Theory of Psychiatry*, New York: Norton.

Tart, C. T. (1975) 'Science, states of consciousness and spiritual experiences: the need for state-specific sciences', in C. T. Tart (ed.) *Transpersonal Psychologies*, London: Routledge & Kegan Paul.

——— (1986) *Waking Up: Overcoming the Obstacles to Human Potential*, Boston: New Science Library.

Tomkins, S. S. (1978) 'Script theory: differential magnification of effects', in H. E. Howe and R. A. Dienstbier (eds) *Nebraska Symposium on Motivation* 26, Lincoln, NB: University of Nebraska Press.

Vargiu, J. G. (1974) 'Psychosynthesis workbook: subpersonalities', *Synthesis* 1.

Vaughan, F. (1985) *The Inward Arc*, Boston: New Science Library.

Verny, T. (1982) *The Secret Life of the Unborn Child*, London: Sphere.

Wallace, W. (1898) *Prolegomena to the Logic of Hegel*, Oxford: Clarendon Press.

Watanabe, S. (1986) 'Cast of characters work: systematically exploring the naturally organized personality', *Contemporary Family Therapy* 8: 75-83.

Watkins, J. G. (1976) 'Ego states and the problem of responsibility: a psychological analysis of the Patty Hearst case', *Journal of Psychiatry and Law* (Winter): 471-89.

—— (1978) *The Therapeutic Self*, New York: Human Sciences Press.

—— (1978a) 'Ego states and the problem of responsibility II: the case of Patricia W', *Journal of Psychiatry and Law* (Winter): 519-35.

—— (1984) 'The Bianchi (L.A. "Hillside Strangler") case: sociopath or multiple personality?', *International Journal of Clinical and Experimental Hypnosis* 32: 67-111.

Watkins, J. G. and Johnson, R. J. (1982) *We, the Divided Self*, New York: Irvington.

Watkins, J. G. and Watkins, H. H. (1979) 'Ego states and hidden observers', *Journal of Altered States of Consciousness* 5.

—— (1986) 'Hypnosis, multiple personality and ego states as altered states of consciousness', in B. B. Wolman and M. Ullman (eds) *Handbook of States of Consciousness*, New York: Van Nostrand Reinhold.

Watkins, M. (1986) *Invisible Guests: the Development of Imaginal Dialogues*, Hillsdale, NJ: The Analytic Press.

Weishaar, M. L. and Beck, A. T. (1986) 'Cognitive therapy', in W. Dryden and W. Golden (eds) *Cognitive-Behavioural Approaches to Psychotherapy*, London: Harper and Row.

Wessler, R. L. (1986) 'Conceptualizing cognitions in the cognitive-behavioural therapies', in W. Dryden and W. Golden (eds) *Cognitive-Behavioural Approaches to Psychotherapy*, London: Harper and Row.

Whitmore, D. and Hardy, J. (1988) 'Psychosynthesis', in J. Rowan and W. Dryden (eds) *Innovative Therapy in Britain*, Milton Keynes: Open University Press.

Wilber, K. (1977) *Spectrum of Consciousness*, Wheaton, Illinois: Quest Books, Theosophical Publishing House.

—— (1980) *The Atman Project: a Transpersonal View of Human Development*, Wheaton, Illinois: Theosophical Publishing House.

—— (1983) *Eye to Eye*, New York: Anchor Press, Doubleday.

—— (1986) 'The spectrum of development' and 'The spectrum of psychopathology', in K. Wilber, J. Engler, and D. P. Brown, *Transformations of Consciousness*, Boston: New Science Library.

Winnicott, D. W. (1965) *The Maturational Processes and the Facilitating Environment*, London: Hogarth Press.

—— (1971) *Playing and Reality*, Harmondsworth: Penguin.

Wittgenstein, L. (1953) *Philosophical Investigations*, Oxford: Basil Blackwell.

Wurf, E. and Markus, H. (1985) 'Self-schemas and possible selves', Unpublished MS, University of Michigan.

233

Wyckoff, H. (1975) 'Problem-solving groups for women', in Claude
    Steiner, H. Wyckoff, D. Goldstine, P. Lariviere, K. Schwebel, J.
    Marius, and members of the Radical Psychiatry Centre (eds)
    Readings in Radical Psychiatry, New York: Grove Press.
Zinker, J. (1978) *Creative Process in Gestalt Therapy*, New York: Vintage
    Books.

INDEX

34, 35, 42, 155, 184; not-OK- 123,
125, 126, 128, 129, 131, 134, 135;
OK- 123, 125, 128, 131; original, *see*
Real Self; outer 135; panicky 129;
past selves 171; peripheral selves
170; plurality of selves 188; possible
selves 8, 22, 108, 171, 172, 173, 197:
positive and negative 172; potential
selves 29, 189; private 134;
protagonist 179; public-relations
144; pure ego 169; Real *see* Real Self;
singular self-identity 80; social selves
15; society of 83; spiritual 157;
structure of 160, 161, 174: anarchy
205; heterarchy 188, 205; hierarchy
157, 160, 161, 162, 166, 167, 205;
pluralism 205; subjective experience
of 183; total 67; transpersonal *see*
transpersonal; true *see* real self;
unified bodymind 210; unity of 89,
155, 184, 220; unreal 8; whole 204;
with a big S 207, 213–15
self-actualization 211; *see also* realized
level
self-awareness 168, 202
self-concept 156, 169, 170, 172, 215
self-consciousness 176, 185; and
self-conscious subject 187
self-consistency 132
self-control 168
self-deception 196, 218
self-deprecation 179
self-development 135
self-enactment 211
self-esteem 134, 184
self-hater 132, 141
self-hypnosis 218
self-image 143, 211; negative 143
self-knowledge 173, 217
self-prototype *see* prototype
self-reflection 183
self-respect 211
self-statements 108
self-trust 203
Sentis, Keith 159, 160, 161, 163
sexual abuse *see* abuse and trauma
shadow *see* archetypes
Shapiro, Stewart 8, 85–7, 88, 90, 196,
202, 203
Shaw, George Bernard 162
Shepherd, Irma Lee 21
Shorr, Joseph 44
Sidis, Boris 16

Simmons, J. L. 21
Sinason, Valerie 199
Singer, June 203
small minds 8, 167
Smith, J. 170
soul 11, 12, 25, 42, 43, 44, 175, 213–15
Southgate, John 6, 22, 129, 139, 140
Spearman, C. 175
Spinoza 5
spiritual plurality 185, 187
spiritual unity 185, 187
spirituality 211, 213, 218; and spiritual
inflation *see* inflation
splitting 22, 84, 100, 122, 123, 124,
125, 126, 177, 199
spontaneity 71, 136
Stanislavsky, Konstantin 150, 197
state-specific: consciousness 37; tasks
9, 37
Steiner, Claude 22, 163
Stevens, Barry 31
Stone, Hal 8, 22, 69, 70, 85, 90–6, 144,
185, 190, 191, 196, 201, 202, 213
Storm, Hyemenyosts 95
Strauss, A. 8
Strawson, P. F. 177, 178
subidentities 8, 184
subjectivity 121, 125, 129, 131, 134,
136, 138, 151, 195
subselves 8, 85–7, 108, 155, 156;
structure of 156
subtle stage *see* psychospiritual
development
Sullivan, Harry Stack 163
superego 8, 18, 61, 62, 63, 79, 82, 93,
113, 129, 146, 196, 200, 202, 213–14
Swartley, William 6
symbols 65, 127, 140, 148, 216

Taine, Hippolyte 15
Tarde, Gabriel 15
Tart, Charles 8, 9, 30, 37
trances 11, 15
transactional analysis 22, 83, 84, 85,
93, 163
transference 101, 112, 113, 115, 177
transpersonal 122, 147, 208, 209, 211,
217, 218; self 53, 54, 74, 207, 212,
213–15, 218
trauma 84, 121–2, 123, 124, 125, 126,
127, 128, 134, 199, 210; birth 122,
123; conception 121; implantation
121

ultimate stage *see* psychospiritual
development
unconscious 14, 15, 16, 17, 38, 47, 57,
64, 68, 69, 79, 92, 93, 101, 112, 130,
139, 140, 142, 145–8, 176, 219;
archaic 146, 147; collective 23, 69,
139, 143–5, 152, 197; cultural 22,
139–43, 197; definitions of 145;
embedded 146; emergent 147, 148;
ground 146, 147; nonconscious 110;
personal 22, 119 139, 197, 218;
submergent 146; types of 145–7

Vargiu, James 34, 47, 72, 73, 74, 155,
203
Vaughan, Frances 213–16
Verny, Tom 121, 210
visions 66, 68, 73
voice dialogue 22, 57, 90–6, 112, 197
von Franz, Marie-Louise 9, 13, 67

Wallace, William 16
Walsby, Harold 5
Watanabe, S. 56
Watkins, Helen 102

Watkins, John 8, 20, 22, 83, 88-90, 102,
151, 156, 197
Watkins, Mary 8, 15, 35, 64, 71, 72, 74,
100, 148–52, 156, 203
Weishaar, M. L. 109
Wessler, Richard 109–10
Whitmore, Diana 106, 107
Wicklund, R. A. 124
Wilber, Ken 121, 131, 134, 138, 145–7,
207–13, 215, 216, 217
Winkelman, Sidra 8, 22, 69, 70, 85,
90–6, 185, 190, 191, 196, 201, 202,
213
Winnicott, Donald 6, 8, 22, 122, 126,
127, 149
Wittgenstein, Ludwig 169
Woolfe, Thomas 162
women 95, 142
Woolf, Virginia 17, 38
Wurf, E. 173
Wyckoff, Hogie 140

Yardley, Krysia 183, 191

Zinker, Joseph 79

SUBPERSONALITIES

'The notion of "subpersonalities" would seem to be absolutely essential to any psychology or any other approach that seeks to describe what it is to be human. Now, Mr Rowan has written what is likely to remain for some time *the book* on this subject, and his important work should be applauded by representatives of many different disciplines – philosophical, psychological, and spiritual, among them. Here is one of those rare books which really can help the reader to know differently, and more comprehensively, himself or herself as well as other people.'

– Robert E. L. Masters, Ph.D, psychologist and author, Director of Research, The Foundation for Mind Research, Pomona, New York, USA.

'It is not often that we find a bridge-building book like this, which spans so many of the gaps between different psychotherapies, different disciplines (psychotherapy, psychology, philosophy) and different frameworks of thought. John Rowan has produced one of those integrative books which we need every twenty years or so to bring together work which has been going on in many different fields, and make sense of it. This book deserves a place on the shelf of anyone seriously concerned with issues of personality, identity, and self.'

– Professor Arnold Keyserling, Vienna. First President, European Association for Humanistic Psychology, Head of the Kriterion Centre, and author of many books.